Transformational Dimensions of
Cyber Crime

Transformational Dimensions of Cyber Crime

by

Dr. M. N. Sirohi

ALPHA EDITIONS

New Delhi (India)

Published by

Alpha Editions
(Publishers and Distributors)
2/19, Ansari Road
Delhi – 110 002
Phones: 91-11-43596460, 91-11-47340674
Fax: 91-11-47340674
e-mail: alphaed@rediffmail.com

Copyright © 2015, *Reserved*

First Published in 2015

ISBN   : 978-81-931422-3-3

Contents

Preface

Cyber Crime can be defined as nay crime with the help of computer and telecommunication technology with the purpose of influencing the functioning of computer or computer system.

The information infrastructure is increasingly under attack by cyber criminals. The number, cost, and sophistication of attacks are increasing at alarming rates. They threaten the substantial and growing reliance of commerce, governments, and the public upon the information infrastructure to conduct business, carry messages, and process information. Some forms of attack also pose a growing threat to the public, and to critical infrastructures.

The general misconception that cyber crime is another variant of crime does not hold good. As in normal classification of crime, from pick pocketing to murder for gain to organised crime to terrorism, cyber crime has in its fold not just the microcosm of the world, but the world itself. From money laundering to medical insurance to providing public platform for ISIS, lot needs to be done to classify these crimes from the techno-legal angle, leave aside providing an effective legal framework and stringent enforcement of the same.

There are a good number of cyber crime variants. A few varieties are discussed for the purpose of completion. This book is not intended to expose all the variants. The readers are directed to other resources. This book makes an serious attempt to understand the Cyber Crime which involves activities like Credit Card Frauds, unathorised excess to other's computer system, Pornography, Software piracy and Cyber stalking etc.

—*Editor*

Introduction

DEFINITIONS OF CYBER CRIME

Most reports, guides or publications on cyber crime begin by defining the term "cyber crime". One common definition describes cyber crime as any activity in which computers or networks are a tool, a target or a place of criminal activity. One example for an international approach is Art. 1.1 of the Draft International Convention to Enhance Protection from Cyber Crime and Terrorism (CISAC) that points out that cyber crime refers to acts in respect to cyber systems. Some definitions try to take the objectives or intentions into account and define cyber crime more precisely, defining cyber crime as "computer-mediated activities which are either *illegal or considered illicit* by certain parties and which can be conducted *through global electronic networks*". These more refined descriptions exclude cases where physical hardware is used to commit regular crimes, but they risk excluding crimes that are considered as cyber crime in international agreements such as the "Convention on Cyber crime".

For example, a person who produces USB -devices containing malicious software that destroy data on computers when the device is connected commits a crime as defined by Art. 4 Council of Europe Convention on Cyber crime. However, the act of deleting data using a physical device to copy malicious code has not been committed through global electronic networks and would not qualify as cyber crime under the narrow definition.

This act would only qualify as cyber crime under a definition based on a broader description, including acts such as illegal data interference. This demonstrates that there are considerable difficulties in defining the term "cyber crime". The term "cyber crime" is used to describe a range of offences including traditional computer crimes, as well as network crimes.

As these crimes differ in many ways, there is no single criterion that could include all acts mentioned in the Stanford Draft Convention and the Convention on Cyber crime, whilst excluding traditional crimes that are just committed using hardware. The fact that there is no single definition of "cyber crime" need not be important, as long as the term is not used as a legal term.

CYBER CRIME VARIANTS

There are a good number of cyber crime variants. A few varieties are discussed for the purpose of completion. This chapter is not intended to expose all the variants. The readers are directed to other resources.

Cyber Stalking

Cyber stalking is use of the Internet or other electronic means to stalk someone. This term is used interchangeably with online harassment and online abuse. Stalking generally involves harassing or threatening Behaviour that an individual engages in repeatedly, such as following a person, appearing at a person's home or place of business, making harassing phone calls, leaving written messages or objects, or vandalizing a person's property.

Hacking

"Hacking" is a crime, which entails cracking systems and gaining unauthorised access to the data stored in them. Hacking had witnessed a 37 per cent increase this year.

Phishing

Phishing is just one of the many frauds on the Internet, trying to fool people into parting with their money. Phishing refers to the receipt of unsolicited emails by customers of financial institutions, requesting them to enter their username, password or other personal information to access their account for some reason. Customers are directed to a fraudulent replica of the original institution's Web site when they click on the links on the e-mail to enter their information, and so they remain unaware that the fraud has occurred. The fraudster then has access to the customer's online bank account and to the funds contained in that account. F-Secure Corporation's summary of 'data security' threats during the first half of 2007 has revealed that the study found the banking industry as soft target for phishing scams in India.

Cross-site Scripting

Cross-site scripting (XSS) is a type of computer security vulnerability typically found in web applications which allow code injection by malicious web users into the web pages viewed by other users. Examples of such code include HTML code and client-side scripts. An exploited cross-site scripting vulnerability can be used by attackers to bypass access controls.

Vishing

Vishing is the criminal practice of using social engineering and Voice over IP (VoIP) to gain access to private personal and financial information from the public for the purpose of financial reward. The term is a combination of "voice" and phishing. Vishing exploits the public's trust in landline telephone services, which have traditionally terminated in physical locations which are known to the telephone company, and associated with a bill-payer. The victim is often unaware that VoIP allows for caller ID spoofing, inexpensive, complex automated systems and anonymity for the bill payer. Vishing is typically used to steal credit card numbers or other information used in identity theft schemes from individuals.

Cyber Squatting

Cyber squatting is the act of registering a famous domain name and then selling it for a fortune. This is an issue that has not been tackled in IT act 2000. Bot Networks A cyber crime called 'Bot Networks', wherein spamsters and other perpetrators of cyber crimes remotely take control of computers without the users realising it, is increasing at an alarming rate. Computers get linked to Bot Networks when users unknowingly download malicious codes such as Trojan horse sent as e-mail attachments. Such affected computers, known as zombies, can work together whenever the malicious code within them get activated, and those who are behind the Bot Neworks attacks get the computing powers of thousands of systems at their disposal.

Attackers often coordinate large groups of Bot-controlled systems, or Bot networks, to scan for vulnerable systems and use them to increase the speed and breadth of their attacks. Trojan horse provides a backdoor to the computers acquired. A 'backdoor' is a method of bypassing normal authentication, or of securing remote access to a computer, while attempting to remain hidden from casual inspection. The backdoor may take the form of an installed Programme, or could be a modification to a legitimate Programme. Bot networks create unique problems for organisations because they can be remotely upgraded with new exploits very quickly, and this could help attackers pre-empt security efforts.

Vulnerability

The Open-Source Vulnerability Database (OSVDB) project maintains a master list of computer - security vulnerabilities, freely available for use by security professionals and projects around the world. Vulnerability information is critical for the protection of information systems everywhere: in enterprises and other organizations, on private networks and intranets, and on the public Internet.

Indian Crime Scene

The major cyber crimes reported, in India, are denial of services, defacement of websites, SPAM, computer virus and worms, pornography, cyber squatting, cyber stalking and phishing. Given the fact that nearly $ 120 million worth of mobiles are being lost or stolen in the country every year, the users have to protect information, contact details and telephone numbers as these could be misused. Nearly 69 per cent of information theft is carried out by current and ex-employees and 31 per cent by hackers. India has to go a long way in protecting the vital information. Symantec shares the numbers from its first systematic survey carried out on the Indian Net Security scene: The country has the highest ratio in the world (76 per cent) of outgoing spam or junk mail, to legitimate e-mail traffic. India's home PC owners are the most targeted sector of its 37.7 million Internet users: Over 86 per cent of all attacks, mostly via 'bots' were aimed at lay surfers with Mumbai and Delhi emerging as the top two cities for such vulnerability.

Phishing

Phishing attacks were more popular among Indian users due to rising Internet penetration and growing online transactions. India has now joined the dubious list of the world's top 15 countries hosting "phishing" sites which aims at stealing confidential information such as passwords and credit card details. A non-resident Malayali, had an account in a nationalised bank in Adoor, lost $ 10,000 when the bank authorities heeded a fake e-mail request to transfer the amount to an account in Ghana.

In Mangalapuram, a person transferred a large sum of money as "processing charge" to a foreign bank account after he received an e-mail, which said he had won a lottery [Kerala: The Hindu Monday Oct 30 2006]. Reports of phishing targeted at customers of banks appear to be on the rise. Web sense Security Labs, in a statement released recently, said it had received reports of such attacks from customers of AXIS Bank.

The Economic Offences Wing (EOW), Crime Branch, Delhi Police, unearthed a major phishing scam involving fake emails and websites of UTI Bank, An analysis of the accounts of the four arrested Nigerian nationals indicated financial transactions of over ₹ 1 crore in an eight-month period till December 2006. Investigations revealed that the scam is multi-layered with pan-India and international characteristics The Lab went on to say that it found a mal ware in the Web site of Syndicate Bank. The users through a spoofed e-mail were asked to renew certain services and claiming that failure to do so would result in suspension or deletion of the account. The e-mail provided a link to a malicious site that attempted to capture the personal and account information.

Phishing emails have increased by approximately twenty five percent over the last year but are harder to detect as they increasingly trick unsuspecting people with ordinary scenarios instead of improbable ones such as sudden cash windfalls.

It has been six months since the phishing attack on ICICI bank customers became public, and during that period, two more such attacks were reported on customers of financial institutions in India, one of UTI Bank and the other.

State Bank of India. RSA's 24/7 Anti-Fraud Command Centre of AFCC has just uncovered a 'Universal man-in-the middle Phishing Kit' in online forums which helps quickly create the fraudulent websites, often borrowing code from the original site.

Cyber Cafes—E-mails

Cyber cafes have emerged as hot spots for cyber crimes. Even terrorists prefer the anonymity of a cyber cafe to communicate with each other.

The mushrooming of cyber cafes in the city, which provide the secrecy through cabins constructed for users, has also made the porn literature easily accessible to the people visiting them. A 23-year-old person from Tiruchi was arrested by the City Cyber Crime police on Thursday on charges of sending an e-mail threat to the Chief Minister and his family.

In another case, the police team investigating the e-mail threat on the lives of the President and the Prime Minister has prepared a sketch of the suspect, who had sent the e-mail from a cyber cafe in the city. The Case of The State of Tamil Nadu vs Suhas Katti is notable for the fact that the conviction was achieved successfully.

The case related to posting of obscene, defamatory and annoying message about a divorcee woman in the yahoo message group. E-Mails were also forwarded to the victim for information by the accused through a false e-mail account opened by him in the name of the victim. The posting of the message resulted in annoying phone calls to the lady. A travel agent was arrested for allegedly sending a threatening mail to blow up the National and Bombay stock exchanges in Kolkata.

Stalking

A tenth standard boy from Bangalore got into trouble when a girl much older than him started stalking him. She pasted 'I Love You' slips on his gate and called his On reviewing his Orkut profile, it was realised that he had accepted chat invites from more than 20 people; only two of who were his real-life friends.

Hacking

A case of suspected hacking of certain web portals and obtaining the residential addresses from the e-mail accounts of city residents had recently come to light. After getting the addresses, letters were sent through post mail and the recipients were lured into participating in an international lottery that had Australian $ 23 lakhs at stake.

Computer hackers have also got into the Bhaba Atomic Research Centre (BARC) computer and pulled out important data. Some computer professionals who prepared the software for MBBS examination altered the data and gave an upward revision to some students in return for a hefty payment. A key finding of the Economic Crime Survey 2006 of Price water house Coopers (PwC) was that a typical perpetrator of economic crime in India was male (almost 100 per cent), a graduate or undergraduate and 31-50 years of age. Further, over one-third of the frauds in the country were perpetrated by insiders and over 37 per cent of them were in senior managerial positions.

Global Anti-Malware Market

Malware is software designed to infiltrate or damage a computer system without the owner's informed consent. The expression is a general term used by computer professionals to mean a variety of forms of hostile, intrusive, or annoying software or Programme code. The global anti-malware market is driven by cyber criminal threats. The commercialisation of cyber crime is spurring malware-writing activity and leading to more threats of this nature. In the consumer space, this translates into identity theft and stolen passwords Growth opportunities have led to intensified competition in both consumer and enterprise segments.

On the other hand, loss of intellectual property and customer data coupled with extortion with the threat of taking down Web sites or revealing sensitive information are on the rise in the enterprise space. Organised crime is now employing KGB-style tactics to ensnare the next generation of hackers and malware authors. Cyber-criminals are actively approaching students and graduates of IT technology courses to recruit a fresh wealth of cyber skill to their ranks Today's worms are the handiwork of malcontents for whom cyber crime affords lucrative returns. A flourishing market exists where large blocks of infected machines that can be controlled remotely are for sale.

So big demonstrated the close nexus between malware writers and spammers, machines infected by the Sobig mass mailing worm were offered to spammers for price. The thriving market for subverted PCs has swung the underworld into hyperactivity. The past ten months have seen several hacker groups and cyber crime syndicates setting up attack networks (botnets) and releasing remote attack tools through increasingly crafty malware such as Blaster, Sinit, MyDoom, Phatbot, Bagle and Netsky. New analysis from Frost and Sullivan, World Anti-Malware Products Markets, finds that the world market for antivirus solutions reached $4,685 million in 2006, up 17.1 per cent from $4,000.7 million in the previous year and expects this market to grow at a 10.9 per cent compound annual growth rate (CAGR) from 2006 to 2013, reaching $9,689.7 million by 2013.

Anti-Cyber crime Initiatives

In a first of its kind initiative in India to tackle cyber crime, police have taken the initiative to keep an electronic eye on the users of the various cyber cafes spread over the city. The Kerala State IT Mission has launched a Web portal and a call centre to tackle cyber crime. The Central Bureau of Investigation (CBI) and the Mumbai police have recommended issuance of licenses to cyber cafe owners. Many countries, including India, have established Computer Emergency Response Teams (CERTs) with an objective to coordinate and respond during major security incidents/events. These organisations identify and address existing and potential threats and vulnerabilities in the system and coordinate with stakeholders to address these threats. Policy initiatives on cyber crime are as yet lethargic because of a general sense that it is nothing more than juvenile hackers out to have fun or impress someone. Prateek Bhargava, cyber law expert says, "There is huge potential for damage to national security through cyber attacks. The Internet is a means for money laundering and funding terrorist attacks in an organised manner. In the words of Pavan Duggal, Supreme Court Lawyer, "Cyber crime is omnipresent and although cyber crime cells have been set up in major cities, most cases remain unreported due to lack of awareness."

THE FUTURE OF CYBER CRIME ACTIVITY

During an eight day period in August of 2003, three separate worms cost the U.S., economy close to two billion dollars in lost production. Later that summer, the east coast of the United States experienced a massive blackout that might have been exacerbated by a worm called Blaster.

Robert Cringley believed that same year that "the cost to society of identity theft is in the range of $4-5 billion per year and may be even higher." With the convergence of organised crime and technically savvy cyber criminals, the growing fear of cyberterrorism, the inability to understand security from major software vendors and the slow footedness of the government, the future seems to point to an Internet that is not only vulnerable to major attacks, but also infested with scams, thieves, and ever increasing opportunities for exploitation.

Although inherently difficult to predict trends within the field of technology, there are some eventualities that seem certain, like the growth of extortion and fraud though the Internet. These difficulties will of course result in new responses that better protect customers and force criminals into new realms. Although it is a hackneyed expression, the Internet is still in the Wild West stages. It is important to remember, though, that the Wild West eventually turned into suburbia after successful methods were found to control and police criminals, making their life extremely difficult. An examination of some of the potentialities will help to illustrate how the Internet and cyber crime can be envisioned, at least in the near term future.

Future Trends in Cyber Crime Activity

The pace at which cyber crime is growing is one of the most disturbing trends. Valerie McNiven, a U.S., Treasury Advisor, has proclaimed "last year was the first year that proceeds from cyber crime were greater than proceeds from the sale of illegal drugs, and that was, I believe, over $105 billion." She further added that "cyber crime is moving at such a high speed that law enforcement cannot catch up with it." It seems clear that the issue will only become worse in the next few years, now that professionals have realised the potential windfalls if exploited properly. Recently, there has been significant discussion over the amalgamation of organised criminals and cyber crime. Such a pairing indeed forebodes an ill omen for the near term future. With most of the criminal groups operating out of eastern Europe, Russia and Asia, where laws and enforcement are scanty, there seems little hope in containing and neutralising the threat through traditional means.

Phil Williams, a visiting scientist at CERT, summarised the issue succinctly. "The Internet provides both channels and targets for crime and enables them to be exploited for considerable gain with a very low level of risk. For organised crime it is difficult to ask for more." The result that can then be expected will be an increase in sophisticated phishing attacks and other means for identity theft that may be two pronged. For example, using call centers to notify "customers" ahead of time of some issue, and then following up with e-mails that request personal information. These types of social engineering attacks can be very damaging and have had a long history of success within cyber crime and fraud related transgressions.

The Internet makes it even easier since, a degree of authority can be imparted with official looking e-mails and fraudulent web sites that mimic their legitimate counterparts exactly. In the past, such social engineering relied on interpersonal skills like gaining trust. Now, the same idea has been transferred to technology, which can be done with greater ease by a wider group of people.

Another aspect of fraud will result from the aggregation of personal information in many third party data centers, making them valuable targets to infiltrate.

It is not hard to imagine criminals using data mining techniques to find the most gullible consumers, or tailoring phishing e-mails for specific people based on their medical, financial or personal history. Identify theft will also move in more automated directions. For example, botnets will become vehicles not just for denial of service attacks and spam, but also as giant search platforms for finding personal information, like credit cards and social security numbers. Controllers of the botnets will then receive payment to run queries on their "database." With professional criminals managing the money laundering and organisation of such schemes, it begs to ask where will all the technical know-how come from in order to perform cyber crime? Unfortunately, there are growing numbers of intelligent black-hats with university degrees spread around the globe, many of them operating in countries where legal employment does not pay as well and the chances of being caught are slim. But more troublesome is that it has become easier than ever before to be a hacker capable of inflicting great harm on networks and committing cyber crime.

The Internet has created a repository of knowledge where anyone is able to learn the fundamentals of subverting computer systems, with numerous tutorials available that spell out in nearly layman's terms how to perform a buffer overflow or a man in the middle attack. Interestingly, the greatest problem is not those who will take the time to learn and find new exploits. In fact this group will probably remain a small, highly intelligent network of researchers and security groups focused solely on finding holes in software. In this, it is preordained, that even if someone is motivated to learn how exploits work, finding a new exploit takes a degree of investigation, skill and diligence that most are not willing to invest.

The real threat comes from the profound ease at which anyone can run a programme like "MetaSploit," a framework for running exploits against targets that allows new modules to be imported and run automatically. The attacker literally needs to know nothing about how computers work, besides how to operate one. In fact, for almost all attacks, the hard work is done by a small group of people, and then released into the public domain, allowing almost anyone to just run the attack.

Botnets are no longer handcrafted software made by one group who truly understood the fundamentals, but instead are opensource collaborative efforts that aim to make it as easy as possible to control remote computers, such as BotNET, eggheads and CSharpBot, all available from SourceForge. Thus, the barrier to entry to the field is so low that it allows almost anyone to experiment and join the swelling ranks of cyber criminals. With the learning curve so low, it should prompt discussion on the need for a new paradigm of thought in how to pre-empt and deal with criminals, in a way that is no longer tied to traditional methods. For example, for someone to break into a house, not only do they need to plan the opportune moment, but they may also have to be aware of lock picking, security system evasion and possess a degree of gumption to overcome moral thresholds.

In opposition, the ease of cyber crime seems inversely proportional to the lucrativeness that it bestows and moreover, these trends show signs of accelerating. Beyond the "who" and the "why" of future cyberattacks, the "how" will also change as operating systems become more secure and harder to exploit. With the damage that comes with each new security hole released, Microsoft, Apple and open source vendors have finally begun to seriously focus on security. Of course that hasn't stemmed the flow of vulnerabilities discovered, but techniques such as address space randomisation to stop buffer overflows, advanced and automatic code reviews and more training will reduce the ability to compromise a machine through operating system protocols over time.

The real danger in the future lies with user applications, which are created by individuals or small groups without the knowledge or training required to implement security correctly. Especially dangerous are web applications that can be installed on web servers. The traditional problem with these types of security vulnerabilities was finding susceptible hosts. But with Google, a programme can automatically search for sites with a specific version of a programme installed and then launch an attack.

If remote code can be executed, the programme may not be able to take over the whole system, but it can run programmes as the user which may be enough to install bots and automatically replicate.

The first instance of such an attack occurred in December of 2004 with the Santy worm that attacked a popular bulletin board system by searching through Google to find hosts with a specific file that was vulnerable. Such attacks aim their weapons at the least secure and vetted of software created. Although the installed base of such systems may be small, with "Google Hacking," they can still be quickly located and exploited. Another avenue of attack that will open up will be through embedded systems, such as cell phones, mobile devices and other electronics that may connect to the Internet for the most mundane of purposes. Software is usually recreated for each iteration of a device as it is specifically designed for the hardware.

This allows for security problems to creep back in over time that may have been eliminated before. As these devices start to allow consumers to make purchases, while storing valuable information, they will become more attractive for criminals. The incentives now to do so are low, so security researchers have only seen "proof-of-concept" viruses, like the one that infected cellphones running a version of the Symbian OS that could spread automatically. It appears organised crime has not moved into this area due to the lack of research and understanding of how such attacks can be made profitable. Much as with the Internet, it will take time to exploit successfully.

In the same vein, eventually automobiles, home electronics devices, refrigerators and almost all devices can and will use the Internet in order to perform maintenance, download upgrades or monitor performance. These will present opportunities for maliciousness and blackmail that doesn't equate in the same way as the purely virtual environment of the Internet. If someone enters their car, controlled by a foreign agent that demands a wire transfer or else the car will be crashed at high speeds, a situation arises that people will no longer accept. Whether such a scenario will occur is debatable, but the possibility will certainly exist.

MITIGATING CYBER CRIME ACTIVITY

Although it is inevitable that cyber crime will increase and continue to explore new vectors for undermining privacy, authentication and law enforcement, there will also be valid and useful attempts for mitigating the abilities of criminals, as well as the effects of cyber crime. These solutions will take form in better software, anti-spyware and anti-virus software integrated into operating systems and more user education regarding phishing and identify theft. These solutions will come primarily from software vendors themselves. On the other side, legislators will work with banks to reduce and prevent fraud, putting some of the liability with those most able to prevent it.

Finally, advanced solutions coming out of research and academia will try to inhibit the inherently anonymous and insecure nature of the Internet. With Microsoft's upcoming release of Vista, the latest version of their operating system, they'll have a new chance to focus on not only improving the general security of the system through fundamental changes, but also in providing methods for eliminating common problems, such as botnets, spyware and phishing attacks. In October of 2005, Microsoft began working together with the FTC to educate customers about botnets and the danger of allowing a computer to turn into a zombie. To deal with the problem of phishing, Microsoft released a programme in July of 2005 called the "Microsoft Phishing Filter," which aims to invalidate the ability of phishers to reach Microsoft customers by dynamically notifying them when there is a high chance that what is being viewed is a phishing attack.

Finally, Microsoft released their "AntiSpyware" programme in January of 2005, to be included with Vista as well, that automatically scans your computer for programmes that match spyware signatures or that try to perform suspicious actions, like modifying system functionality or trying to run upon computer start up. If cyber crime continues to grow to epidemic proportions, as all indications seem to point to, legislation will invariably step in, but more importantly, those with the most to lose will become more involved. This includes credit card companies, banks, lending operations and other organisations dealing with monetary transactions. Paypal.com has quickly come to dominate the online payment industry, while also serving as a bank in many capacities. With only an e-mail address and a password required to send money, this low hanging fruit has been one of the most heavily exploited realms for phishing attacks. In response, Paypal has offered at least a thousand dollars of purchase protection and a supposed one hundred percent protection against unauthorised payments sent from an account.

A fraud investigation team responds to queries and according to their web site, they have software that automatically monitors every transaction for inconsistencies. This last measure used by Paypal has also become fertile ground for credit cards companies, as their systems have become powerful at identifying fraudulent purchases though the use of neural networks, a type of software emerging out of the field of artificial intelligence. In some cases, this software has been able to reduce fraud by thirty percent or more. It's important to remember that the systems are not perfect solutions, but do address a large portion of illegal activity. Combined with other efforts, the goal is to reduce the effect of fraud, while making it more difficult to achieve.

Legislation will attempt to do its part as well, even though it has moved notoriously slowly when dealing with cyberthreats. The past few years have seen laws specifically crafted for spam and dealing with attacks that threaten the integrity of the infrastructure of the Internet. If the botnet problem continues to grow, coupled with identify theft, surely more action will be taken. Although, it is still unclear how effective it will be without a significant contribution to cyberforensic development and funding for the various governmental enforcement agencies responsible for handling cyber crime matters.

Another issue discussed in the Legal Policies section is the need for more international cooperation in locating, extraditing and prosecuting foreign criminals when possible, as the current system leaves much to be desired. Finally, as with any dangerous and difficult problem, there will be new and inventive ways to handle security issues coming out of research. One contribution that has limited, but not eliminated many common security flaws that are exploited, is the use of randomisation in dealing with code, data and other programmatic necessities.

By introducing a factor of unpredictability, it can make the work of a hacker much more difficult and prone to error, limiting the ability of those who do not posses the skill to effect a novel attack. Other interesting proposals have included trace back systems that can remove the anonymous identity of data traveling through the Internet, devising a system for fast and accurate discovery of the source of even one packet of data.

Stopping distributed denial of service attacks and worm discovery has also been proposed as a method that can be automated and integrated into the backbone of the Internet, high speed routers.

By analysing similar patterns coming from separate locations, such detectors can realise an attack while it is in its infancy and isolate infected hosts. There is also still room for ISPs to actively monitor and discourage botnets, spam and DDoS attacks from occurring.

As the first link in the chain for many zombie hosts, as well as attackers, they are in a prime position for stopping spam, either by blocking outgoing mail, which most users have no need for, or by identifying when one host is sending out a large amount of data that does not match expected behaviour.

Additionally, if they noticed that a number of hosts were acting in concert, with regards to the data being disseminated from those machines, they may assume with likelihood that they are being controlled remotely. Consequently, the ISPs can examine logs to find who is sending the commands and initiate a complaint with the F.B.I. The problem holding back this kind of proactive approach has not been technical in nature, but rather legalistic, as it can be considered an invasion of privacy. Furthermore, such methods are being used to track down minor copyright violations, instead of focusing on more substantial problems, such as cyber crime and identify theft.

Looking Ahead

The future of the Internet is still up for grabs between criminals and normal users. Fears of a cyber-apocalypse still abound, while the potential extent of damage that can be caused by wide scale fraud is nearly unbounded. These anxieties should be rationally tempered with the knowledge that the problems are being addressed, although perhaps not fast enough. The usefulness of the Internet has proved itself in numerous and myriad ways that will hopefully be enough to ensure it does not become a wasteland of criminal activity and a bastion for the malicious.

The government still has an important role to play, but most of the prevention needs to be done by commercial entities producing software and those with the ability to stop fraud. Relying on consumer education programmes will only affect a percentage of possible victims. The others need to be automatically protected through measures that do not stress and require considerable participation. Security needs to be easy and effective if it is do work. Whether cyber crime is still a pertinent issue ten years from now is unknowable in a sense, but if the Internet will continue to grow, it must be solved so that the realities of cyber crime will be proportional to real-world crimes, if not better.

2

Cyber Crimes and Legal Issues
in Technical Aspects

CYBERCRIME

"Cybercrime" is an amorphous field. It refers broadly to any criminal activity that pertains to or is committed through the use of the Internet. A wide variety of conduct fits within this capacious definition. We will concentrate in this chapter on five activities that have been especially notorious and that have strained especially seriously the fabric of traditional criminal law: use of the Internet to threaten or stalk people; online fraud; "hacking"; online distribution of child pornography; and cyberterrorism.

Threats and Stalking

Unfortunately, the Internet makes it much easier to learn about other people, track their activities, and threaten them. The following excerpt from Radosevich, *Thwarting The Stalker: Are Anti-Stalking Measures Keeping Pace with Today's Stalker?*, 2000 U. Ill. L. Rev. 1371 (2000) describes an especially serious aspect of the problem.

In the United States, recent data suggest that stalkers terrorize approximately one million women each year. Although stalking is not necessarily a gender-specific crime, seventy-five to eighty percent of stalking cases involve a male stalking a female. In addition, only a minority of stalking victims are celebrities; the majority of targets are ordinary citizens. Estimates from the early 1990s indicate ordinary citizens account for fifty-one percent of stalking targets but celebrities comprise only seventeen percent of all stalking victims; the remaining thirty-two percent of stalking victims are lesser-known entertainment figures....

As the Internet and other electronic communications technologies permeate virtually every aspect of society, electronic stalking has been increasing as well, although no detailed statistics have been developed for this phenomenon. However, both electronic harassment and stalking also seem to target women as victims. "In a 1993 survey of 500 members of Systers, an electronic mailing list for women in computer science, twenty percent of the respondents reported having been the targets of sexual harassment on-line."

The term "cyberstalking" has been coined to refer to the use of the Internet, e-mail, or other electronic communications devices to stalk another person. Because of the emerging nature of this form of stalking, the available evidence of cyberstalking is still largely anecdotal, but it suggests that the majority of cyberstalkers are men and the majority of their victims are women. As in off-line stalking, in many on-line cases, the cyberstalker and the victim had a prior relationship, and when the victim attempts to end the relationship, the cyberstalking begins.

Preliminary evidence on cyberstalking has come from incidents handled by state law-enforcement agencies. For example, the Stalking and Threat Assessment Unit of the Los Angeles District Attorney's Office has estimated that e-mail or other electronic communications were a factor in approximately twenty percent of the roughly 600 cases handled by the unit. About twenty percent of the cases handled by the Sex Crimes Unit in the Manhattan District Attorney's Office involved cyberstalking. Finally, by 1999, an estimated forty percent of the caseload in the Computer Investigations and Technology Unit of the New York City Police Department involved electronic threats or harassment, and "virtually all of these... occurred in the past three or four years."...

"Stalkers harness the tremendous power of the Web to learn about their prey and to broadcast false information about the people they target. And the Internet - the same tool they use to investigate and spread terror - provides stalkers with almost impenetrable anonymity." In cyberspace, stalking and harassment may occur via e-mail and through user participation in news groups, bulletin boards, and chat rooms. One major difference from off-line stalking is that cyberstalkers can also dupe other Internet users into harassing or threatening victims.

For example, a cyberstalker may post an inflammatory message to a bulletin board using the name, phone number, or e-mail address of the victim. Each subsequent response to the victim, whether from the actual cyberstalker or others, will have the intended effect on the victim, but the cyberstalker's effort is minimal.

The veil of anonymity offered by the Internet also puts the cyberstalker at an advantage. Internet users can conceal their true identity by using different Internet Service Providers (ISPs) and/ or by adopting different screen names.

When an individual creates an electronic mailbox through a web site on the Internet, most ISPs request some identifying information from the user, but rarely do the ISPs authenticate or confirm this information. If the services require payment, the user can typically pay in advance with a nontraceable form of payment, such as a money order. As long as payment is received in advance, the ISP has little incentive to verify any information given and will simply provide service to the account holder. Cyberstalkers can also change their screen names and use "mail servers that purposefully strip identifying information and transport headers from electronic mail." Stalkers can make the message nearly perfectly anonymous by first forwarding their mail through several of these types of servers.

Although ISPs are beginning to receive more complaints about harassing and threatening behavior on-line, they have yet to pay much attention to these types of complaints. On-line industry associations assert that providing more attentive protection to their customers (informing them as to the ISP's complaint procedures, the policies as to what constitutes prohibited harassment, and the ISP's follow-up procedures) would be costly and difficult. They argue that "no attempt to impose cyberstalking reporting or response requirements should be made unless fully justified," yet they assert that "the decentralized nature of the

Internet would make it difficult for providers to collect and submit such data."

The anonymity of the cyberstalker's threat and potential lack of direct conduct between the stalker and the victim can be particularly ominous to a cyberstalking victim, and make it more difficult for ISPs and law enforcement to identify, locate, and arrest the stalker. Also, with the knowledge that they are anonymous, cyberstalkers might be more willing to pursue their victims, using additional information easily gleaned from the Internet. Furthermore, Internet web sites provide great assistance and resources to off-line stalkers and cyberstalkers alike. Web sites can teach an individual how to stalk a woman and how to research her social security number, her home address, and her driver's license number.

A miscellaneous collection of state and federal statutes can be employed by police and prosecutors in attempting to prevent or punish behavior of these sorts. Some were adopted long before the development of the Internet; others are of more recent vintage.

18 U.S.C. § 875:

(a) Whoever transmits in interstate or foreign commerce any communication containing any demand or request for a ransom or reward for the release of any kidnapped person, shall be fined under this title or imprisoned not more than twenty years, or both.

(b) Whoever, with intent to extort from any person, firm, association, or corporation, any money or other thing of value, transmits in interstate or foreign commerce any communication containing any threat to kidnap any person or any threat to injure the person of another, shall be fined under this title or imprisoned not more than twenty years, or both.

(c) Whoever transmits in interstate or foreign commerce any communication containing any threat to kidnap any person or any threat to injure the person of another, shall be fined under this title or imprisoned not more than five years, or both.

(d) Whoever, with intent to extort from any person, firm, association, or corporation, any money or other thing of value, transmits in interstate or foreign commerce any communication containing any threat to injure the property or reputation of the addressee or of another or the reputation of a deceased person or any threat to accuse the addressee or any other person of a crime, shall be fined under this title or imprisoned not more than two years, or both.

California Penal Code § 646.9:

(a) Any person who willfully, maliciously, and repeatedly follows or harasses another person and who makes a credible threat with the intent to place that person in reasonable fear for his or her safety, or the safety of his or her immediate family, is guilty of the crime of stalking, punishable by imprisonment in a county jail for not more than one year or by a fine of not more than one thousand dollars ($1,000), or by both that fine and imprisonment, or by imprisonment in the state prison.

(e) For the purposes of this section, "harasses" means a knowing and willful course of conduct directed at a specific person that seriously alarms, annoys, torments, or terrorizes the person, and that serves no legitimate purpose. This course of conduct must be such as would cause a reasonable person to suffer substantial emotional distress, and must actually cause substantial emotional distress to the person.

(f) For purposes of this section, "course of conduct" means a pattern of conduct composed of a series of acts over a period of time, however short, evidencing a continuity of purpose. Constitutionally protected activity is not included within the meaning of "course of conduct."

(g) For the purposes of this section, "credible threat" means a verbal or written threat, including that performed through the use of an electronic communication device, or a threat implied by a pattern of conduct or a combination of verbal, written, or electronically communicated statements and conduct made with the intent to place the person that is the target of the threat in reasonable fear for his or her safety or the safety of his or her family and made with the apparent ability to carry out the threat so as to cause the person who is the target of the threat to reasonably fear for his or her safety or the safety of his or her family. It is not necessary to prove that the defendant had the intent to actually carry out the threat. The present incarceration of a person making the threat shall not be a bar to prosecution under this section.

(h) For purposes of this section, the term "electronic communication device" includes, but is not limited to, telephones, cellular phones, computers, video recorders, fax machines, or pagers.

Many messages transmitted over the Internet will clearly violate one or more of these statutes. Determining who sent the message may be difficult, but once the sender is identified, criminal liability is straightforward. A good example is provided by the case of Carl Johnson (as summarized in the U.S. Department of Justice's Computer Crime and Intellectual Property website (1999):

On June 11, 1999, Carl Edward Johnson was sentenced to 37 months of imprisonment on four felony counts of sending threatening e-mail messages via the Internet to federal judges and others. Johnson was convicted of one count of retaliating against a judicial officer, one count of obstructing justice by making a death threat against a judicial officer, and two counts of transmitting threatening communications in foreign commerce. The first three charges were based on death threats posted to the Internet naming two federal judges based in Tacoma and Seattle. The fourth charge was based on an e-mail threat sent directly to Microsoft Chairman Bill Gates.

The conviction and sentence were the culmination of a two-year investigation by U.S. Treasury agents into anonymous threats posted on the Internet and a scheme to assassinate government officials known as "Assassination Politics." As the testimony and evidence at trial showed, the assassination scheme was first promoted by James Dalton Bell, of Vancouver, Washington, who had proposed to murder government employees, had gathered a list of IRS agents' names and home addresses, had contaminated an IRS office with a noxious chemical, and had experimented with other toxic and dangerous chemicals, including nerve agents. Johnson had corresponded with Bell about Bell's "Assassination Politics" concept via Internet e-mail. After Bell's arrest, Johnson vowed in an Internet e-mail message to take "personal action" in support of Bell. On June 23, 1997, Johnson anonymously posted a message on the Internet suggesting that specific sums of money would be paid, in the form of electronic cash, for the deaths of a Federal Magistrate Judge in Tacoma, Washington, and Treasury agents involved in the Bell investigation. Additional threatening messages linked to Johnson continued to appear on the Internet in the months that followed, and Johnson set up a World Wide Web page with a partial prototype of the "Assassination Politics" scheme.

Johnson also issued a death threat to several Judges of the United States Court of Appeals for the Ninth Circuit, again through an anonymous e-mail message. The Government was able to identify Johnson as the author of the threatening messages and the Internet assassination web page through a variety of technical means. In the case of the Ninth Circuit Judges death threat, Treasury agents were able to link the unique characteristics of an encrypted digital signature on the threatening message to encryption "keys" found on Johnson's computer.

The retaliation and threatening communication counts each carried a potential maximum penalty of five years in prison. The obstruction of justice count carried a maximum penalty of 10 years in prison.

Other situations are less straightforward – whether because of jurisdictional complications, questions concerning the substantive reach of these statutes, or the tension between these statutes and the constitutional protection for freedom of speech.

CYBER LAWS AND LEGAL ISSUES

Cyberlaw is a term that encapsulates the legal issues related to use of communicative, transactional, and distributive aspects of networked information devices and technologies. It is less a distinct field of law in the way that property or contract are, as it is a domain covering many areas of law and regulation. Some leading topics include intellectual property, privacy, freedom of expression, and jurisdiction.

Jurisdiction and Sovereignty

Issues of jurisdiction and sovereignty have quickly come to the fore in the era of the Internet. The Internet does not tend to make geographical and jurisdictional boundaries clear, but Internet users remain in physical jurisdictions and are subject to laws independent of their presence on the Internet. As such, a single transaction may involve the laws of at least three jurisdictions: 1) the laws of the state/nation in which the user resides, 2) the laws of the state/nation that apply where the server hosting the transaction is located, and 3) the laws of the state/nation which apply to the person or business with whom the transaction takes place. So a user in one of the United States conducting a transaction with another user in Britain through a server in Canada could theoretically be subject to the laws of all three countries as they relate to the transaction at hand.

Jurisdiction is an aspect of state sovereignty and it refers to judicial, legislative and administrative competence. Although jurisdiction is an aspect of sovereignty, it is not coextensive with it. The laws of a nation may have extraterritorial impact extending the jurisdiction beyond the sovereign and territorial limits of that nation.

This is particularly problematic as the medium of the Internet does not explicitly recognize sovereignty and territorial limitations. There is no uniform, international jurisdictional law of universal application, and such questions are generally a matter of conflict of laws, particularly private international law. An example would be where the contents of a web site are legal in one country and illegal in another. In the absence of a uniform jurisdictional code, legal practitioners are generally left with a conflict of law issue.

Another major problem of cyberlaw lies in whether to treat the Internet as if it were physical space (and thus subject to a given jurisdiction's laws) or to act as if the Internet is a world unto itself (and therefore free of such restraints). Those who favour the latter view often feel that government should leave the Internet community to self-regulate. John Perry Barlow, for example, has addressed the governments of the world and stated, "Where there are real conflicts, where there are wrongs, we will identify them and address them by our means.

We are forming our own Social Contract. This governance will arise according to the conditions of our world, not yours.

Our world is different".· A more balanced alternative is the Declaration of Cyber secession: "Human beings possess a mind, which they are absolutely free to inhabit with no legal constraints. Human civilization is developing its own (collective) mind. All we want is to be free to inhabit it with no legal constraints. Since you make sure we cannot harm you, you have no ethical right to intrude our lives. So stop intruding!" Other scholars argue for more of a compromise between the two notions, such as Lawrence Lessig's argument that "The problem for law is to work out how the norms of the two communities are to apply given that the subject to whom they apply may be in both places at once" (Lessig, Code 190).

Though rhetorically attractive, cyber secession initiatives have had little real impact on the Internet or the laws governing it. In practical terms, a user of the Internet is subject to the laws of the state or nation within which he or she goes online.

Thus, in the U.S., Jake Baker faced criminal charges for his e-conduct, and numerous users of peer-to-peer file-sharing software were subject to civil lawsuits for copyright infringement. This system runs into conflicts, however, when these suits are international in nature. Simply put, legal conduct in one nation may be decidedly illegal in another. In fact, even different standards concerning the burden of proof in a civil case can cause jurisdictional problems. For example, an American celebrity, claiming to be insulted by an online American magazine, faces a difficult task of winning a lawsuit against that magazine for libel. But if the celebrity has ties, economic or otherwise, to England, he or she can sue for libel in the British court system, where the standard of "libelous speech" is far lower.

Net Neutrality

Another major area of interest is net neutrality, which affects the regulation of the infrastructure of the Internet. Though not obvious to most Internet users, every packet of data sent and received by every user on the Internet passes through routers and transmission infrastructure owned by a collection of private and public entities, including telecommunications companies, universities, and governments, suggesting that the Internet is not as independent as Barlow and others would like to believe. This is turning into one of the most critical aspects of cyberlaw and has immediate jurisdictional implications, as laws in force in one jurisdiction have the potential to have dramatic effects in other jurisdictions when host servers or telecommunications companies are affected.

Free Speech in Cyberspace

In comparison to traditional print-based media, the accessibility and relative anonymity of cyber space has torn down traditional barriers between an individual and his or her ability to publish.

Any person with an internet connection has the potential to reach an audience of millions with little-to-no distribution costs. Yet this new form of highly-accessible authorship in cyber space raises questions and perhaps magnifies legal complexities relating to the freedom and regulation of speech in cyberspace.

Recently, these complexities have taken many forms, three notable examples being the Jake Baker incident, in which the limits of obscene Internet postings were at issue, the controversial distribution of the DeCSS code, and Gutnick v Dow Jones, in which libel laws were considered in the context of online publishing. The last example was particularly significant because it epitomized the complexities inherent to applying one country's laws (nation-specific by definition) to the internet (international by nature). In 2003, Jonathan Zittrain considered this issue in his paper, "Be Careful What You Ask For: Reconciling a Global Internet and Local Law".

In many countries, speech through cyberspace has proven to be another means of communication which has been regulated by the government. The Open Net Initiative, whose mission statement is "to investigate and challenge state filtration and surveillance practices" in order to "...generate a credible picture of these practices," has released numerous reports documenting the filtration of internet-speech in various countries.

While China has thus far proven to be the most rigorous in its attempts to filter unwanted parts of the internet from its citizens, many other countries-including Australia, Singapore, Iran, Saudi Arabia, and Tunisia-have engaged in similar practices of internet censorship. In one of the most vivid examples of information-control, the Chinese government for a short time transparently forwarded requests to the Google search engine to its own, state-controlled search engines.

These examples of filtration bring to light many underlying questions concerning the freedom of speech, namely, does the government have a legitimate role in limiting access to information? And if so, what forms of regulation are acceptable? The recent blocking of "blogspot" and other websites in India failed to reconcile the conflicting interests of speech and expression on the one hand and legitimate government concerns on the other hand. In the UK the case of Keith-Smith v Williams confirmed that existing libel laws applied to internet discussions.

Governance

The unique structure of the Internet has raised several judicial concerns. While grounded in physical computers and other electronic devices, the Internet is independent of any geographic location. While real individuals connect to the Internet and interact with others, it is possible for them to withhold personal information and make their real identities anonymous. If there are laws that could govern the Internet, then it appears that such laws would be fundamentally different from laws that geographic nations use today.

In their essay "Law and Borders — The Rise of Law in Cyberspace", David Johnson and David Post offer a solution to the problem of Internet governance. Given the Internet's unique situation, with respect to geography and identity, Johnson and

Post believe that it becomes necessary for the Internet to govern itself.

Instead of obeying the laws of a particular country, Internet citizens will obey the laws of electronic entities like service providers. Instead of identifying as a physical person, Internet citizens will be known by their usernames or email addresses. Since the Internet defies geographical boundaries, national laws will no longer apply. Instead, an entirely new set of laws will be created to address concerns like intellectual property and individual rights. In effect, the Internet will exist as its own sovereign nation.

Even if the Internet represents a legal paradigm shift, Johnson and Post do not make clear exactly how or by whom the law of the Internet will be enforced. Instead, the authors see market mechanisms, like those that Medieval merchants used, guiding Internet citizens' actions like Adam Smith's invisible hand. Yet, as more physical locations go online, the greater the potential for physical manifestation of electronic misdeeds. What do we do when someone electronically turns off the hospital lights?

However, there is also substantial literature and commentary that the internet is not only "regulable," but is already subject to substantial regulation, both public and private, by many parties and at many different levels. Leaving aside the most obvious examples of internet filtering in nations like China or Saudi Arabia or Iran (that monitor content), there are four primary modes of regulation of the internet described by Lawrence Lessig in his book, Code and Other Laws of Cyberspace:

1. Law: Standard East Coast Code, and the most self-evident of the four modes of regulation. As the numerous statutes, evolving case law and precedents make clear, many actions on the internet are already subject to conventional legislation (both with regard to transactions conducted on the internet and images posted). Areas like gambling, child pornography, and fraud are regulated in very similar ways online as off-line. While one of the most controversial and unclear areas of evolving laws is the determination of what forum has subject matter jurisdiction over activity (economic and other) conducted on the internet,

particularly as cross border transactions affect local jurisdictions, it is certainly clear that substantial portions of internet activity are subject to traditional regulation, and that conduct that is unlawful off-line is presumptively unlawful online, and subject to similar laws and regulations. Scandals with major corporations led to US legislation rethinking corporate governance regulations such as the Sarbanes-Oxley Act.

2. Architecture: West Coast Code: these mechanisms concern the parameters of how information can and cannot be transmitted across the internet. Everything from internet filtering software (which searches for keywords or specific URLs and blocks them before they can even appear on the computer requesting them), to encryption programs, to the very basic architecture of TCP/IP protocol, falls within this category of regulation. It is arguable that all other modes of regulation either rely on, or are significantly supported by, regulation via West Coast Code.

3. Norms: As in all other modes of social interaction, conduct is regulated by social norms and conventions in significant ways. While certain activities or kinds of conduct online may not be specifically prohibited by the code architecture of the internet, or expressly prohibited by applicable law, nevertheless these activities or conduct will be invisibly regulated by the inherent standards of the community, in this case the internet "users." And just as certain patterns of conduct will cause an individual to be ostracised from our real world society, so too certain actions will be censored or self-regulated by the norms of whatever community one chooses to associate with on the internet.

4. Markets: Closely allied with regulation by virtue of social norms, markets also regulate certain patterns of conduct on the internet. While economic markets will have limited influence over non-commercial portions of the internet, the internet also creates a virtual marketplace for information, and such information affects everything from the comparative valuation of services to the traditional valuation of stocks. In addition, the increase in popularity

of the internet as a means for transacting all forms of commercial activity, and as a forum for advertisement, has brought the laws of supply and demand in cyberspace.

LEGAL POLICIES ON CYBER CRIME

In its nascent stages, cyber crime enjoyed a special legal status that belied common practice used in adjudicating crimes. Hacking was commonly perceived as a prank perpetrated by teenagers. Later, the lone, highly skilled attacker working against a high value target was mythologised and revered in some ways. The media and movie industry continued to foster the notion, so that when Kevin Mitnick was arrested in 1995, there was a relative groundswell of support for his release, despite having broken into systems, stolen millions of dollars in proprietary software, "altered information, corrupted system software, and eavesdropped on users, sometimes prevented or impeded legitimate use."

The idea that cyber crime was "different" from regular crime persisted into the dawn of the Internet age, helped along by an unwillingness among police to get involved in patrolling and investigating cyberspace. Such reluctance may have been due to lack of reference points in law, low rates of successful prosecutions and international resistance to help track cross-border crimes. The perception that cyber criminals are different entities has now been thoroughly discouraged. Indeed, "prosecutors are starting to make aggressive use of the Computer Fraud and Abuse Act, which carries penalties of up to 20 years in prison. The lengthiest sentence so far has been nine years, issued in December." There is no longer any calls to be lenient on a those who use computers to exploit, steal and abuse privileges, such as the Californian software executive who conspired to steal trade secrets from a competitor by illegally accessing network and computer systems.

The change in these commonly held notions happened gradually, but importantly, there is now a strong sense of civic empowerment given to the government to apprehend cyber criminals, which when coupled with the renewed diligence attributed to preventing terrorism, has allowed legislation to evolve rapidly in the past few years. As computers have become more integral to daily life, allowing users to conduct higher value operations, they have naturally become targets for those imbued with the criminal tendency.

Most users have recognised the threat and the need for protection, even if they ignore certain precautions, like maintaining the secrecy of passwords. If users notice that they can no longer effectively use their workstations, legislation has usually been proposed, albeit after a lengthy period of discussion. For example, a few years ago, spam was threatening to overwhelm the usefulness of e-mail. Subsequently, congress passed the CAN-SPAM Act of 2003, which made certain practices, like harvesting e-mail addresses, illegal, while imposing maximum fines of up to one million dollars.

Despite flaws that some detractors have brought up, such as continuing to allow e-mail addresses to be sold to third parties, the act has provided a legal threshold to base decisions upon and brought notoriously flagrant spammers to justice. In a broader sense, the government has reacted to the demand for better enforcement and the need to extend legal jurisdiction over crimes that may have not been crimes before. The Cyber Security Enchancement Act of 2002, which fell under the Homeland Security Act, and the USA PATRIOT Act both instituted changes to deal with cyber crime. Other, more comprehensive laws, like the Fraud and Related Activity in Connection with Computers, located in the the US Criminal Code and Unlawful Access to Store Communications have been codified for a longer period of time.

The increase in awareness of cyber criminality has begun to manifest itself with the passage of laws, creation of organisations and advisory committees and powers granted to enforcement agencies. Their application to current cyber crime has found varying degrees of success. What needs to then be examined and discussed with the aforementioned issues in mind are the crafting of laws, enforcement and effectiveness. These have to be multiplexed across national and international settings, while being interpreted within a framework of technology and trends that are rapidly evolving. Only then can a broad understanding of the legal policies surrounding cyber crime be achieved.

International Cyber Crime

A significant problem that arises when working with cyber crime is that most crimes transit data through a multititude of international borders before reaching the final, intended target. Such circuitousness has a deleterious effect on investigating cyber crimes as well as the application of laws. An illustrative example of the legal hurdles faced with international incidents comes from the "Searching and Seizing Computers and Obtaining Electronic Evidence in Criminal Investigations" manual for the United State Department of Justice. The manual reports that when seeking assistance from ISPs overseas, officers must work "with the consent of that country," which means certain formalities need to be resolved before proceeding.

First, prior permission of the foreign government must be obtained. Next, approval from the Justice Department's Office of International Affairs, and finally a clear indication that the actions would not be objectionable in the foreign country. The process is long and unwieldy, especially since, by the time the necessary paper work is filed, ISPs may have already deleted the information. Or in a worse case, after the information is obtained, it will then be discovered that the attacker went through another country, forcing the process to be repeated. Many developing countries are short on the resources and technical knowledge needed to expedite this process, causing the investigation to fail.

By 1997, the problem was being recognised internationally and the G-8 Justice and Interior Ministers noted that to be "consistent with the principles of sovereignty and the protection of human rights, nations must be able to collect and exchange information internationally, especially within the short time frame so often required when investigating international high-tech crimes." To aid this process they created a Point of Contact network which required participating countries to specify a specific group that could assist 24 hours a day, 7 days a week. By 2002, twenty countries were participating. These types of mutual legal assistance treaties (MLATs) have been effective where in the past law enforcement has been stymied.

For example, in 1992, the US government required assistance from Switzerland regarding an attack in the U.S., but since, Switzerland had no such laws regarding hacking on the books, they refused to help. In devising MLATs, a country can either create bilateral or multilateral relationships, each having its own benefits and drawbacks. Traditionally, sovereign nations have entered bilateral agreements with countries that they trust and are willing to accept each other's legal characteristics. They are quicker to negotiate, produce more detailed documents, are easier to change and allow nations to feel more comfortable sharing sensitive information. In fact, after the 2001 terrorist attacks, the US was eager to more quickly establish such ties and has concluded over 45 such agreements.

The drawbacks of course are that separate, and perhaps unequal, agreements must be reached, resulting in varying interpretations of crime and legal precedent. Multilateral pacts seem more suited to issues that are global in scale, much like cyber crime. Thus, it was with great fanfare that in November of 2001, thirty countries signed the Council of Europe's Convention on Cyber crime. The convention had been five years in the making and represents the first truly multinational attempt at defining, regulating and providing a framework for the legal issues in relation to cyber crime.

Briefly, it established conduct that is prohibited, identified required national legal processes and addressed international cooperation. At the U.S., Senate hearings on ratifying the treaty, Swartz noted "in the past, if an electronic transmission's trail led to another country, the chances were slim of successfully tracking the communication to its source or securing the evidence before deletion. With the tools provided for under the Convention, however, the ability of U.S., law enforcement to obtain international cooperation in identifying major offenders and securing evidence of their crimes so that they can be brought to justice will be significantly enhanced." Although the Senate Foreign Relations Committee approved the treaty, it has stalled in the Senate for nearly two years, as certain groups have opposed it for reasons related to civil liberties.

The current state of multinational legislation thus remains a patchwork of bilateral treaties put together piece by piece. Establishing transnational treaties is a difficult task and remains as an open policy debate. What can be agreed upon is that all nations need multilateral assistance in a global sense, not just a limited group, as cyber criminals can route through any country. Treaties, then, need to harmonise laws, while building capabilities. Most importantly, such treaties should not be used to violate human rights, even though to do so may be legal in some countries.

For example, with the current Convention on Cyber crime, China could ask the U.S., to assist in finding political dissidents and supporters of democracy and the U.S., would be obliged, under the terms of the Convention, to provide assistance. More often than not, even if a successful conviction can be obtained, extraditing a criminal is still a tough legal battle. For example, in October of 2001, a Pakistani man was charged with defacing an American-Israeli organisation's web site. The FBI, working with the U.S., Embassy in Pakistan, was able to identify the attacker and get a warrant issued for his arrest in Pakistan, yet three years later he is still at large. Clearly, there is a need for a more comprehensive international plan.

Future Trends in Legislation

The direction of legislation has slowly been proceeding to more severe and serious punishments for cyber crime. November 3 saw the first prosecution for owning and operating a botnet system. It seems probable as legislatures, federal and state, become aware of threat posed by botnets, and as methods become more advanced in discerning botcontrollers, legislation aimed at the problem will follow.

Whether it will become an effective deterrent probably rests with the ability to investigate and prosecute. Another area of concern is identity theft, a process facilitated to a large degree through the Internet. California has been the first to create legislation aimed at companies with lax security regarding the protection of personal information they may store. The California Security Breach Information Act (SB-1386), which went into effect in July of 2003, forces organisations to notify individuals if there is such a security breach.

It has been a powerful method for not only making people aware of the issue, but also applying a force for change in policy within many organisations, lest they be branded as uncaring and incompetent. With more sensitive information being stored by a greater number of third parties, more states will come to the conclusion California has and indirectly apply pressure to organisations to reform. In another example, a recent piece of county legislation in Westchester, New York proposed to make it illegal for companies storing personal information to allow insecure access to their networks. In a sense, it would criminalise using a wireless network with no security measures. Although, many have pointed out specific weaknesses in the bill, the idea has been praised as a step in the right direction and an important conduit for educating the public.

Cyber crime presents a challenging position for lawmakers, as they struggle to keep up with changes in technology and in the methods used to exploit those technologies for maliciousness. Unfortunately, legal wrangling leaves the judicial system in a state that can be behind the times. It should be realised that in the end, laws can only do so much to regulate an activity. Proactive security, user education and vigilance, combined with effective forensics and enforcement remain the best remedies for combating cyber crime. Legislation still needs to enact appropriate punishments and establish frameworks, though and in that sense it has a crucial role to play in the mitigation of cyber crime.

ILLEGAL ACCESS (HACKING)

Since the development of computer networks, their ability to connect computers and offer users access to other computer systems, computers have been used by hackers for criminal purposes. There is substantial variation in hackers' motivations. Hackers need not be present at the crime scene; they just need to circumvent the protection securing the network.

In many cases of illegal access, the security systems protecting the physical location of network hardware are more sophisticated than the security systems protecting sensitive information on networks, even in the same building. The illegal access to computer systems hinders computer operators from managing, operating and controlling their systems in an undisturbed and uninhibited manner. The aim of protection is to maintain the integrity of computer systems.

It is vital to distinguish between illegal access and subsequent offences (such as data espionage), as legal provisions have a different focus of protection. In most cases, illegal access (where law seeks to protect the integrity of the computer system itself) is not the end-goal, but rather a first step towards further crimes, such as modifying or obtaining stored data (where law seeks to protect the integrity and confidentiality of the data).

The question is whether the act of illegal access should be criminalised, in addition to subsequent offences?

Analysis of the various approaches to the criminalisation of illegal computer access at the national level shows that enacted provisions sometimes confuse illegal access with subsequent offences, or seek to limit the criminalisation of the illegal access to grave violations only.

Some countries criminalise mere access, while others limit criminalisation to offences only in cases where the accessed system is protected by security measures, or where the perpetrator has harmful intentions, or where data was obtained, modified or damaged. Other countries do not criminalise the access itself, but only subsequent offences. Opponents to the criminalisation of illegal access refer to situations where no dangers were created by mere intrusion, or where acts of "hacking" have led to the detection of loopholes and weaknesses in the security of targeted computer systems.

Convention on Cyber crime

The Convention on Cyber crime includes a provision on illegal access protecting the integrity of the computer systems by criminalising the unauthorised access to a system. Noting inconsistent approaches at the national level, the Convention offers the possibility of limitations that – at least in most cases – enable countries without legislation to retain more liberal laws on illegal access.

The Provision

- Article 2 – Illegal access: Each Party shall adopt such legislative and other measures as may be necessary to establish as criminal offences under its domestic law, when committed intentionally, the access to the whole or any part of a computer system without right. A Party may require that the offence be committed by infringing security measures, with the intent of obtaining computer data or other dishonest intent, or in relation to a computer system that is connected to another computer system.

The Covered Acts

The term "access" does not specify a certain means of communication, but is open-ended and open to further technical developments.

It shall include all means of entering another computer system, including Internet attacks, as well as illegal access to wireless networks. Even unauthorised access to computers that are not connected to any network (*e.g.*, by circumventing a password protection) are covered by the provision.

This broad approach means that illegal access not only covers future technical developments, but is also covers secret data accessed by insiders and employees. The second sentence of Article 2 offers the possibility of limiting the criminalisation of illegal access to access over a network. The illegal acts and protected systems are thus defined in a way that remains open to future developments. The Explanatory Report lists hardware, components, stored data, directories, traffic and content-related data as examples of the parts of computer systems that can be accessed.

Mental Element

Like all other offences defined by the Convention on Cyber crime Art. 2 requires that the offender is carrying out the offences intentionally. The Convention does not contain a definition of the term "internationally". In the Explanatory Report the drafters pointed out that the definition of "intentionally" should happen on a national level.

Without Right

Access to a Computer can only be prosecuted under Article 2 of the Convention, if it should happen "without right". Access to a system permitting free and open access by the public or access to a system with the authorisation of the owner or other rights-holder is not "without right".

In addition to the subject of free access, the legitimacy of security testing procedures is also addressed. Network administrators and security companies that test the protection of computer systems in order to identify potential gaps in the security measures were wary of the possibility of criminalisation under illegal access. Despite the fact that these professionals generally work with the permission of the owner and therefore act legally, the drafters of the Convention emphasised that "testing or protection of the security of a computer system authorised by the owner or operator, are with right". The fact, that the victim of the crime handed out a password or similar access code to the offender does not necessary mean that the offender then acted with right when he accessed the computer system of the victim.

If the offender persuaded the victim to disclose a password or access code due to a successful social engineering approach it is necessary to verify if the authorisation given by the victim does cover the act carried out by the offender. In general this is not the case and the offender therefore acts without right.

Restrictions and Reservations

As an alternative to the broad approach, the Convention offers the possibility of restricting criminalisation with additional elements, listed in the second sentence. The procedure of how to utilise this reservation is laid down in Article 42 of the Convention. Possible reservations relate to security measures, special intent to obtain computer data, other dishonest intent that justifies criminal culpability, or requirements that the offence be committed against a computer system through a network. A similar approach can be found in the EU Framework Decision on Attacks against Information Systems.

Commonwealth Computer and Computer Related Crimes Model Law

A similar approach can be found in Sec. 5 of the 2002 Commonwealth Model Law:

- Sec. 5.: A person who intentionally, without lawful excuse or justification, accesses the whole or any part of a computer system commits an offence punishable, on conviction, by imprisonment for a period not exceeding, or a fine not exceeding or both.

The main difference to the Convention on Cyber crime is the fact that Sec. 5 of the Commonwealth Model Law does, unlike Art. 2 Convention on Cyber crime, not contain options to make reservations.

Stanford Draft Convention

The informal 1999 Stanford Draft Convention recognises illegal access as one of those offences the signatory states should criminalise.

The Provision

- Art. 3 – Offences:
  - 1. Offenses under this Convention are committed if any person unlawfully and intentionally engages in any of the following conduct without legally recognised authority, permission, or consent:
  - (c) enters into a cyber system for which access is restricted in a conspicuous and unambiguous manner;

The Covered Acts

The draft provision shows a number of similarities to Art. 2 of the Convention on Cyber crime. Both require an intentional act that is committed without right/without authority. In this context requirement of the draft provision (*"without legally recognised authority, permission, or consent"*) is more precise than the term "without right" used Convention on Cyber crime and explicitly aims to incorporate the concept of selfdefence. The main difference to the Convention is the fact that the draft provision uses the term "cyber system".

The cyber system is defined in Art. 1, paragraph 3 of the Draft Convention. It covers any computer or network of computers used to relay, transmit, coordinate, or control communications of data or Programmes.

This definition shows many similarities to the definition of the term 'computer system" provided by Art. 1 a) Convention on Cyber crime. Although the Draft Convention refers to acts related to the exchange of data and does therefore primarily focus on network based computer systems both definitions include interconnected computer as well as stand alone machines.

TECHNICAL AND PROCEDURAL MEASURES

Cyber crime-related investigations very often have a strong technical component. In addition the requirement of maintaining the integrity of the evidence during an investigation requires precise procedures. The development of the necessary capacities as well as procedures is therefore a necessary requirement related to fight against cyber crime. Another issue is the development of technical protection systems.

Well-protected computer systems are more difficult to attack. Improving technical protection by implementing proper security standards is an important first step. For example, changes in the online banking system (*e.g.,* the switch from TAN to ITAN) have eliminated much of the danger posed by current "phishing" attacks, demonstrating the vital importance of technical solutions. Technical protection measures should include all elements of the technical infrastructure – the core network infrastructure, as well as the many individually connected computers worldwide.

Two potential target groups can be identified for protecting Internet users and businesses:

1. End users and businesses (direct approach); and
2. Service providers and software companies.

Logistically, it can be easier to focus on protection of core infrastructure (*e.g.,* backbone network, routers, essential services), rather than integrating millions of users into an Anti-Cyber crime Strategy. User protection can be achieved indirectly, by securing the services consumers use – *e.g.,* online banking. This indirect approach to protecting Internet users can reduce the number of people and institutions that need to be included in steps to promote technical protection. Although limiting the number of people that need to be included in technical protection might seem desirable, computer and Internet users are often the weakest link and the main target of criminals. It is often easier to attack private computers to obtain sensitive information, rather than the well-protected computer systems of a financial institution.

Despite these logistical problems, the protection of end-user infrastructure is vital for the technical protection of the whole network. Internet Service Providers and product vendors (e.g. software companies) play a vital role in the support of anticyber crime strategies. Due to their direct contact with clients, they can operate as a guarantor of security activities (*e.g.,* the distribution of protection tools and information on the current status of most recent scams).

Organizational Structures

An effective fight against cyber crime requires highly developed organizational structures. Without having the right structures in place that avoids overlapping and is based on clear competences it will hardly be possible to carry out complex investigations that require the assistance of different legal as well as technical experts.

Capacity Building and User Education

Cyber crime is a global phenomenon. In order to be able to effectively investigate offences harmonisation of laws and the development of means of international cooperation needs to be established. In order to ensure global standards in developed countries as well as in developing countries capacity building is necessary.

In addition to capacity building user education is required. Certain cyber crimes – especially those related to fraud, such as "phishing" and "spoofing" – do not generally depend on a lack of technical protection, but rather lack of awareness by victims. There are various software products that can automatically identify fraudulent websites, but until now, these products cannot identify all suspicious websites. A user protection strategy based only on software products has limited ability to protect the users. Although the technical protection measures continue to develop and the products available are updated on a regular basis, such products cannot yet substitute for other approaches. One of the most important elements in the prevention of cyber crime is user education. For example, if users are aware that their financial institutions will never contact them by e-mail requesting passwords or bank account details, they cannot fall victim to phishing or identity fraud attacks. The education of Internet users reduces the number of potential targets.

Users can be educated through:

• Public campaigns;
• Lessons in schools, libraries, IT centres and universities;
• Public Private Partnerships (PPPs).

One important requirement of an efficient education and information strategy is the open communication of the latest cyber crime threats. Some states and/or private businesses refuse to emphasize that citizens and clients respectively are affected by cyber crime threats, in order to avoid them losing trust in online communication services. The United States Federal Bureau of Investigation has explicitly asked companies to overcome their aversion to negative publicity and report cyber crime. In order to determine threat levels, as well as to inform users, it is vital to improve the collection and publication of relevant information.

International Cooperation

In a large number of cases data transfer processes in the Internet affect more than one country. This is a result of the design of the network as well as the fact the protocols that ensures that successful transmissions can be made, even if direct lines are temporarily blocked. In addition a large number of Internet services (like for example hosting services) are offered by companies that are based abroad.

In those cases where the offender is not based in the same country at the victim, the investigation requires cooperation between law enforcement agencies in all countries that affected. International and transnational investigations without the consent of the competent authorities in the countries involved are difficult with regards to the principle of National Sovereignty.

This principle does in general not allow one country to carry out investigations within the territory of another country without the permission of the local authorities.

Therefore, investigations need to be carried out with the support of the authorities in all countries involved. With regard to the fact that in most cases there is only a very short time gap available in which successful investigations can take place, the application of the classic mutual legal assistance regimes involves clear difficulties when it comes to cyber crime investigations.

This is due to the fact that mutual legal assistance in general requires time consuming formal procedures. As a result improvement in terms of enhanced international cooperation plays an important and critical role in the development and implementation of cyber security strategies and anti-cyber crime strategies.

LEGAL CHALLENGES

Challenges in Drafting National Criminal Laws

Proper legislation is the foundation for the investigation and prosecution of cyber crime. However, law-makers must continuously respond to Internet developments and monitor the effectiveness of existing provisions, especially given the speed of developments in network technology.

Historically, the introduction of computer-related services or Internet-related technologies gave rise to new forms of crime, soon after the technology was introduced. One example is the development of computer networks in the 1970s – the first unauthorised access to computer networks occurred shortly afterwards.

Similarly, the first software offences appeared soon after the introduction of personal computers in the 1980s, when these systems were used to copy software products.

It takes time to update national criminal law to prosecute new forms of online cyber crime – some countries have not yet finished with this adjustment process. Offences that have been criminalised under national criminal law need to be reviewed and updated – for example, digital information must have equivalent status as traditional signatures and printouts.

Without the integration of cyber crime-related offences, violations cannot be prosecuted. The main challenge for national criminal legal systems is the delay between the recognition of potential abuses of new technologies and necessary amendments to the national criminal law. This challenge remains as relevant and topical as ever as the speed of network innovation accelerates. Many countries are working hard to catch up with legislative adjustments.

In general, the adjustment process has three steps: Adjustments to national law must start with the recognition of an abuse of new technology.

Specific departments are needed within national law enforcement agencies, which are qualified to investigate potential cyber crimes. The development of computer emergency response teams (CERTs), computer incident response teams (CIRTs), computer security incident response teams (CSIRTs) and other research facilities have improved the situation.

The second step is the identification of gaps in the penal code. To ensure effective legislative foundations, it is necessary to compare the status of criminal legal provisions in the national law with requirements arising from the new kinds of criminal offences.

In many cases, existing laws may be able to cover new varieties of existing crimes (*e.g.,* laws addressing forgery may just as easily be applies to electronic documents). The need for legislative amendments is limited to those offences that are omitted or insufficiently covered by the national law. The third step is the drafting of new legislation.

Based on experience, it may be difficult for national authorities to execute the drafting process for cyber crime without international cooperation, due to the rapid development of network technologies and their complex structures.

Drafting cyber crime legislation separately may result in significant duplication and waste of resources and it is also necessary to monitor the development of international standards and strategies.

Without the international harmonisation of national criminal legal provisions, the fight against trans-national cyber crime will run into serious difficulties due to inconsistent or incompatible national legislations. Consequently, international attempts to harmonise different national penal laws are increasingly important. National law can greatly benefit from the experience of other countries and international expert legal advice.

New Offences

In most cases, crimes committed using ICTs are not new crimes, but scams modified to be committed online. One example is fraud – there is not much difference between someone sending a letter with the intention to mislead another person and an e-mail with the same intention. If fraud is already a criminal offence, adjustment of national law may not be necessary to prosecute such acts. The situation is different, if the acts performed are no longer addressed by existing laws.

In the past, some countries had adequate provisions for regular fraud, but were unable to deal with offences where a computer system was influenced, rather than a human. For these countries, it has been necessary to adopt new laws criminalising computer-related fraud, in addition to the regular fraud. Various examples show how the extensive interpretation of existing provisions cannot substitute for the adoption of new laws.

Apart from adjustment for well-known scams, law-makers must continuously analyse new and developing types of cyber crime to ensure their effective criminalisation. One example of a cyber crime that has not yet been criminalised in all countries is theft and fraud in computer and online games.

For a long time, discussions about online games focused on youth protection issues (*e.g.*, the requirement for verification of age) and illegal content (*e.g.*, access to child pornography in the Online game "Second Life"). New criminal activities are constantly being discovered – virtual currencies in online games may be "stolen" and traded in auction platforms. Some virtual currencies have a value in terms of real currency (based on an exchange rate), giving the crime a 'real' dimension. Such offences may not be prosecutable in all countries. In order to prevent safe havens for offenders, it is vital to monitor developments worldwide.

Increasing Use of ICTs and the Need for New Investigative Instruments

Offenders use ICTs in various ways in the preparation and execution of their offences. Law enforcement agencies need adequate instruments to investigate potential criminal acts. Some instruments (such as data retention) could interfere with the rights of innocent Internet users. If the severity of the criminal offence is out of proportion with the intensity of interference, the use of investigative instruments could be unjustified or unlawful. As a result, some instruments that could improve investigation have not yet been introduced in a number of countries. The introduction of investigative instruments is always the result of a trade-off between the advantages for law enforcement agencies and interference with the rights of innocent Internet users. It is essential to monitor ongoing criminal activities to evaluate whether threat levels change. Often, the introduction of new instruments has been justified on the basis of the "fight against terrorism", but this is more of an far-reaching motivation, rather than a specific justification *per se*.

Developing Procedures for Digital Evidence

Especially due the low costs compared to the storage of physical documents, the number of digital documents is increasing. The digitalisation and emerging use of ICT has a great impact of procedures related to the collection of evidence and its use in court. As a consequence of the development digital evidence was introduced as a new source of evidence.

It is defined as any data stored or transmitted using computer technology that supports the theory of how an offence occurred. Handling digital evidence is accompanied with unique challenges and requires specific procedures. One of the most difficult aspects is to maintain the integrity of the digital evidence.

Digital data is highly fragile and can easily be deleted or modified. This is especially relevant for information stored in the system memory RAM that is automatically deleted when the system is shut down and therefore requires special preservation techniques.

In addition, new developments can have great impact on dealing with digital evidence. An example is cloud-computing. In the past investigators were able to focus on the suspects premise while searching for computer data. Today they need to take into consideration that digital information might be stored abroad and can only be accessed remotely, if necessary. Digital evidence plays an important role in various phases of cyber crime investigations.

It is in general possible to separate between four phases:
1. Identification of the relevant evidence;
2. Collection and preservation of the evidence;
3. Analysis of computer technology and digital evidence; and,
4. Presentation of the evidence in court.

In addition to the procedures that relate to the presentation of digital evidence in court, the ways in which digital evidence is collected requires special attention.

The collection of digital evidence is linked to computer forensics. The term 'computer forensics' describes the systematic analysis of IT equipment with the purpose of searching for digital evidence.

With regard to the fact that the amount of data stored in digital format constantly increases, highlights the logistic challenges of such investigations. Approaches to automated forensic procedures by, for example, using hash-value based searches for known child pornography images or a keyword search therefore play an important role in addition to manual investigations.

Depending on the requirement of the specific investigation, computer forensics could for example include the following:

- Analysing the hardware and software used by a suspect;
- Supporting investigators in identifying relevant evidence;
- Recovering deleted files;
- Decrypting files; and,
- Identifying Internet users by analysing traffic data.

3

Cyber Crimes and Its Law

CYBER LAWS

Cyber law is a term that encapsulates the legal issues related to use of communicative transactional, and distributive aspects of networked information devices and technologies.

It is the law governing cyber space. Cyber space is a very wide term and includes computers, networks, software, data storage devices (such as hard disks, USB disks etc.), the Internet, websites, emails and even electronic devices such as cell phones, ATM machines etc.

The Information Technology (IT) Act, 2000, specifies the acts which have been made punishable. Since the primary objective of this Act is to create an enabling environment for commercial use of I.T., certain omissions and commissions of criminals while using computers have not been included.

With the legal recognition of Electronic Records and the amendments made in the several sections of the IPC vide the IT Act, 2000, several offences having bearing on cyber-arena are also registered under the appropriate sections of the IPC.

DEVELOPING CYBER LAW

The main feature of an application that would ideally realise the above principles and successfully implement them online would be the direct incorporation of law in the network's software protocol mechanisms. An example could be the TCP/IP set of protocols for Internet communications, which are structured on mathematical logic and patterns chosen for their technical adequacy. However, the latter are not immutable, and new, different models of communication protocols have been proposed and are currently under development.

Two different elements will contribute to achieving the aspired goals. The first is the careful selection of legal rules that will regulate appropriately online environments. The second is the effective, accurate transfer of legal methodology into computer language.

Restructuring the virtual Space

Before going through these successive steps, it is crucial to define, in advance, the regulated area's dimensions, as successful application of law is indissolubly bound up with both the natural and social parameters of a given and potentially regulated space. The community is, therefore, assumed to operate on a shared online platform, open in membership, though closed in access (meaning, active via typing allocated passwords), and in general performing similarly to a typical Web browser. This then allows e-mail communications and stereotypical data exchange, graphical on-screen representation of websites and an additional set of assisting applications and accessory tools.

Additionally, it is important to identify entities that represent subjects and objects within this electronic world. The online social structure, as a real-world metaphor, includes active participants and static objects in analogously operating digitised projections. Both users and their autonomous software, which may execute a variety of prearranged tasks on the formers' behalf, are defined as "actors". According to typical online functionalism, documents, pictures, sounds, programmes and contiguous exchangeable information are classified as "movable objects", while IP addresses, including single web-sites and hosted secondary platforms, constitute a class of "immovable objects".

Codification

Common use of the word "codification" originally captured the lexical confusion between a certain method for legislating and the graphic expression of written law, leading today to a dual-conception of both the method of codification and the instrument of code.

In the legal world, codification serves a number of substantial needs, offering:

- Accessibility,
- Completeness and cohesion in representation,
- Consistency and
- Certainty.

However, in developing a networking protocol that will articulate legal norms through automated transmissions, "Codification" means actually "encoding" into computer language the existing legal norms, changing them from passive text into an active, automated regulatory framework. In other words, it means cutting the text of law into pieces and reinstating it in the form of processible code.

Objectives and Method of Implementation

Codification requires the development of a translatable legal logic that preserves law's desired regulatory impact on social behaviour and interaction. As these pre-set rules reflect the distinctive character of the electronic reality and, at the same time, direct its operation, codification's objectives may be summarised as follows:

- "Scalable" clarity, thus requiring a complete and comprehensive regulatory framework that maximises internal compatibility between the variety of inducted legal themes,
- Open provisional structure for assimilating future file formats and models of data distribution,
- Precise representation of real-world legal knowledge, in processible, mathematically arranged logical sequences, and
- Creation of a uniquely identifiable and well ordered interactive setting, capable of preventing online participants' evasive behaviour while exercising their exchange practices.

The first two objectives are realised through the first step of the codification procedures, and define the selection of law that will eventually run through the online community. As online activities substantially remodel real-world patterns of contact and association, the claim is made here that the required framework, from which the most suitable legal rules will be extracted, already exists in the form of statute law. Continental codifications carry the advantage of exhibiting ordered text-layout in concise logical sequences, which can easily be transcribed in computer language patterns as shown previously with the "obligations" example. Moreover, they bring to the point common universal "abstract rules and principles which apply to all of the specific circumstances."

A scheme for efficiently running online environments would incorporate the core protocol of these codifications. At the same time, however, it would allow the online community to evolve through more relaxed common law practices that take place within the platform's software sequences.

While the platform's legal evolution will be implemented through online interactivity, with the extended use of autonomous agents, the computer code will progressively integrate precedents with the potential for altering the community's "legal" standards. This issue will be explained and addressed briefly in the last part of the paper.

The third of the above objectives reflects the second step of the codification procedure.

In short, it includes formation of a legal ontology, assessed by evaluating the induced concepts along with the individual objects and variables that they prescribe (persons, items, quantitative elements etc.) Following the analysis and adaptation of legal concepts to the community's standards, a finite number of common key notions are revealed to the protocol's designers/creators. These key notions are essentially determined by the frequency and functionality of the used terminology. Therefore, simple or complex terms consisting of different sub-notions are easily marked down to complete a legal ontology that will eventually be transcribed as computer code.

An idea of what this ontology would look like can be gained through the previous Boolean rephrasing of "obligation". "Obligation" shares certain aspects with concepts like "contract" or "ownership". Moreover, variables like "item" (varying in the electronic environment from audio files to executable programmes) or "creditor" (emerging from an e-commerce agreement as the seller or the buyer), frequently appear in everyday online communications. A concept itself may include another concept, or may also use shared legal terminology.

While determining the applied law's structure involves mainly assistance from legal experts, the second step requires additional technological support, A.I. expertise in the field of ontological modelling and the relevant computer programming skills. Practically, this is the part of the procedure where the law becomes essentially encoded.

CYBER CRIME LAW IN INDIA

The general laws in India were drafted and enacted in the 19th century. Whilst each of the general laws have undergone modifications and amendments, the broad and underlying provisions have withstood the test of time, including unimaginable advancements in technology, which speaks to the dynamism of the General laws. The general laws referred to in this Article are the Indian Penal Code, 1860 ("IPC"), which is the general penal law of India and the Indian Evidence Act, 1872 ("Evidence Act"), the general law pertaining to admissibility of evidence in civil and criminal trials. The manner in which trial of criminal cases are to be conducted is dealt with under the Criminal Procedure Code, 1973 ("Cr. P. C"). India got its first codified Act in the Information Technology Act, 2000 ("IT Act), which fell far short of the Industry's requirements to meet global standards. The focus if the IT Act was however recognition of electronic records and facilitation of e - commerce. Barely ten sections were incorporated in the IT Act to deal with Cyber Crime. At the time when the IT Act was passed several acts deemed to be illegal in most jurisdictions including virus attacks, data theft, illegal access to data/ accessing and removal of data without the consent of the owner, etc., were listed as civil penalties under the IT Act. The IT Industry continued to rely on self –regulation and contractual undertakings to appease its global clients, as it had done before the passing of the IT Act.

The primary offences under the IT Act were:

- Tampering with source code;
- Deleting, destroying or altering any data on any computer resource with mala fide intent to cause wrongful loss or to diminish its value;
- Publishing or transmitting pornographic material through a computer resource;
- Provisions pertaining to encryption technology, the right of the Government authorities to intercept and decrypt such data and to call upon any entity or individual to decrypt such data were also included in the IT Act. Certain acts affecting the integrity and sovereignty of the nation were classified as offences.

The saving grace of the IT Act were the amendments carried out to the IPC and Evidence Act, which to some extent provided for prosecution of rampant offences like the Nigerian Scams, Phishing and other Banking frauds may be prosecuted. Cyber Crime prosecution was however not resorted to in many instances due to lack of awareness (amongst both the victims and the enforcement authorities) about the applicability of such general Laws to cyber crimes (like Phishing). To add to this, administrative delegation of powers treated offences under the IT Act differently to those falling under general laws! Further, crimes like data theft; illegally accessing/ removal of data; virus attacks etc., could not be prosecuted due to the lack of relevant penal provisions.

S.66 of the Act misleadingly titled "hacking" is one of the most misused and abused provisions in India. Recently *i.e.,* in September 2009, the Delhi High Court has quashed the criminal proceedings initiated in or about July 2005, under S.66 of the IT Act by M/s. Parsec Technologies Ltd., against some of its former employees, who left and started their own Company, holding that the continuation of the proceedings would amount to abuse of process of law.

Likewise the IT Act did not provide sufficient recourse for women and child victims of cyber crimes like Cyber Stalking and paedophilia. Controversy has dogged the IT Act from its inception. The Ministry of Information Technology prepared and posted proposed draft amendments to the IT Act in 2005.

In 2006, the IT Bill with substantial changes brought about as a result of the objections to the proposed amendments of 2005 was tabled before the Parliament.

In December 2008 as a knee–jerk reaction to the November 2008 terror attacks in Mumbai, India, the Information Technology (Amendments) Act, 2008 ("ITA, 2008") was hastily tabled before the Parliament and was passed hastily and without any debate whatsoever. Unlike the IT Act of 2000, the focus of the new ITA 2008 is clearly on Cyber Terrorism and to a significant extent, Cyber Crime. This paper deals with some important provisions of ITA, 2008 relating to data protection, privacy, encryption and cyber crime and to what extent it arms one against emerging trends in Cyber Crime.

Definitions

The replacement of the word "Digital" with the word "Electronic", which makes the IT Act more technology neutral and expands its applicability beyond just the digital medium.

- Inclusion of cell phones, personal digital assistants and other such devices in the definition of "Communication Devices" broadens the scope of the statute.
- The modified definition of "Intermediary" includes all service providers in respect of electronic records again broadens the applicability while inclusion of Cyber cafes in the definition of Intermediaries removes the need to interpret the statute.

The extensive definition of "cyber security" as including protection of both data and the equipment from unauthorised access, use, disclosure etc., is another vital inclusion that impacts the new Data Protection provisions included under the ITA, 2008. The relevance of these definitions, where applicable are set out below.

Data Protection

The IT industry has been lobbying for a law to protect Data and the new legislation has addressed the industry's demands to a certain extent particularly since Mphasis Limited, a Pune based Company suffered the notoriety of puncturing the Indian BPO fairy tale in April 2004, when some of its employees stole confidential credit card information of clients and used it to siphon substantial amounts. Apart from highlighting the security lapses within the Company, this case also brought to the limelight the lack of suitable Data Protection Laws in India. Several cases have now been reported where former employees are accused of data theft and misuse of Confidential and proprietary Information and data. In one instance, a BPO Company purportedly closed down due to rampant data theft.

The Indian Legislature's response to the hue and cry raised is the transposition of certain civil penalties into criminal offences and the addition of one section under civil penalties as set out hereunder:

- The only provision under the IT Act for data protection was S.43, which only imposed Civil Penalties in the event of the commission of certain acts without the permission of the owner or person in charge of the computer or computer systems such as:
  - Securing access (without permission);
  - Downloading or copying of data stored in a computer or computer system;
  - Introducing computer viruses;
  - Damaging computers and or data stored therein;
  - Disrupting computers;
  - Denial of access;
  - Abetting such acts; or
  - Illegal charging for services on another's account.

S.43A has now been added under the ITA 2008 to address the data protection requirements of the Industry. S.43A stipulates that any "Body Corporate" possessing, dealing with or handling any "sensitive personal data or information" in a computer resource it owns, controls or operates, is liable for negligence, if it fails to maintain "reasonable security practices and procedures" and thereby causes wrongful loss or wrongful gain to any person. What amounts to reasonable security practices and procedures remains to be finalised by the Central Government.

Apart from the above addition under Civil Penalties, the Civil wrongs set out under S.43 of the IT Act have now been qualified as criminal offences under the ITA 2008 under S. 66. A reverse transposition has further been carried out under the ITA 2008 of two criminal provisions from the IT Act (S.66 and S.65) as civil penalties under S.43 (i) & S.43 (j), respectively. Any act set out under S.43, if committed "dishonestly or fraudulently", would amount to a criminal offence, punishable with punishment of up to three years or fine of a maximum of Rupees Five Lakhs or both, under the ITA 2008.

Though S.66 of the IT Act has purportedly been deleted, the addition of S.43 (i) under the ITA 2008 has in effect resulted in the retention of the contentious S.66 of the IT Act. However retention of S.65 of the IT Act without any modification despite its transposition into S.43 appears to be a tautology, which could be due to oversight. S.66B inserted by the ITA, 2008 is on the lines of similar provisions in the Indian Penal Code ("IPC"), which provides for punishment of the receiver of stolen property. S.66B makes the receipt or retention of a stolen computer resource or communication device punishable with imprisonment up to three years or with fine up to Rupees One Lakh or both.

Whilst S.66B may seem to also apply to hardware, which is also covered under the IPC, the term "computer resource" is defined under the IT Act as a "Computer, computer system, computer network, data, computer database or software." The extension of the above provision to the receiver of stolen data, software etc., may prove to be substantially useful when faced with issues of Corporate Espionage.

Further Analysis of the Data Protection Legislation

Although the data protection provisions introduced by the ITA, 2008 may not comprehensively address the industry specific requirements applicable to data providers and handlers;

nevertheless this is an important head start towards introduction of specific data protection legislation in India, which is absolutely essential in today's business environment. One of the important outcomes of the ITA, 2008 amendments is the clarity on whether Data theft is considered a criminal offence. Commission of acts provided in S.43 to 66 dishonestly or fraudulently, clearly implies "Data Theft" as an offence in such instances.

However these acts would amount to a punishable offence only if such data is "downloaded, copied or extracted" from a computer resource. Therefore it may be argued that the provisions of S.43 (b) are not inclusive, as they do not provide for removal of data through uploading. Criminal provisions give rise to liability only in cases of unambiguity.

If a provision has to be applied through interpretation, then such interpretation, which favours the Accused, would have to be applied. With the addition of S.43A by the ITA, 2008, the onus of implementing "Reasonable Security Practices" is on the business entity. Whilst this may be a known liability that parties agree upon, unsuspecting companies or firms may get mulcted with liability if duties and obligations are not specified, as the Central Government guidelines will then become applicable. As of now, violations under S.43 A are however not criminal offences.

Confidentiality and Privacy

India was shocked out of its complacent conservatism due to the widespread circulation of a MMS clip shot by a Delhi schoolboy. This case took an unexpected twist when this clip was circulated on Bazee.com and its Chief Executive Officer of American origin was arrested. S.66E has now been introduced under the ITA, 2008 for the protection of physical or personal privacy of an individual.

This section makes intentional capturing of the images of a person's private parts without his or her consent in any medium and publishing or transmitting such images through electronic medium, a violation of such person's privacy punishable with imprisonment of up to three years or with fine up to Rupees Two Lakhs, or both. A case of posting of the personal information and obscene material on a Yahoo! Site was touted as the fastest trial and conviction of a cyber crime case in Chennai. It appears that this conviction has recently been reversed.

S.72 A of the ITA, 2008 now explicitly provides recourse against dissemination of personal information obtained without the individual's consent through an intermediary or under a services contract, with intent to cause wrongful loss or wrongful gain. The maximum punishment prescribed for this offence is three years imprisonment, or fine up to Rupees Five Lakhs or both. Service providers on the Internet, social networking sites, Companies, firms, individuals and other intermediaries ought to now be careful in the collection, retention and dissemination of personal data. Interactive websites and P2P site operators also have to be extremely careful to ensure that the provisions of S.66E and S.72 A are not violated.

Other Cyber Crimes Including Cyber Terrorism

Provisions to combat cyber frauds have now been introduced under the ITA 2008. However certain issues relating to protection against banking frauds such as Phishing, money transfers through online hacking, e-mail frauds and cyber squatting (including through wilfully misleading domain names) to name a few have not been addressed separately in the ITA, 2008, even though these are significantly increasing problems.

S.66C inserted by the ITA, 2008 makes dishonest or fraudulent use of a person's electronic signature or identity, password or any other unique identification feature punishable as theft with imprisonment of up to three years and fine up to Rupees One Lakh.

S.66D inserted by the ITA, 2008 makes cheating by personating through a computer resource punishable with imprisonment of up to three years and fine up to One Lakh Rupees. It may be noted that S.419 of IPC already provides for punishment for cheating by personating but does not provide for the maximum fine imposable. In addition to S.67 of the IT Act, S.67A and S.67B have been included by the ITA, 2008 *inter alia* to combat child pornography. S.67A makes transmission of a sexually explicit act or conduct punishable and S.67B makes publishing and transmission of child pornography an offence, punishments for which range from five to seven years and fine.

Several exceptions have also been set out to S.67 and S.67A, including for depictions in any book, pamphlet, paper, writing, drawing, painting representation or figure in electronic form. Further, S.67C introduced by the ITA, 2008 imposes liability on Intermediaries for retention and production of information. However the duration, manner and formats of retention of such information are still subject to prescription by the Central Government. This section appears to be directed mainly against Cyber Cafes and has already been subject to dissension. Failure to comply with such requirements is punishable with imprisonment up to three years and also fine.

Observations on the Cyber Crime Provisions under the ITA, 2008

- S.43 was included in the IT Act, 2000 to address certain kinds of illegal acts. However, the Legislature has not looked beyond S.43 to address recent trends in Cyber Crimes and for dealing with such issues.
- S.66 of the IT Act, under the heading "Hacking" which was misleading was criticised for its ambiguity and for the possibility of abuse. However, whilst the proposed amendments sought for its deletion, this section has been transposed to not only being applicable as a civil penalty but is also retained as a criminal offence. With the retention of S.66 of the IT Act, one of the main issues that need to be addressed is the criminality of actions resulting in "diminishing of value" of any information residing in a computer resource. Even if the law – makers thought fit to retain this provision, its use and abuse Since, 2000 ought to have been evaluated when re-defining this provision.
- S.66C only addresses some kinds of cyber frauds and not all such frauds committed without using digital or electronic signatures. Further S.66D may be considered redundant in the light of the amendments made to the IPC after the enactment of the IT Act in 2000, save and except

for the maximum fine imposable under the ITA, 2008.

- S.67A is a much – needed introduction to the IT Act and would help in combating the pernicious offences of child pornography as observed in some recent shocking incidents involving school children. Several new provisions have been introduced under the ITA 2008 to combat Cyber Terrorism. These provisions appear to be a necessary and welcome addition though there are apprehensions about their abuse and whether the Government authorities are well equipped to handle and protect the information, acquired by it in compliance with such provisions.

- S.66A inserted by the ITA, 2008 is an essential provision from the perspective of combating Cyber Terrorism and to address several instances of cyber stalking, cyber harassment, etc. However this provision can also be easily abused. S.66A provides for punishment of three years and fine against any person found guilty of: (i) sending information through a computer resource or devise, which is grossly offensive or of menacing character; (ii) false information intended to annoy, inconvenience, deceive or mislead the addressee or recipient about the origin of such message; or (iii) endanger, obstruct, insult, injure, intimidate or to cause enmity, hatred or ill will. This would not only help the police against anonymous and false messages etc., and harassed individuals, but also corporate bodies, which could rework their internal policies in consonance with this provision.

- S.66F directly addresses the issue of cyber terrorism. Acts intended to: (i) threaten the unity, integrity, security or sovereignty of India; (ii) to strike terror in the people or any section of the people by denial of access, hacking and virus attacks; and (iii) by such means does or may cause death or injuries to persons or damage to property or disrupts supplies or services essential to the life of the community; or (iv) adversely affects the critical information infrastructure; is the commission of Cyber Terrorism, the punishment for which ranges from imprisonment from three years to life and fine depending upon the seriousness of the crime.

CUSTOMARY LAW IN CYBERSPACE

As they implemented the mediation program they instituted for eBay, Katsh, et al. (2000: 728) report discovering that: "As we encountered disputants and observed them as they participated in our process, we began to see eBay not from eBay's perspective, which assumes that eBay is the equivalent of a landlord with little power over how a transaction is finalized, but form the user's perspective. The more we saw of this, the more we became persuaded that disputants were, indeed, participating as if they wee 'in the shadow of the law.' The law whose shadow was affecting them, however, was eBay's law rather than the shadow of any other law." That is, eBay is not just a marketing arrangement. It also is a legal jurisdiction. Parties agreed to participate in mediation "at a very high rate" because of eBay law. Their primary concern was in maintaining their eBay reputations. As Katsh, et al. (2000: 729) explain,

Ebay's response to this public safety problem was not to install a police force to deal with problems after they occurred but to use an information process to try to prevent disputes from occurring. Since the public safety problem largely focused on unknown and perhaps untrustworthy sellers and buyers, eBay put in place a process for sellers and buyers to acquire reputations as trustworthy parties.... Protecting one's feedback rating looms large in any eBay user's mind. As one guidebook to eBay points out, "on eBay, all you have is your reputation."

.... While online auctions try to limit potential liability by creating distance between the auction site and those doing business in the auction site, the site owners are the designers and administrators of the process of creating identities and establishing reputations. This is a formidable power and, while it might appear that the auction site owners are merely making a process available and then letting users employ it, there are terms and conditions governing these data collection and data distribution processes, and these rules are made and administered by eBay and other proprietors of auction sites. Ebay's rules are not simply created at the arbitrary prerogative of eBay management, of course.

Many of the rules develop as a consequence of interactions with users. Recall the response to customer complaints about fraud by sellers in travel auctions, for instance. As a result of these complaints, a new rule was introduced that required all sellers of travel services to register with SquareTrade, the privately owned seller-verification company. Even the dispute resolution process was experimental, intended to see how eBay users reacted to its availability. If users find the arrangement to be unattractive, it will not last in its initial form. Indeed, Ebay law is not, and cannot be, imposed through coercion. After all, there are many other auction service providers that eBay customers could choose. As Post (1996: 167) notes, "Mobility - our ability to move unhindered into and out of these individual networks with their distinct rule-sets - is a powerful guarantee that the resulting distribution of rules is a just one." Ebay dominates the market because its rules and procedures produce a legal environment that is conducive to trust building and voluntary exchange.

Polycentric Cyber Governance

Ebay law, or more generally the alternative legal arrangements of auction sites, is far from unique in cyberspace. As Gibbons, et al. (2002: 41) note, "many traditional businesses have learned that existing institutions such as contract law (private law making) and its corollary alternative non-judicial dispute resolution (private adjudication or ADR) may be used in new and creative ways. Both traditional and ebusiness synergistically couple the efficiency and flexibility of private law and private adjudication with the technological and communicative nature of cyberspace, achieving, in many instances, an economically optimal result." But the same is true of non-commercial groups. The fact is that numerous "online legal cultures containing what might be considered to be legal doctrine and legal processes already are emerging in many online 'places'".

When AOL decides to filter e-mail in order to reject mail arriving from a blacklisted address it has promulgated a rule about spam. Subscribers who believe it is a good rule remain in the AOL community, subject to AOL law, while those who believe it is a bad rule, perhaps because it infringes on the spammer's freedom of speech, or the right of individuals to receive the spammer's advertising, are free to leave the community and enter another ISP's jurisdiction. If AOL survives in this market with this rule, the implication is that its subscribers prefer the rule (or more accurately, the set of rules that characterize AOL law) over alternatives. As Post (1996: 169) suggests, in cyberspace, users are free to "vote with their electrons." Furthermore, "Cyberspace is not a homogeneous place; groups and activities found at various on-line locations possess their own unique characteristics and distinctions, and each area will likely develop its own set of distinct rules".

Cyberspace has many boundaries, even though they do not correspond to the political boundaries of geographic space. These boundaries can slow or block the flow of information.

As Johnson and Post (1996: 1395) note, these boundaries are marked by distinct names and addresses, required passwords, entry fees, and various visual cues created by software that distinguish one part of cyberspace from another: "The Usenet newsgroup 'alt.religion.scientology' is distinct from alt.misc.legal,' each of which is distinct from a chat room on Compuserve or America Online which, in turn, are distinct from the Cyberspace Law Institute listverver or Counsel Connect.

Users can only access these different forums through distinct addresses ..., often navigating through login screens, the use of passwords, or the payment of fees." The existence of such borders separating very different kinds of activities allow different internet communities to develop their own distinct sets of rules, and allow those rules to evolve over time. Indeed, rules can change very quickly as online communication and information flows are so rapid. On-line firms and membership clubs can control participation and even prevent outsiders from learning about their activities. The behavior that may be acceptable in one cyber community need not be tolerated in another community. Rules about who can enter and under what conditions they can copy or redistribute data, can be established and enforced. Violators can be excluded. Indeed, while many of these boundaries can be breached by some hackers, "Securing online systems from unauthorized intruders may prove an easier task than sealing physical borders from unwanted immigration [or smuggling]". Cyber law clearly is polycentric law.

A great deal of internet activity crosses cyber boundaries, of course. E-mail goes for a sender in one ISP to an in box that is served by another ISP. Web searches take individuals all over cyberspace. Individuals download information from distant locations, enter eBay to trade and then leave, perhaps to go to a listserver or a chat room, and so on. The ease with which individuals can move from one jurisdiction to another has important implications. For one thing, individuals can be members of many of the different customary law communities, as long as they behave according to the rules of each community.

For another, "In Cyberspace, ... any given user has more accessible exit option, in terns of moving form one virtual environment's rule set to another's, thus providing a more legitimate 'selection mechanism' by which differing rule sets will evolve over time". Individuals can compare the rules offered by different communities and choose those that best meet their preferences. Competition between different firms and organizations providing similar services will either lead to similar rules if consumers all have similar preferences, or to different rules to accommodate the divergent preferences of different people.

Furthermore, technological change that alters the ability ot travel and/or create boundaries may require significant changes in both boundaries and rules. Finally, inter-jurisdictional arrangements can be expected to develop.

Thus, for instance, MAAWG, the organization of ISPs is establishing rules for behavior that involves communications between their subscribers. This organization is not attempting to "harmonize" the rules that operate within each ISP except to the degree that they might affect inter-ISP transactions. Thus, the polycentric nature of cyber law remains, with the added development of second order clustering, as predicted by Vanberg and Buchanan's (1990) analysis, and illustrated by various real space examples. While this may sound like a very complex and confusing system of rules, it must be recognized that most of these customary communities are very narrowly focused in a functional sense. Therefore, the set of rules that a community develops only applies to those kinds of interactions that are relevant to the community function. Each community's rules are likely to be quite simple, since their purpose is to facilitate the voluntary interactions of community members and protect those members from harm. One community's rules may be quite different from another community's rules but that does not mean that the two sets of rules are conflict, as they can arise in the context of vary different kinds of interactions. In contrast, a nation state that attempts to monopolize all law will have to have a very large and complex set of rules, these rules often can have conflicting purposes. Thus, polycentric law is not necessary any more complex and difficult to deal with than monocentric law, and it may be much less complex.

ANIMATING CYBER LAW

The following example illustrates the ideal performance of an online community operating with the CyberLaw networking protocol and using the appropriate software platform.

Mr L, a famous photographer, uploads on his platform portal (his webpage) pictures from his upcoming book to "tease" consumers/community participants. The site contains explicit warnings against unauthorised online retrieval.

M, a user, intrigued by the images, tries to copy two pictures. Her software asks the hosting platform for authorisation to deliver visual material to M. Since there is no prior relevant input/ instructions from the rightful owner, the platform responds negatively to M's demand. Next, the autonomous software inspects M's personal settings for any previous legal relationship that would justify a claim for transferring the pictures; it conducts a quick "legal" search through the full range of the online "allowed" concepts. Failing to discover any valid link between M and L, the shared platform is alerted, informing M's personal browser that there is no authorisation and, thus, the terminal is unable to perform the requested transfer.

M does not give up. She e-mails L asking for permission; L, however, declines until the book is published. Alerted by the email, he "reads" on his software all recent attempts to download his pictures and he instructs it (via his browser's interface) to communicate with corresponding platforms in order to enforce an obligation against deprivation of his property.

Furthermore, he institutes the same condition *erga omnes*, in order to prevent further attempts to download the indicated material in the future. His agents travel across the platform and impose the condition on all participants, notifying them against specific contact with L's website.

M persists and she sends her agents in search of a picture using L's name and an additional description "y" that accompanied the photo on the previous site. The agents discover "L's unofficial fan club" URL, which supports fanatically L's work and has been rewarded with a sneak preview of his new material. Unable to contain their enthusiasm, L's fans have uploaded by chance picture "y", the very same that M desires, without adjusting the necessary restrictions for banning its further transfer.

M's agents converse with the file and they demand acquisition, which, resembling BGB §854, follows the pattern: "NOT<obtain> IF (NOT<consent><other possessor>)". Since there is no restriction from the Fans' URL, M's autonomous agents pick the file without further denial.

However, as the file comes into M's possession, the application identifies import of the marked item "y" and detects direct conflict with L's previous conditional rule, which, alerted in turn, immediately identifies import of the marked item "y". Thereafter, through the application, L is informed about the conducted breach. Under the scope of the "default by debtor" concept another subsequent "compensation for default" concept comes automatically into effect to demand compensation from M. Ultimately, the same procedure would take place simultaneously between L and an infinite number of users/participants.

In terms of community structure and operation, the practical nature of "compensation" would need to be explicitly defined. It might constitute online payment, destruction of a specific file's copy, or a ban from distributing it online. Failure to comply with the "creditor's" notice, possibly within a certain period of time, would cause the software to process and impose "communal" measures against the "debtor". However, a system-placed blockade, for example, could be terminated automatically if M complied with the requested "compensation".

Conclusions: potential and applicability

These simplified examples underline the key element of this distinctive merging of law into technology: the automation of regulating interactivity.

From the lawyer's perspective, within this new system resides inherent potential:

(a) For overcoming legislative ambiguities that emerge from transnational networking communications, and

(b) For shaping global regulatory frameworks.

The CyberLaw protocol's structural logic facilitates the introduction of indirect legal harmonisation for the online community's various participants, regardless of their national origin or status. In this respect, typical conflicts of international private law that emerge from the global online context (e.g. jurisdiction) give way to the CyberLaw's main operation of precluding disputes through computer code by keeping behavioural activity in compliance with the law at the precise moment of its execution.

Additionally, as the adopted legal policies are merely a minimalist restatement of the fundamental principles of private law, they are easily understandable across the network community. Exploring the protocol's functionality on this basis, a wide range of areas and issues of law that have required additional legislation for their Internet manifestations (and the institution of further, more complex and ambiguous terminology) revert to familiar legal concepts that outline and prescribe the fundamental proportions of fixed social systems, e.g. copyright in CyberLaw is ideally dealt with in the traditional ownership context.

However, the creation of electronic-legal hybrids that would substitute and eventually circumvent the effect of real-world law, is not the intent of the CyberLaw protocol. On the contrary, the protocol provides a practical prevention mechanism against the increasing Internet-related litigiousness that places unsuspecting individual users in costly judicial battles with gigantic international entities.

Moreover, the transparency of the automatically imposed behavioural limits and restrictions over online interactivity is brought under narrow scrutiny. Law enforcement within democratic structures is characterised by clarity and its availability to the public for criticism and debate, a principle social institution, which the "invisible" computer language sequences presumably challenge in practice. However, the protocol does not constitute an administration of justice mechanism but, rather, an interactivity management system which replicates private law methodology.

Since CyberLaw acknowledges the community system in a Luhmannian sense the CyberLaw protocol's explicit incorporation of law enhances the respect for the human participant as legal actor, unlike the arbitrarily created software platforms, which currently monopolise the global electronic market. Protection and security through the protocol, though, are provided equally for both the individual and the service provider, reflecting the universality of Law in the electronic environment. Therefore, in assessing the added value for international online transactions, the private sector as well as state authorities are invited to contribute to the development of the CyberLaw protocol, in pursuit of satisfactory regulatory schemes for the Internet.

Referring initially to basic legal modules, the law through the protocol becomes alive: a collective autonomous innovation that, by hosting a series of small cross-operational tasks, evolves ultimately only through the initiative of its masters/subjects. In this respect, cyber-democracy, capable of presenting its own tailor-made law, is not just a digital utopia.

Beyond the above-explored option of building local, independent communities, the Internet as a whole is the protocol's ultimate and most ambitious challenge. It is arguable whether the

Web has the capacity to integrate globally new socio-legal solutions, especially since a framework of universally shared formal laws was not ab initio cultivated across the users' community. In addition, the commercialisation of the Web has led to the fragmented administration of cyberspace by innumerable, and thus uncontrollable, private operators. Encouragingly, however, as long as many, and technically more advanced, electronic network constructions are still underway, the CyberLaw protocol proposal offers the promising potential for future interactive systems to construct their operational basis concretely towards human law, predicting and escaping the already encountered ambiguities on the "two-dimensional" Internet.

SIDES OF INDIAN CYBER LAW OR IT ACT OF INDIA

Cyber laws are meant to set the definite pattern, some rules and guidelines that defined certain business activities going on through internet legal and certain illegal and hence punishable. The IT Act 2000, the cyber law of India, gives the legal framework so that information is not denied legal effect, validity or enforceability, solely on the ground that it is in the form of electronic records.One cannot regard government as complete failure in shielding numerous e-commerce activities on the firm basis of which this industry has got to its skies, but then the law cannot be regarded as free from ambiguities.

MMS porn case in which the CEO of bazee.com(an Ebay Company) was arrested for allegedly selling the MMS clips involving school children on its website is the most apt example in this reference. Other cases where the law becomes hazy in its stand includes the case where the newspaper Mid-Daily published the pictures of the Indian actor kissing her boyfriend at the Bombay nightspot and the arrest of Krishan Kumar for illegally using the internet account of Col. (Retd.) J.S. Bajwa.

The IT Act 2000 attempts to change outdated laws and provides ways to deal with cyber crimes. Let's have an overview of the law where it takes a firm stand and has got successful in the reason for which it was framed.

1. The E-commerce industry carries out its business via transactions and communications done through electronic records. It thus becomes essential that such transactions be made legal. Keeping this point in the consideration, the IT Act 2000 empowers the government departments to accept filing, creating and retention of official documents in the digital format. The Act also puts forward the proposal for setting up the legal framework essential for the authentication and origin of electronic records / communications through digital signature.

2. The Act legalizes the e-mail and gives it the status of being valid form of carrying out communication in India. This implies that e-mails can be duly produced and approved in a court of law, thus can be a regarded as substantial document to carry out legal proceedings.

3. The act also talks about digital signatures and digital records. These have been also awarded the status of being legal and valid means that can form strong basis for launching litigation in a court of law. It invites the corporate companies in the business of being Certifying Authorities for issuing secure Digital Signatures Certificates.

4. The Act now allows Government to issue notification on the web thus heralding e-governance.

5. It eases the task of companies of the filing any form, application or document by laying down the guidelines to be submitted at any appropriate office, authority, body or agency owned or controlled by the government. This will help in saving costs, time and manpower for the corporates.

6. The act also provides statutory remedy to the coporates in case the crime against the accused for breaking into their computer systems or network and damaging and copying the data is proven. The remedy provided by the Act is in the form of monetary damages, not exceeding Rs. 1 crore($200,000).

7. Also the law sets up the Territorial Jurisdiction of the Adjudicating Officers for cyber crimes and the Cyber Regulations Appellate Tribunal.

8. The law has also laid guidelines for providing Internet Services on a license on a non-exclusive basis.

The IT Law 2000, though appears to be self sufficient, it takes mixed stand when it comes to many practical situations. It looses its certainty at many places like:

1. The law misses out completely the issue of Intellectual Property Rights, and makes no provisions whatsoever for copyrighting, trade marking or patenting of electronic information and data. The law even doesn't talk of the rights and liabilities of domain name holders, the first step of entering into the e-commerce.

2. The law even stays silent over the regulation of electronic payments gateway and segregates the negotiable instruments from the applicability of the IT Act, which may have major effect on the growth of e-commerce in India. It leads to make the banking and financial sectors irresolute in their stands.

3. The act empowers the Deputy Superintendent of Police to look up into the investigations and filling of charge sheet when any case related to cyber law is called. This approach is likely to result in misuse in the context of Corporate India as companies have public offices which would come within the ambit of "public place" under the Act. As a result, companies will not be able to escape potential harassment at the hands of the DSP.

4. Internet is a borderless medium ; it spreads to every corner of the world where life is possible and hence is the cyber criminal. Then how come is it possible to feel relaxed and secured once this law is enforced in the nation??

The Act initially was supposed to apply to crimes committed all over the world, but nobody knows how can this be achieved in practice, how to enforce it all over the world at the same time.

* The IT Act is silent on filming anyone's personal actions in public and then distributing it electronically. It holds ISPs (Internet Service Providers) responsible for third party data and information, unless contravention is committed

without their knowledge or unless the ISP has undertaken due diligence to prevent the contravention.

* For example, many Delhi based newspapers advertise the massage parlors; and in few cases even show the 'therapeutic masseurs' hidden behind the mask, who actually are prostitutes. Delhi Police has been successful in busting out a few such rackets but then it is not sure of the action it can take...should it arrest the owners and editors of newspapers or wait for some new clauses in the Act to be added up?? Even the much hyped case of the arrest of Bajaj, the CEO of Bazee.com, was a consequence of this particular ambiguity of the law. One cannot expect an ISP to monitor what information their subscribers are sending out, all 24 hours a day.

Cyber law is a generic term, which denotes all aspects, issues and the legal consequences on the Internet, the World Wide Web and cyber space. India is the 12th nation in the world that has cyber legislation apart from countries like the US, Singapore, France, Malaysia and Japan.

But can the cyber laws of the country be regarded as sufficient and secure enough to provide a strong platform to the country's e-commerce industry for which they were meant?? India has failed to keep in pace with the world in this respect, and the consequence is not far enough from our sight; most of the big customers of India 's outsourcing company have started to re-think of carrying out their business in India.Bajaj's case has given the strongest blow in this respect and have broken India 's share in outsourcing market as a leader. If India doesn't want to loose its position and wishes to stay as the world's leader forever in outsourcing market, it needs to take fast but intelligent steps to cover the glaring loopholes of the Act, or else the day is not far when the scenario of India ruling the world's outsourcing market will stay alive in the dreams only as it will be overtaken by its competitors.

CYBER CRIME IN INDIA AND ITS LAWS

Cyber crime is a new term for most of the people in india. The laws are also new better say evolving. The sole purpose of this blog is to creat awareness among people and try to help them to understand the law by answaring their mails.

Cybercrime is more Effective than Drug Trading

Global cybercrime generated a higher turnover than drug trafficking in 2004 and is set to grow even further with the wider use of technology in developing countries.

No country is immune from cybercrime, which includes corporate espionage, child pornography, stock manipulation, extortion and piracy.

"Last year was the first year that proceeds from cybercrime were greater than proceeds from the sale of illegal drugs, and that was, I believe, over \$105 billion."

"Cybercrime is moving at such a high speed that law enforcement cannot catch up with it."

Cyber Evidence Collection..a Major Challenge to Law Enforcement in India

Whether in the case of a Cyber Crime pursued by the Police or a Computer Audit pursued by an auditor, "Evidence" plays a vital part in securing the interests of the Information Asset owner. Naavi discusses the legal requirements and the devices required for the purpose of collecting judicially acceptable Cyber Evidence. It is more than three years since law was passed in India to recognize electronic documents as admissible evidence in a Court of law. The necessary amendments were made to the Indian Evidence Act 1872 by the Information Technology Act 2000 (ITA-2000).

In the case of electronic documents produced as "Primary Evidence", the document itself must be produced to the Court. However, such electronic document obviously has to be carried on a media and can be read only with the assistance of an appropriate Computer with appropriate operating software and application software.

In many cases even in non-electronic documents, a document may be in a language other than the language of the Court in which case it needs to be translated and submitted for the understanding of the Court by an "Expert". Normally the person making submission of the document also submits the translation from one of the "Experts". If the counter party does not accept the "Expert's opinion", the court may have to listen to another "Expert" and his interpretation and come to its own conclusion of what is the correct interpretation of a document.

In the case of the Electronic documents, under the same analogy, "Presentation" of document is the responsibility of the prosecution or the person making use of the document in support of his contention before the Court. Based on his "Reading" of the documents, he submits his case. This may however be disputed by the counter party. In such a case, it becomes necessary for the Court to "Get the document Read by an expert" to its satisfaction. It is necessary to have some clarity on the legal aspects of such documents presented to the Court because most of the court battles are expected to revolve around "Proper Reading " of the documents and "Possible manipulation of the documents".

In making presentation of an "Electronic Document", the presentor may submit a readable form of the document in the form of a "Print Out". Question arises in such a case whether the print out is a "Primary Evidence" or a "Secondary Evidence".

According to Indian Evidence Act, section 65 refers to "Cases in which secondary evidence relating to documents may be given". However, the modifications made to this section by ITA-2000 have added Sections 65 A and Section 65 B.

Though these sections have been numbered as A and B of 65, these are not to be treated as sub sections of Section 65. As per schedule II to ITA-2000, serial number 9, it appears that 65A and 65B are to be treated as independent sections. According to Section 65 A therefore, " Contents of electronic records may be proved in accordance with the provisions of Section 65B".

Whether by design or otherwise, Section 65B clearly states that " Not withstanding anything contained in this (Ed:Indian Evidence Act) Act, any information contained in an electronic record which is printed on a paper, stored, recorded or copied in optical or magnetic media produced by a computer (herein after called the Computer Output) shall be deemed to be also a document...."

However, for the "Computer Output" to be considered as admissible evidence, the conditions mentioned in the Section 65 B (2) needs to be satisfied.

Section 65B(2) contains a series of certifications which is to be provided by the person who is having lawful control over the use of the Computer generating the said computer output and is not easy to be fulfilled without extreme care.

It is in this context that the responsibility of the Law Enforcement Authorities in India becomes onerous while collecting the evidence.

In a typical incident when a Cyber Crime is reported, the Police will have to quickly examine a large number of Computers and storage media and gather leads from which further investigations have to be made. Any delay may result in the evidence getting obliterated in the ordinary course of usage of the suspect hard disk or the media.

Any such investigation has to cover the following main aspects of Cyber Forensics, namely,

1. Collection of suspect evidence
2. Recovery of erased/hidden/encrypted data
3. Analysis of suspect evidence.

If the process of such collection, recovery and analysis is not undertaken properly, the evidence may be rejected in the Court of law as not satisfying the conditions of Section 65B of the Indian Evidence Act.

In the evolution of the Indian challenge to Cyber Crimes, it may be said that during the last three years, Police in different parts of the Country have been exposed to the reality of Cyber Crimes and more and more cases are being registered for investigation. However, if the Law enforcement does not focus on the technical aspects of evidence collection and management, they will soon find that they will be unable to prove any electronic document in a Court of Law.

Cyber Evidence Management

In the previous article, we had discussed the requirements of Indian Evidence Act for the admissibility of Electronic Evidence. In this article we shall discuss the hardware required for making copies of hard disks for further analysis.

In most of the incidents of Cyber Crime investigation by the Police or suspected fraud in a Corporate network, it becomes necessary to seize the suspect Computer or its hard disk for a detailed examination.

Some times even in an "Intelligence gathering Mission" it may be necessary to subject a hard disk for a detailed examination. The practical problem in most such cases is that if the computer is seized immediately, it may disrupt the operations of the enterprise seriously. If the Police make this as a common practice, then no Company would be comfortable in preferring a complaint in case of a computer crime.

A similar problem also arises in case of an auditor who suspects some fraud in a hard disk but needs access to the same for a prolonged time for further analysis.

It therefore becomes necessary for the investigator or the auditor to make a "Copy" of the original "Evidence" and carry on his investigations on the "Copy". The question then arises that if he stumbles upon some evidence during his examination and then comes back to seize the original hard disk, the data on the original hard disk may no longer contain the evidence he had unearthed during the investigation.

Even assuming that the "Original Hard Disk" itself had been seized and the investigations have unearthed some evidence, there would be a charge from the accused that the evidence was in the custody of the Police/Auditor and could have been tampered with.

It becomes absolutely essential therefore for the investigator to preserve the original evidence and at the same time subject it to any type of analysis he may like besides not disrupting the regular user of the system and the hard disk.

A device required for this purpose is one which makes a "Bit Image Copy" of the suspect hard disk, creates a "hash code" for the "original" being copied so that the original can be preserved, the "Clone" can be subjected to analysis and in case of necessity prove with the hash code that the data as captured from the "Original" has not been tampered with during the process of "analysis".

Ineffective Law Enforcement, Bad Economy Fueling Cybercrime

Cyber-criminals operating worldwide are benefitting from ineffective law enforcement and a growing economic recession that could make jittery people more susceptible to cybercrime scams.

So concludes security firm McAfee in its new report, "Virtual Criminology Report—Cybercrime vs. Cyberlaw." published Tuesday. The report pulls together the opinions of about two dozen legal experts, academic researchers and security-response professionals working as far afield as Britain, continental Europe, the Baltic countries, Brazil, India, Japan, Australia, New Zealand and North America.

"There have been a few cases where Cyber-criminals have been promptly arrested, but they're usually responsible for the small attacks," says Paulo Lima, a Brazilian lawyer specializing in computer-related crime. "Those responsible for the large operations have never been arrested. The public sector has usually acted in a mitigating manner, attacking the symptom and not the illness — there is an antiquated system and a completely unprepared law enforcement body."

Lima's sentiment is echoed in Britain, India and elsewhere by those involved in trying to combat a worldwide cybercrime spree that includes phishing, denial-of-service (DoS) extortion rackets, botnets, spam, cyber-espionage and national attacks of a political nature.

"Cybercrime has become a big problem in India this year," says Vijay Mukhi, president of the Foundation of Internet Security and Technology in India. "However, politicians and judges do not understand how to deal with it, and in fact few of them ever use the Internet. Police are reluctant to register cases because they prove too difficult to prosecute."

The view among some in the United Kingdom is only slightly more optimistic. Peter Sommer, a British professor and consultant whose main research field is the reliability of digital evidence, says there's some progress being made in how the U.K. courts address technology-related crimes, but the computer forensics piece of the puzzle is not yet complete. "The Council for Registered Forensics Practitioners scheme to accredit experts is still not yet working," he adds.

Anther problem is talent: In many places around the world, private industry is siphoning the cybercrime fighting talent from government, offering them more money to work in the private sector.

In addition, many worry that the growing economic recession and banking fiscal crisis is being exploited by Cyber-criminals to prey upon jittery consumers.

Politics is also an issue. China, Russia and Moldova are often blamed as international sources for all kinds of cybercrime, and the McAfee report takes up the issue of whether there are places around the world where prosecution of cybercrime is thought to be especially lax.

"Criminal behaviour is still receiving political cover," says Eugene Spafford, professor of computer sciences at Purdue University and executive director of the Center for Education and Research in Information Assurance and Security in the United States.

One example Spafford cites is the July cyberattack on Web sites protesting the Burmese military regime, in which the government in Myanmar was thought to have had a hand. "In the case of the Myanmar denial-of-service attacks, they took place with local Eastern European and Russian support," he says.

"Russia and China are especially reluctant to cooperate with foreign law enforcement bodies for reputation and intelligence reasons," Spafford adds.

Another contributor to the report, Dmitri Alperovitch, says he believes that Russian's President Vladimir Putin and political influence within the Federal Security Service (Russia's successor to the Soviet KGB) are hampering efforts to prosecute cyber-crimes, such as those related to the Storm botnet.

Alperovitch is director of intelligence analysis and hosted security at Secure Computing (recently acquired by McAfee). McAfee says Russia is the predominant source of the most sophisticated, well-designed malware.

"The vast percentage of 'professional' malware we see today is, frankly, coming out of Russia," acknowledges Dave Marcus, director of security research and communication at McAfee Avert Labs.

"We find it on Russian hosting sites and the read-me documents are in Russian."

National concerns about political uses of malware and denial-of-service attacks are growing, according to the McAfee report.

Estonia, which suffered massive and crippling DoS attacks in April 2007, this year established a "top-secret cyber security hub," which has been "operational as of August 2008 and backed by NATO and seven EU countries (Estonia, Germany, Italy, Latvia, Lithuania, Slovakia and Spain)," the McAfee report states.

Estonia also is said to have pledged 50,000 Euros to back the Council of Europe Convention on Cybercrime.

But while some countries end up as high-tech crime scapegoats, the report notes, in reality it's very difficult to precisely identify origination points.

"In fact, obfuscation seems to be the name of the game," says Alana Maurushat, acting director of the Cyberspace Law and Policy Centre of the University of New South Wales in Australia. "It is easy to make it appear as if malware or espionage activities are originating from a county other than the original source. There is considerable misdirection as to origin of attacks. Much traffic is misdirected as a decoy.

The actual attack may originate in the same city as the target. This is often done with cases of country espionage and corporate espionage."

Those out on the Web front lines say they can only speak about what they witness daily.

"We're getting hacking attempts constantly," says Clay Hill, Web site manager at the libraries division at Mississippi State University, which allows authorized access to research. "And most of it is from China."

4

Computer Crime Techniques

BACKGROUND

What is a cyber-crime? Law enforcement experts and legal commentators are divided. Some experts believe that computer crime is nothing more than ordinary crime committed by high-tech computers and that current criminal laws on the books should be applied to the various laws broken, such as trespass, larceny, and conspiracy. Others view cyber-crime as a new category of crime requiring a comprehensive new legal framework to address the unique nature of the emerging technologies and the unique set of challenges that traditional crimes do not deal with; such as jurisdiction, international cooperation, intent, and the difficulty of identifying the perpetrator. Another source of confusion is the meaning of "hacker" and "cracker" and the distinction behind their motivations. The differences between the two and their relevance to federal criminal statutes.

The State of the Law

Congress has approached computer crime as both traditional crime committed by new methods and as crime unique in character requiring new legal framework. For example, Congress has amended the Securities Act of 1933 to include crimes committed by a computer. However, Congress has also enacted a comprehensive new computer fraud and abuse section that can easily be amended to reflect changes in technology and computer use by criminals. In fact, the U.S. Congress has enacted statutes that widen the scope of traditional crimes to specifically include crimes involving computers, or categorize them as entirely separate offenses. For example, the main federal statutory framework for many computer crimes is the Computer Fraud and Abuse Act ("CFAA"). The statute is structured with an eye to the future so that it can be easily amended to reflect changes in technology and criminal techniques. The statute has already been amended several times to close unintended loopholes created by judicial interpretation. In its current form, the statute is very broad in scope, reflecting the government's resolve to combat cyber-crime at every level.

THE PERPETRATORS—HACKERS AND CRACKERS

Hackers

"Hacker" is a term commonly applied to a "computer user who intends to gain unauthorized access to a computer system." Hackers are skilled computer users who penetrate computer systems to gain knowledge about computer systems and how they work. The traditional hacker does not have authorized access to the system.

Hacking purists do not condone damage to the systems that are hacked. According to The Jargon Dictionary, the term "hacker" seems to have been first adopted as a badge in the 1960s by the hacker culture surrounding The Tech Model Railroad Club ("TMRC") at Massachusetts Institute of Technology when members of the group began to work with computers. The TMRC resents the application of the term "hacker" to mean the committing of illegal acts, maintaining that words such as "thieves," "password crackers," or "computer vandals" are better descriptions.

In the hacking "community," it is considered better to be described as a "hacker" by others than to describe oneself as a "hacker." Hackers consider themselves members of an elite meritocracy based on ability and trade hacker techniques and "war stories" amongst themselves in Usenet forums, local or regional clubs, and national conferences, such as the annual Def Con Computer Underground Convention held in Las Vegas.

Crackers

A "cracker" is a hacker with criminal intent. According to The Jargon Dictionary, the term began to appear in 1985 as a way to distinguish "benign" hackers from hackers who maliciously cause damage to targeted computers. Crackers maliciously sabotage computers, steal information located on secure computers, and cause disruption to the networks for personal or political motives.

Estimates made in the mid-1990's by Bruce Sterling, author of *The Hacker Crackdown: Law and Disorder on the Electronic Frontier*, put "the total number of hackers at about 100,000, of which 10,000 are dedicated and obsessed computer enthusiasts. A group of 250-1,000 are in the so-called hacker 'elite', skilled enough to penetrate corporate systems and to unnerve corporate security."

In the eyes of the law, hacking and cracking are not always treated the same way. Depending upon the method of intrusion, the type of computer that was broken into, the hacker's intent, and the type and amount of damage, different statutes and penalties will apply. There are many ways to approach a discussion on hacking.

We will structure the discussion on hacking techniques within the framework of the statutory elements to provide an understanding of how the different techniques trigger different statutes and penalties. We begin with an overview of hacking and an explanation of several common hacking techniques. Then, we discuss the relevant criminal code that can be applied depending on the nature of the hack.

Why People Hack

Hactivism

In recent years, according to the Department of Justice's National Infrastructure Protection Center, there has been a rise in what has been dubbed "hacktivism." Hacktivists launch politically motivated attacks on public web pages or e-mail servers. The hacking groups and individuals, or Hacktivists, overload e-mail servers by sending massive amounts of e-mail to one address and hack into web sites to send a political message. In 1999, for example, the homepages for the White House, the U.S. Department of the Interior, White Pride, the United States Senate, Greenpeace, and the Klu Klux Klan were attacked by political activists protesting the site's politics.One such group is called the "Electronic Disturbance Theater," which promotes civil disobedience on-line to raise awareness for its political agenda regarding the Zapatista movement in Mexico and other issues. Also, during the 1999 NATO conflict in Yugoslavia, hackers attacked web sites in NATO countries, including the United States, using virus-infected e-mail and other hacking techniques. On February 7, 2000, the official web site of the Austrian Freedom Party was hacked to protest the inclusion of Jörg Haider and his party into a coalition Austrian government.

Employees

According to a study conducted in 1999 by Michael G. Kessler & Associates Ltd., disgruntled employees are the greatest threat to a computer's security. Employees that steal confidential information and trade secrets account for thirty-five percent of the theft of proprietary information.

In fact, data suggests that serious economic losses linked to computer abuse have been and continue to be attributed to current and former employees of the victimized organization rather than to outside hackers with modems. Internet Security Systems' Chris Klaus estimates that over eighty percent of the attacks on computer systems are committed by employees.

According to recent FBI assessments, disgruntled insiders are a principal source of computer crimes. Insiders do not need a great deal of knowledge about their target computers, because their inside knowledge of the victim's system allows them unrestricted access to cause damage to the system or to steal system data. A Computer Security Institute/FBI report notes that fifty-five percent of survey respondents reported malicious activity by insiders. Employees who exceed their authorized use and intentionally cause damage are just a liable as an outside hacker who intentionally causes damage. However, § 1030(a)(5) of the CFAA does not criminalize damage caused by authorized persons and company insiders that was reckless or negligent. Only outside non-authorized hackers are liable for *any* damage caused, whether it was negligent, reckless, or intentional.

Recreational Hackers

"Recreational hackers" break into computer networks for the thrill of the challenge or for bragging rights in the hacking community. While hacking once required a fair amount of skill or computer knowledge, the recreational hacker today can now download attack scripts and protocols from the Internet and launch them against victim sites with little knowledge of the systems they are attacking. There are countless web sites on the Internet that provide "newbies" (inexperienced hackers, or "wannabes") with detailed instructions on hacking techniques and downloadable, do-it-yourself hacking tools. In recent years, the hacker's attack tools have become more sophisticated and easier to use. For example, in 1999 hackers defaced the Anniston Army Depot, Lloyd's of London, the U.S. Senate and Yahoo home pages to demonstrate to the hacking community their ability to hack into third-party servers and to highlight the servers' vulnerabilities.

Web Site Administrators and Web Pages

It is usually considered a passive and harmless exercise to visit a web site. The user requests information and the server responds to the request by sending out packets of requested data back to the user's computer. However, web sites can also access a lot of hidden background information from the user. For example, Privacy.net has a web site that will show users all of the information that can be taken from their individual computer.

The remote web site can determine the following information about a visitor:

(a) The IP address the user is accessing the web site from;
(b) The number of prior visits to the web site, and the dates;
(c) The URL of the page that contained the link to get the user to the web site;
(d) The user's browser type and operating system and version;
(e) The user's screen resolution;

(f) Whether JavaScript and VBScript are enabled on the user's computer;

(g) How many web pages the user has visited in the current session;

(h) The local time and date; and

(i) FTP username and password, if there is one.

Privacy advocates have pressured web browser developers to address security concerns by enabling users to significantly enhance their privacy by adjusting the security level on their browsers. The extent of information that a web site can retrieve from a visitor without violating the CFAA is still uncertain.

Section 1030(a)(2)(C) proscribes the intentional access of a computer without, or in excess of authority to obtain information. When a person visits a web site, how much information has that person reasonably "authorized" the web site to obtain? This question may be answered by a court in one of the cases filed against RealNetworks over its gathering of user data.

It is also possible for a web programmer to enable a web page to send an e-mail to a predetermined address just by visiting the page through a JavaScript exploit in Netscape Navigator Versions 2.0 through 4.0b1. For example, if a person visits such a web site, hidden within the hypertext markup language ("HTML") is code that will cause the person's e-mail program to send an e-mail to the web site with the person's e-mail address in the "from" slot. Theoretically, this exploit would allow a web site to collect all of the e-mails from persons who visit their web site. Internet Explorer and Netscape Navigator provide security warnings to users before they send the mail if the security level is set at a higher level.

BASIC HACKING TECHNIQUES

There are as many hacking techniques as there are hackers. One common technique that is technically not a "hacking" technique, but is nevertheless a criminal violation, is the "cookie" exploit. A cookie is simply an HTTP header that consists of a text-only string that gets entered into the "memory" of a browser. This string contains the domain, path, lifetime, and value of a variable that a web site sets. If the lifetime of this variable is longer than the time the user spends at that site, then this string is saved to file for future reference. For example, when a person signs up with a password and user name on a web site, the user's identification information is placed on the user's computer in the form of a cookie. When the user revisits the web site, the web site recognizes the user so that the user does not have to re-enter identifying information. However, some older web browsers allow remote sites to retrieve cookies that were not planted by them, enabling malicious web site operators to "steal" the cookie, effectively retrieving the username and password. For example, Buysellzone.com allows registered users to place ads and have access to the various classified ad centers on their server. However, the cookie on the user's computer holds the user's name and password in text format, not encrypted, so anyone with access to the user's cookie.txt file can access the user's account.

Depending upon the purpose of the intrusion, the risk level the hacker is willing to assume, the type of server, the remote and local operating systems, and countless other variables, there is a different hacking technique that can be deployed. Rather than exploring the details of several different techniques, for the purposes of gaining enough knowledge to understand the applicable provisions in 18 U.S.C. § 1030(a), it should be adequate to walk the reader through two hypothetical hacks.

Regardless of whether the hacker intends to deface a web site or steal information, the ultimate technical objective is to "get root." The "root level" is also often referred to as the "god" account, where the "god" account has access to the entire system. The root level provides the hacker with the same permissions and privileges as the system administrator. If the hacker can "penetrate" to the root level, he will be able to, amongst countless other possibilities, change passwords, access files, change web site files, re-route server traffic, and steal credit card numbers if the server is reckless enough to store unencrypted credit card numbers on its site. Once the hacker "gets root," he must eliminate traces of his intrusion — his digital footprints — so the system administrator is unaware of his access.

However, not all hacks require "root access" to damage or change files on the server. Our first example is a relatively unsophisticated hack that only requires access to a user's account on the server. We will refer to this as a "user-level hack." The second example demonstrates a "root access" hack that is significantly more dangerous to the integrity of the machine, although the statutes do not make the distinction. According to 18 U.S.C. § 1030(a), "access" is not defined by the level of penetration. Breaching the system in any manner to obtain information, obtain something of value or cause damage is enough to trigger the statutory liability. For the terms of this chapter, we will refer to this type of hack as a "root access hack."

One way to explain the difference between the two hacks is to compare them to a non-technical example—a hotel. On "hosted" web sites, where the user "rents" web space on another company's server, there are two different levels of access: that of the system administrator and that of the lessee. In a hotel, there are also two main levels of access: the hotel management and the hotel guest. A guest only has a key to access a room (user access), while management has keys to access all of the rooms, as well as the back office, front door and the storeroom (system administrator's root access). A hacker who is able to "get root" has access to the management's keys, thereby gaining full access to everything in the hotel. However, just because someone has the hotel's "all access" key, does not necessarily mean they can enter the restricted areas freely because there are security guards (system administrators) and security cameras (server access logs). The goal of the "root hacker" is to enter unnoticed, compromise the security, and depart the scene without leaving any traces of his visit.

Example of a User-level Hack

Hacker wants to access a computer to deface a web site that was developed using Microsoft FrontPage. Hacker employs a technique that exploits a "bug" in FrontPage web sites that use FrontPage server extensions. The first thing that Hacker must address is how to prevent his access from being traced. There are many ways to hide the origination of the hack, such as spoofing. In this case, because Hacker does not want the victim to be able to trace him back to his point of origin, Hacker uses a laptop computer and a converted telephone lineman's handset to tap into the outside box of a neighbor's house by connecting two alligator clips to the appropriate box terminals. Hacker conducts the attack in the daytime, when the owner of the phone is not home, and the network traffic on the target site is more active.

The next objective is to ascertain the user name and password for the site's webmaster, or the lessee, so he can access the web files on the server. Hacker dials into a free ISP located in another region of the country to complicate the multi-company tracing investigation. Once he is on-line, Hacker enters an exploitative URL address that contains the "service.pwd." Most web sites that use FrontPage server extensions locate the service.pwd in a predictable directory. If the server administrator was careless in setting up the "chmod" command that tells the server who can do what in a directory, such as granting the owner, groups or the public to read, write and execute files within the directory, then Hacker will be able to read a string of text that looks like the following: "kathy:paB.1Mg4MB6MF." Hacker can already determine that the webmaster's username is "kathy." Now all that Hacker has to do is add a few commands to the password string, insert the password string into a DES decrypting password cracker and viola, Hacker has the webmaster's password as well. From there, Hacker downloads the web page he wants to deface, alters the web page with his favorite web editor, and uploads the file to the server and the web page is "owned."

TYPES OF COMPUTER CRIME

We begin by providing an overview of cyber-crime and criminal techniques used to penetrate protected computer networks. The CFAA, how it is applied, and how it has changed over the past decade. Then we will look at other laws that are on the books that the federal government uses to control computer crimes. Due to the international nature of cyber-crimes, we discuss briefly some of the international cooperative developments.

A computer can be the target of the offense, the tool used in the offense, or may contain evidence of the offense. An understanding of the different uses of a computer will provide the foundation of the application of the criminal statutes.

The computer is an indispensable tool for almost all cyber-crimes. However, as more devices are enabled to communicate with the Internet, the hackers arsenal of tools is likely to multiply.

When a computer is the target of the offense, the criminal's goal is to steal information from, or cause damage to, a computer, computer system, or computer network. Hacking, cracking, espionage, cyber-warfare, and malicious computer code viruses are common forms of crimes that target the computer. The perpetrators range from teenage "cyber-joyriders" to organized crime operations and international terrorists. According to a survey conducted by Michael G. Kessler & Associates Ltd., a New York security firm, computer theft of proprietary information is committed by discontented employees (35%), outside hackers (28%), other U.S. companies (18%), foreign corporations (11%), foreign governments (8%), and miscellaneous (10%).

The computer may also be a tool of the offense. The criminal uses the computer to commit a traditional crime, such as counterfeiting. For example, a counterfeiter that used to engrave plates to create the counterfeit currency can now use sophisticated graphic computers with advanced color printers. An example of a computer used to perpetrate a traditional crime is the extortion attempt by George Matos Rocha from North Carolina. Mr. Rocha was charged with bombing three home improvement stores and subsequently threatened the retail chain to continue the bombings unless he received $250,000. Using the Internet, Mr. Rocha set up a bank account in Latvia and instructed the company to wire the extortion money to his Latvian account. The FBI was able to identify the account and trace its origin back to the United States with the help of his Internet Service Provider. Mr. Rocha pleaded guilty in December to explosives charges and extortion. He could have faced life in prison.

Computers can also be incidental to the offense, but are nevertheless important because they contain the evidence of a crime. Money launderers, for example, may use a computer to store details of their laundering operation instead of relying on paper accounting records. Child pornographers' computers are often seized as the key evidence that the defendant produced, possessed, received, and/or distributed child pornography.

Denial of Service

A Denial of Service ("DoS") attack is a rather primitive technique that overwhelms the resources of the target computer which results in the denial of server access to other computers. There are several different techniques that hackers use to "bring down" a server. As the network administrators learn how to limit the damage of one technique, hackers often create more powerful and more sophisticated techniques that force system administrators to continually react against assaults. In order to understand how to apply the law to these attacks, a basic understanding of the anatomy of the attacks is necessary.

There are basically three main network exploits that are used to overwhelm a system's server: SYN Flood Attacks, UDP Flood Attacks and ICMP Flood Attacks. Each technique exploits a weakness in the way computers communicate amongst each other over the Internet. A basic understanding of the TCP/IP Internet protocols is helpful to differentiate between the techniques.

Internet Protocols

The Internet is a network of computers that are connected so they can exchange information amongst each other. The computer that is asking for information from another computer is the "client" and the computer that is receiving the request is the "server." When the client wants to receive information that is located on the server, it sends a request for the information. However, the computers must establish a connection before data can be exchanged.

The server needs to know who it is going to send the information to and needs to make sure the client computer is ready to receive the information. This is considered a "3-way handshake." The first part of the handshake occurs when the client computer sends a message to the server with a "SYN flag" that tells the server how to identify it. Second, upon receiving the request, the server will send out its own identification number, called an Initial Sequence Number ("ISN") in a SYN for this request and an acknowledgement ("ACK") of the client's request.

In the third part of this "handshake," the client computer receives the SYN and ACK from the server and sends back the ACK with the server's numbers, like a secret code the two of them share so the server can keep track of multiple clients. Now the data transfer can take place.

In summary, the client sends a message to the server, the server sends back a message to the client that the server is "awake" and ready to process the requests, then the client sends back an acknowledgement that they are ready.

This may seem redundant, but the need to establish the connection on both sides is very important because the data is broken up into small pieces by the server and sent out over the Internet to the client. The client needs to know how to organize the data puzzle as the packets arrive and the client also needs to know if any packets are missing. As each piece of the puzzle arrives, the client lets the server know the piece has been received, so the server knows if it has to re-send it.

TCP/IP stands for Transmission Control Protocol and Internet Protocol. Basically, the TCP is the workhorse of the communication on both sides. If a file is requested by the client, the server locates the file on its computer and breaks the file into tiny pieces. The tiny pieces are called datagrams. Each datagram is "wrapped" in a bundle of instructions that tells it where to go. These little bundles are called "packets." The TCP assigns a sequence number to every byte transferred so it can track what it has sent and eliminate the need to duplicate sending the same piece twice unless the piece is lost somewhere along the line to the client. The "packet header," contains the sequence numbers that also tells the client the next sequence number to expect after each packet, so the client can start arranging the packets and conduct a rolling inventory. The TCP acts as a digital shipping and receiving department.

The job of the Internet Protocol ("IP") is easier. The IP's job is to route the packets across the Internet to the client. Each computer on the Internet has an IP address that tells the computers where the other is located.

The IP address is very similar to a zip code. For example, a zip code that begins with a 9, belongs to an address located on the west coast of the United States.

If the next number is a 4, the location is in the San Francisco area, and so on until the precise region is located. However, to parallel the IP addresses, each house in the zip code area would be assigned a number, instead of an address.

So when a client or server sends a packet out over the Internet, the packet is "routed" through many other servers to reach its final destination.

The IP tacks on the numerical address and ships it out, hoping the packet arrives where it is supposed to go. If the server does not receive a response that the packet was received on the other end, the IP can send an error message to the client, called an Internet Control Message Protocol, or ICMP, letting the client know that the packet did not get there. It is this system of trust and cooperation between the computers that is exploited by a denial of service attack.

SYN Flood Attacks

One of the weaknesses in the system is the amount of SYN requests the TCP can handle. When the TCP receives more requests than it is programmed to handle, it puts the other incoming SYN requests in a queue. When the queue is filled to capacity, there is no more room to put the other incoming SYN requests and they are turned back. Hence, they are "denied service."

Another technique is to slow down the TCP process by making the TCP wait for all of the ACKs it sent out to be acknowledged by the client. When the attacker sends a message to the server requesting data, the server sends out a SYN and an ACK and waits to hear back from the attacker's client, as part of the third part of the 3-way handshaking. However, the attacker has "spoofed" his return address so that the server sends a "self-addressed and stamped" envelope to an address that is either false or belongs to a computer that is not responding. If enough of these "spoofed"

SYN messages are sent, the server is paralyzed by its wait for non-existent confirmations. "SYNK" is a common SYN flood program that is widely downloadable on the Internet.

UDP Flood Attacks

User Datagram Protocol ("UDP") flood attacks work in very much the same manner as the SYN Flood attacks. In a server, the UDP provides information about the server to other computers, such as the server's local time, echo, chargen, etc. When the server is hit with multiple requests for information about itself, the server can be quickly overwhelmed by its inability to process so many UDP packets.

The result is total consumption of the server's processing power and bandwidth, thereby "denying service" to others who are trying to access the server. The problem is multiplied when a hacker connects one computer's chargen port with another's echo port. The result is the generation of a massive amount of packets that overwhelm the system and render it useless.

ICMP Flood Attack

The Internet Control Message Protocol ("ICMP") flood attack is also similar to the above flood attacks. The ICMP is used to handle errors and "pings."

Pings are small "feelers" that are sent out to other computers to see if they are turned on and connected to the same network. Ping is also used to determine if there is network congestion and other network transport problems. When a ping packet is sent to an IP broadcast address from a computer outside of the remote computer's network, it is broadcast to all machines on the target network.

The ICMP attack begins when a large number of forged ping requests are sent to a broadcast address on a third-party's server. These packets contain the return address of the intended victim. The flood of ping requests causes the targeted server to answer with a flood of responses which can cause both the target site and third-party sites to crash. A variation on the ICMP attack is the "Ping of Death." The Ping of Death is a large ICMP packet that is sent to the target server. The target receives the ping in fragments and starts to re-assemble the packets as they arrive. However, the completed size of the packet is larger than the buffer, or than the room the computer has allocated to such packets, and the computer is overwhelmed, often resulting in the server shutting down or freezing up.

COMPUTER CRIME LEGISLATION

Because of the versatility of the computer, drawing lines between criminal and noncriminal behaviour regarding its use can be difficult. Behaviour that companies and governments regard as unwanted can range from simple pranks, such as making funny messages appear on a computer's screen, to financial or data manipulation producing millions of dollars in losses. Early prosecution of computer crime was infrequent and usually concerned Embezzlement, a crime punishable under existing laws. The advent of more unique forms of abuse, such as computer worms and viruses and widespread computer hacking, has posed new challenges for government and the courts.

The first federal computer crime legislation was the Counterfeit Access Device and Computer Fraud and Abuse Act (18 U.S.C.A. § 1030), passed by Congress in 1984. The act safeguards certain classified government information and makes it a misdemeanor to obtain through a computer financial or credit information that federal laws protect. The act also criminalizes the use of computers to inflict damage to computer systems, including their hardware and software.

In the late 1980s, many states followed the federal government's lead in an effort to define and combat criminal computer activities. At least 20 states passed statutes with similar definitions of computer crimes. Some of those states might have been influenced by studies released in the late 1980s. One report, made available in 1987 by the accounting firm of Ernst and Whinney, estimated that computer abuse caused between $3 billion and $5 billion in losses in the United States annually. Moreover, some of those losses were attributable to newer, more complicated crimes that usually went unprosecuted.

The number of computer crimes continued to increase dramatically in the early 1990s. According to the Computer Emergency and Response Team at Carnegie-Mellon University, the number of computer intrusions in the United States increased 498 percent between 1991 and 1994. During the same time period, the number of network sites affected by computer crimes increased by 702 percent. In 1991, Congress created the National Computer Crime Squad within the Federal Bureau of Investigation (FBI). Between 1991 and 1997, the Squad reportedly investigated more than 200 individual cases involving computer hackers.

Congress addressed the dramatic rise in computer crimes with the enactment of the National Information Infrastructure Act of 1996 as title II of the Economic Espionage Act of 1996, Pub. L. No. 104-294, 110 Stat. 3488. That Act strengthened and clarified provisions of the original Computer Fraud and Abuse Act, although lawmakers and commentators have suggested that as technology develops, new legislation might be necessary to address new methods for committing computer crimes. The new statute also expanded the application of the original statute, making it a crime to obtain unauthorized information from networks of government agencies and departments, as well as data relating to national defense or foreign relations.

Notwithstanding the new legislation and law enforcement's efforts to curb computer crime, statistics regarding these offenses remain stag-gering. According to a survey in 2002 conducted by the Computer Security Institute, in conjunction with the San Francisco office of the FBI, 90 percent of those surveyed (which included mostly large corporations and government agencies) reported that they had detected computer-security breaches. Eighty percent of those surveyed acknowledged that they had suffered financial loss due to computer crime. Moreover, the 223 companies and agencies in the survey that were willing to divulge information about financial losses reported total losses of $455 million in 2002 alone.

Concerns about Terrorism have also included the possibility that terrorist organizations could perform hostile acts in the form of computer crimes. In 2001, Congress enacted the Uniting and

Strengthening America by Providing Appropriate Tools Required to Intercept and Obstruct Terrorism Act (USA PATRIOT ACT), Pub. L. No. 107-56, 115 Stat. 277, to provide law enforcement with the necessary tools to combat terrorism. The Act includes provisions that allow law enforcement greater latitude in hunting down criminals who use computers and other communication networks. The Homeland Security Act of 2002, Pub. L. No. 107-296, 116 Stat. 2135 also directed the UNITED STATES SENTENCING COMMISSION to review, and possibly to amend, the sentencing provisions that relate to computer crimes under 18 U.S.C.A. § 1030.

The Department of Justice's Computer Crime and Intellectual Property Section prosecutes dozens of computer-crime cases each year. Many of those cases involve instances of computer hacking and other unauthorized intrusions, as well as software Piracy and computer fraud.

One set of especially destructive crimes—internal computer crimes—includes acts in which one computer's program interferes with another computer, thus hindering its use, damaging data or programs, or causing the other computer to crash (i.e., to become temporarily inoperable). Two common types of such programs are known in programming circles as "worms" and "viruses." Both cause damage to computer systems through the commands written by their authors. Worms are independent programs that create temporary files and replicate themselves to the point where computers grow heavy with data, become sluggish, and then crash. Viruses are dependent programs that reproduce themselves through a computer code attached to another program, attaching additional copies of their program to legitimate files each time the computer system is started or when some other triggering event occurs.

The dangers of computer worms and viruses gained popular recognition with one of the first cases prosecuted under the Computer Fraud and Abuse Act. In *United States v. Morris*, 928 F.2d 504 (2d Cir. 1991), Cornell University student Robert T. Morris was convicted of violating a provision of the act that punishes anyone who, without authorization, intentionally accesses a "federal interest computer" and damages or prevents authorized use of information in such a computer, causing losses of $1,000 or more. Morris, a doctoral candidate in computer science, had decided to demonstrate the weakness of security measures of computers on the Internet, a network linking university, government, and military computers around the United States. His plan was to insert a worm into as many computers as he could gain access to, but to ensure that the worm replicated itself slowly enough that it would not cause the computers to slow down or crash. However, Morris miscalculated how quickly the worm would replicate. By the time he released a message on how to kill the worm, it was too late: Some 6,000 computers had crashed or become "catatonic" at numerous institutions, with estimated damages of $200 to $53,000 for each institution. Morris was sentenced to three years' Probation and 400 hours of community service, and was fined $10,500.

Computer hackers often share Morris's goal of attempting to prove a point through the clever manipulation of other computers. Hackers, who, typically, are young, talented, amateur computer programmers, earn respect among their peers by gaining access to information through Telecommunications systems. The information obtained ranges from other individuals' E-Mail or credit histories to the Department of Defense's secrets.

A high-profile case in 1992 captured national headlines. In what federal investigators called a conspiracy, five young members of an underground New York City gang of hackers, the Masters of Deception (MOD), faced charges that they had illegally obtained computer passwords, possessed unauthorized access devices (long-distance calling-card numbers), and committed wire fraud in violation of the Computer Fraud and Abuse Act. Otto Obermaier, the U.S. attorney who prosecuted the youths, described their activities as "the crime of the future," and said that he intended to use the case to make a critical statement about computer crime. The indictment contained 11 counts, each punishable by at least five years in prison and individual fines of $250,000. Supporters of MOD's civil liberties questioned whether the gang members had done anything truly illegal.

MOD members Paul Stira and Eli Ladopoulos pleaded guilty to the charges against them. They confessed that they had broken the law but insisted that they had not done anything for personal profit. They were sentenced to six months in a federal penitentiary, followed by six months' home detention. John Lee and Julio Fernandez faced specific charges of illegally selling passwords for personal profit. Lee pleaded guilty and received a year behind bars, followed by 300 hours of community service. Fernandez bargained with prosecutors, offering them information on MOD activities, and thus received no jail time. Gang leader Mark Abene, who was notorious in computer circles by his handle Phiber Optik, pleaded guilty to charges of fraud. A U.S. District Court judge sentenced Abene to a year in federal prison, hoping to send a message to other hackers. However, by the time Abene was released from prison in 1995, his notoriety had grown beyond the hacker underground. Many in the computer world hailed him as a martyr in the modern web of computer technology and criminal prosecution. Abene subsequently found employment as a computer technician at a New York-based on-line service.

Computer crime can become an obsession. Such was the case for Kevin Mitnick, a man federal prosecutors described prior to his arrest as the most wanted computer hacker in the world. In the early 1980s, as a teenager, Mitnick proved his mettle as a hacker by gaining access to a North American Air Defense terminal, an event that inspired the 1983 movie *War Games*. Like the MOD gang, Mitnick gained access to computer networks through telecommunications systems. In violation of federal law, he accessed private credit information, obtaining some 20,000 credit numbers and histories. Other break-ins by Mitnick caused an estimated $4 million in damage to the computer operations of the Digital Equipment Corporation. The company also claimed that Mitnick had stolen more than one million dollars in software.

Mitnick was convicted, sentenced to one year in a minimum-security prison, and then released into a treatment program for compulsive-behaviour disorders. Federal investigators tried to keep close track of him during his probation, but in November 1992, he disappeared. Authorities caught up with his trail when Mitnick broke into the system of computer-security expert Tsutomu Shimomura at the San Diego Supercomputer Centre—a move that was clearly intended as a challenge to another programming wizard. Shimomura joined forces with the Federal Bureau of Investigation to pursue their elusive quarry in cyberspace. Using a program designed to record activity in a particular database that they were sure that Mitnick was accessing, while monitoring phone activity, Shimomura and authorities narrowed their search to Raleigh, North Carolina. A special device detecting cellular-phone use ultimately led them to Mitnick's apartment. Mitnick was arrested and was charged on 23 federal counts. He pleabargained with prosecutors, who agreed to drop 22 of the counts in exchange for Mitnick's guilty plea for illegally possessing phone numbers to gain access to a computer system. Mitnick was sentenced to eight months in jail.

Mitnick's case illustrates the difficulties that legislatures and courts face when defining and assigning penalties for computer crime. Using a computer to transfer funds illegally or to embezzle money is clearly a serious crime that merits serious punishment. Mitnick broke into numerous services and databases without permission and took sensitive information, in violation of federal laws; however, he never used that information for financial gain. This type of behaviour typically has no counterpart outside of cyberspace—for example, people do not break into jewelry stores only to leave a note about weak security.

Some instances of computer crimes demonstrate the way in which small computer files that require relatively little effort on the part of the perpetrator can cause millions of dollars' worth of damage to computer networks. In March 1999, David L. Smith of New Jersey created a virus that lowered the security levels of certain word-processing programs and caused infected computers to send e-mail messages containing attachments with the virus to e-mail addresses contained in the infected computer's e-mail address book. The virus was activated on an infected computer when the user opened the word-processing program.

Smith posted a message on March 26, 1999, to an Internet newsgroup called "Alt.Sex." The message claimed that if a user opened an attachment, it would provide a list of passcodes to pornographic websites. The attachment contained the virus, which became known as the "Melissa" virus. Smith was arrested by New Jersey authorities on April 1, 1999, but not before the virus had infected an estimated 1.2 million computers and affected one-fifth of the country's largest businesses.

The total amount of damages was $80 million. Smith pleaded guilty in December 1999 to state and federal charges. He faced 20 months in a federal prison and a fine of approximately $5,000 for his crime. He faced additional time in state prison. According to U.S. Attorney Robert J. Cleary, "There is a segment in society that views the unleashing of computer viruses as a challenge, a game. Far from it; it is a serious crime. The penalties Mr. Smith faces—including potentially five years in a federal prison—are no game, and others should heed his example." Others have continued to commit such crimes. In February 2000, a computer hacker stunned the world by paralyzing the Internet's leading U.S. web sites. Three days of concentrated assaults upon major sites crippled businesses like Yahoo, eBay, and CNN for hours, leaving engineers virtually helpless to respond. When the dust had settled, serious doubts were raised about the safety of Internet commerce. An international hunt ensued, and web sites claimed losses in the hundreds of millions of dollars. After pursuing several false leads, investigators ultimately charged a Canadian teenager in March 2000 in one of the attacks.

On February 7, engineers at Yahoo, the popular portal web site, noticed traffic slowing to a crawl. Initially, suspecting faulty equipment that facilitates the thousands of connections to the site daily, they were surprised to discover that it was receiving many times the normal number of hits. Buckling under exorbitant demand, the servers—the computers that receive and transmit its Internet traffic—had to be shut down for several hours. Engineers then isolated the problem: Remote computers had been instructed to bombard Yahoo's servers with automated requests for service. Over the next two days, several other major web sites suffered the same fate. Hackers hit the auction site eBay, the bookseller Amazon.com, the computer journalism site ZDnet, stock brokerages E*Trade and Datek, the computer store Buy.com, the web portal Excite at Home, and the flagship site for news giant CNN. As each site ground to a halt or went offline, engineers tried in vain to determine where the digital bombardment had originated.

Experts expressed amazement at the attacks' simplicity as well as at the inherent vulnerabilities that they exposed in the Internet's architecture. Hackers had launched what quickly came to be known as a distributed Denial-of-Service (DOS) attack—essentially a remote-controlled strike using multiple computers. First, weeks or months in advance, they had surreptitiously installed commonly available hacking programs called "scripts" on 50 or more remote computers, including university systems chosen for their high-speed connections to the Internet. Later, they activated these scripts, turning the remote computers into virtual zombies that were ordered to send unfathomably large amounts of data—up to one gigabyte per second—continuously to their victims. These data asked the target web sites to respond, just as every legitimate connection to a web site does. The sheer multitudes of requests and responses overwhelmed the victim sites. To escape detection, the "zombies" forged their digital addresses.

Federal investigators were initially stymied. They had legal authority to act under 18 U.S.C.A. § 1030, which criminalizes "knowingly transmit(ting) a program information code or command" that "intentionally causes damage." Sleuthing was difficult, however. Not only had the hackers covered the trail well, but also the FBI had suffered numerous personnel losses to private industry.

The bureau had to hire consultants and had to develop special software to assist in its manhunt. Moreover, as FBI official Ron Dick told reporters, the proliferation of common hacking tools meant that even a teenager could have orchestrated the crime. In early March 2000, authorities arrested 17-year-old New Hampshire resident Dennis Moran, allegedly known online as "Coolio." The lead proved false. In mid-April, claiming to have found "Mafia boy," Royal Canadian Mounted Police arrested a 15-year-old Montreal hacker. The youth, whose real name was not divulged, allegedly had boasted of his exploits online while trying to recruit helpers. Officials charged him with a misdemeanor for launching the attack upon CNN's website.

Although the DEPARTMENT OF JUSTICE continued its hunt, this denial-of-service attack was never completely resolved. Analysts have noted that DOS attacks have occurred for several years, although not to the extent as that of February 2000. In May 2001, for instance, the White House's web page was hit with a DOS attack that blocked access to the site for about two hours.

Based upon the sheer number of cases involving computer crime, commentators remain puzzled as to what is necessary to curb this type of activity. Clearly, technology for law enforcement needs to stay ahead of the technology used by the hackers, but this is not an easy task. A number of conferences have been held to address these issues, often attracting large corporations such as Microsoft and Visa International, but the general consensus is that the hackers still hold the upper hand, with solutions still elusive.

NEW COMPUTER CRIME LEGISLATION

Senators Charles Schumer and Jon Kyl have introduced new legislation, S 2092, aimed at addressing some of the perceived weaknesses in the CFAA. The three main provisions addressed by this new legislation propose the following: trap and trace orders, federal jurisdiction requirements, and sentencing.

First, the new legislation would make it easier for cyber-investigators to obtain "trap and trace" orders. "Trap and trace" devices are used to capture incoming IP packets to identify the packet's origins. Due to the ease with which hackers are able to "spoof" their true origin, the most effective way to reconstruct the path of a virus, DoS or hacking assault is to follow a chain of trapping devices that logged the original malicious packets as they arrived at each individual router or server. In the case of a single telephone company, it has been relatively easy for investigators to obtain trap and trace orders. According to Congresswoman Scott of Virginia, "one communication is being carried by several different [ISPs], by a telephone company or 2, local or long distance, by a cell company or 2, and soon enough by a satellite company or 2." Once the segment of the route goes beyond the court's jurisdiction, investigators must then go to the next jurisdiction and file a request for a trap and trace order for the next segment. The new legislation would authorize the issuance of a single order to completely trace an on-line communication from start to finish.

The second provision would lower the monetary barrier for federal jurisdiction. Currently, the CFAA requires a damage threshold in excess of $5,000. However, the $5,000 is often difficult to establish when there is no fixed monetary value to the information. For example, how do you put a price on the value of medical records? Also, investigators must currently wait for a damage assessment before they can initiate an investigation, which can cause expensive delays. The new legislation would permit federal jurisdiction at the outset of an attack. Crimes that exceed $5,000 will still be treated as felonies. However, attacks that cause less than $5,000 in damage would be defined as misdemeanors. Finally, the legislation clarifies what is included in the calculation of "damage," making it easy to reach the $5,000 threshold. It provides for the costs of responding to the offense, the damage assessment costs, restoration costs, and any lost revenue or costs incurred from the interruption of service.

The third provision would modify the strict sentence directives contained in the Antiterrorism and Effective Death Penalty Act of 1999 which required a mandatory incarceration for a minimum of six months for any violation of 18 U.S.C. § 1030(a). Some hacking crimes have gone unprosecuted because the six month sentence was considered excessive. The new legislation would provide lesser sentences for lesser crimes, helping to ensure that all levels of hacking cases will be prosecuted.

Finally, the proposed legislation would make juvenile perpetrators fifteen years of age and older eligible for federal prosecution in serious computer crime cases at the Attorney General's discretion.

However, the proposed changes have raised privacy concerns. A report written by the President's Working Group on Unlawful Conduct on the Internet entitled "The Electronic Frontier: the Challenge of Unlawful Conduct Involving the Use of the Internet" has raised the concerns of privacy advocates. The groups are particularly concerned about the potential for trap and trace abuse by authorities. The American Civil Liberties Union ("ACLU"), would like to raise the standards for trap and trace devices, rather than lower them. According to the ACLU, law enforcement currently only needs to overcome "minimum obstacles" to obtain trap and trace devices. The ACLU is concerned that an expansion of the government's power to obtain trap and trace orders will enhance the government's power to "surreptitiously intercept even more personal electronic communications." The current standard for a trap and trace order is that the investigator must assert in writing to the court that the information is "relevant" to an ongoing investigation. According to the ACLU, the "judge to whom the application is made *must* approve the application, *even if he disagrees* with the assertions of law enforcement."

Additionally, the ACLU is concerned that an expansion of the substance of the orders will erode privacy. The ACLU speculates that an expansion of the powers "might allow law enforcement agents to access a variety of data, including dial-up numbers, Internet Protocol ("IP") addresses, electronic mail logs, uploaded files, and so on.... without a court order."

The CFAA is broad enough to cover most computer crimes. The Act protects government and private computers against inside and outside threats to information, fraud, and damage. Continued pro-active legislative changes to keep the Act up to date in the escalating cyber-war between secure web sites and hackers will be critical to maintaining the integrity of our increasingly inter-networked society.

One challenge in the near future will be the expansion of devices that are able to access the Internet. For example, as televisions become "web-enabled," allowing users to access the Internet from their televisions, will televisions be considered "high-speed data processing devices" as defined under the Act's "computer" definition? Would passwords taken from the television's cookie storage be protected under the Act? As Wireless Application Protocol ("WAP") brings the Internet to hand-held devices and mobile telephones, will the devices and telephones be considered "protected computers"? Will refrigerators that are wired to the Internet be covered? Cyber-crime prosecutors are also facing the difficulty of attacks that originate overseas beyond their jurisdiction. If part of a hacking trail is routed overseas, unless the U.S has an agreement with the foreign jurisdiction, that trail could lead to a dead end if investigators do not have access to the server's logs. The world of individual national jurisdictions will need to address the increasingly borderless crimes committed in cyberspace. However, the CFAA provides a solid foundation upon which we can develop new cyber-crime laws for the coming century.

CRIMINAL AND LEGAL ASPECTS OF FIGHTING COMPUTER CRIME

Nowadays, intensive use of computer technologies in various spheres of human activity has significantly changed an idea of a place and a role of information in present-day society. National information resources have appeared as a new economic category. They became one of the most important factors of post industrial world development. Society is getting features of an information society. This happens owing to development of computer technologies processing information.

Unfortunately, new kinds of crime as "computer crime", "cyber terrorism" and "information war" appeared. Special anxiety is related to crimes in sphere of computers. Number of computers in developed countries is constantly growing. Trend of increase in such crimes is extending. We have a number of cases illustrating computer technologies use for criminal purposes. Serious problems of information security constantly arise as homeland is integrating in the Internet.

A united policy is realized at the state level on purpose of national interests security maintenance from threats in information sphere; a balance of need for free information exchange and admissible restrictions for its distribution are established; the legislation is being improved; activity of state authorities on safety in the information environment is being coordinated; state information resources are being protected at defence enterprises; native telecommunication and information means are being developed; information structure of IT development is being improved; means of search, collecting, storage, processing and the analysis of information are being unified on purpose of entering global information infrastructure.

The urgency of research in this issue is caused also by a problem of increase in efficiency of fighting computer criminality on the part of law enforcement. Creating of the corresponding legal base in law enforcement agencies is of high priority.

In process of studying the legislative experience in foreign countries, some separate scientists drafted recommendations and offers on criminal legal regulation of this field in native legislation.

According to D. Azarov "regulations in the new Criminal Code concerning responsibility for crimes in sphere of computers and computer systems demand a careful analysis. We consider that it is necessary to take into account experience of other European countries in this sphere. Issues of criminalization and, probably, decriminalization of certain actions in sphere of computers, systems and networks demand a further studying. The international experience shows a presence of certain actions that belong to a category of computer crimes, and crimes of some other character, rather than those which attributes are determined in the Criminal Code".

Especially, European Council experts in criminal law suggest to criminalize such socially dangerous acts in sphere of computer information:

1) computer fraud;
2) computer forgery;
3) damage of computer information or software;
4) computer sabotage;
5) unauthorized access;
6) unauthorized interception.

The analysis of law that regulates public information relations in Ukraine, allows to assert that our government takes measures of stimulating the infrastructure development on the basis of the newest technologies, along with necessary measures of containment and counteraction to negative events in sphere of computer technologies.

Among top-priority steps of state policy in sphere of counteraction to computer criminality is an appearance of new Section 16 in the Criminal Code of Ukraine-"Crimes in Sphere of Computers, Systems and Networks". Having recognized information as a subject of theft, assignment, extortion and other criminal acts, criminal law has confirmed status of information as an object of the property right that is coordinated with substantive regulations of information legislation. Till recently, criminal legal doctrine unreasonably unfilled information from the list of possible subjects of theft or other property crimes.

In this connection, appearance of the mentioned section in the Code is natural and objective necessity of legal means in process of solving problems related to fundamental modification of technology, world outlook of people, international relationship under conditions of a wide scope computerization of information sphere.

As is well-known, "Illegal interference with operation of computers, systems and networks", that is an illegal interference with operation of automated computers, systems or networks resulted in distortion or erasing of computer information or destroying its carriers, and also to spreading of computer viruses by using software and hardware designed for illegal penetration into these machines, systems or networks and capable of distortion or erasing computer information or destroying its carriers";

"Theft, misappropriation, extortion of computer information or its capture by swindling or abusing official position" and the "Violation of automated electronic computer operating rules": violation of operating rules of automated computers, systems or networks on the part of a person responsible for their operation, if it has entailed theft, distortion or erasing of computer information, security means, or illegal copying of computer information, or essential infringement of such facilities, systems or networks operation.

The components of crimes defined in the mentioned section are correlated with existing needs of public legal actuality. Also, they are aimed at protection maintenance of the corresponding rights, liberties and legitimate interests of individuals and legal entities. Unfortunately, these legal norms have some weaknesses at the same time.

The owner of automated system is any person that legally uses services of information processing as the proprietor of such system (computer, systems or networks) or as the person that has the right to use such system.

It always has a character of fulfilment of certain actions, and it can be a penetration into computer system by use of special technical means or software, allowing to overcome installed systems of protection from illegal application of obtained passwords or masking under a kind of a legal user with purpose of penetration into computer system.

So, "illegal interference with operation of automated computers, systems and networks that has led to distortion or destruction of computer information or carriers of such information" as penal action. This component of crime is of material character. Consequences are obligatory element of the crime. The person who has performed the specified actions in forms, not defined in the Article 361, is not subject to criminal liability.

The Criminal Code has established the responsibility for distribution of computer viruses. But an obligatory element of the objective side of this crime lies in the way of its commitment, namely: by application a software and/or other means with intent of illegal penetration into automated machines, systems and networks and capable to cause distortion or destruction of computer information or carriers of such information. If the person distributes a computer virus in a different way or by application of other instruments and means which are not bearing the above-stated attributes in aggregate, such person is not subject to the responsibility according to the Criminal Code.

Direct object of a crime is the information property right, that is the broken right of the proprietor's ownership, use or control over information. Interpretation of this term in a context of automated systems is placed in the Article 1 of the Automated Systems Information Security Law "... information in automated systems is a set of all data and programs used in automated systems, irrespectively of means of their physical and logic representation... ".

Displays of the objective side of crime components are: actions like distortion or destruction of computer information or carriers of such information, and also distribution of... carriers of such information, and also distribution of computer virus.

As used here, destruction of information is its loss, when information in sphere of computers, systems and networks ceases to exist for individuals and legal entities that have full or limited property right to it. Termination of access to information should be considered as blocking of information. Such actions can be performed, for example, with the help of electromagnetic, laser and other effect on data carriers in which info is materialized or with the help of which it is transferred; by forming of signals of means and blocks of programs effecting information, its carriers and means of technical protection that causes violation of integrity of information, its distortion or destruction.

Distortion of information is a modification of its contents, violation of its integrity, including partial destruction. Establishing of a mode of access to information is regulated by the Information Law. It defines the order of reception, use, distribution and retention of information. Depending on a mode of access, information is divided into open information and information with restricted access (confidential and secret). According to the Article 30 of the mentioned law, confidential information is data which is in ownership, use or order of separate individuals or legal entities and is distributed, at their will, according to the terms provided for by them.

Citizens and legal entities that own information of professional, business, industrial, commercial and other character, having obtained it due to own means, or such which is a subject of their professional, business, industrial, commercial and other interest and does not break secret provided for by law, have the right to define independently a mode of access to it, including its belonging to the confidential category, and establish a system (ways) of its protection.

Secret information is information containing data, making state and others secret defined by the law, disclosure of which cause damage to the person, society and the state.

We offer to understand the damage caused by criminal acts (direct and indirect losses) which size is equal or exceeds 100 minimal free incomes of citizen as heavy consequences.

The components of this crime are characterized by presence of the general subject. Commitment of such actions by the person which professional duties include preservation or processing of such information should be admitted as the attribute that burdens the responsibility.

Material components structure of the crime is chosen for developing of the first part of this norm. The structure establishes the necessity of criminal consequences approach, like distortion or destruction of computer information or carriers of such information.

The Article directly defines mental attitude of the person to own actions, therefore the guilt form of such person is intention only.

Unfortunately, the Criminal Code does not adjust a situation when interference with operation of automated computers, systems or networks is performed owing to careless actions.

Thus, the significant amount of possible infringements and even actions which are really performed with intent, as it is hard to prove the intent of the computer criminal during investigation of circumstances of intervention (e.g. a person that usually uses e-mail in the Internet, probably not deliberately but also owing to carelessness, may distribute computer viruses).

Theft, assignment, extortion of computer information or its abstraction by swindle or official position abusing (referring to the Article 362) concerns only "computer" crimes. They make the majority among files of offences in sphere of computers, systems and networks.

The definition of "computer information", introduced by the legislation, is very important. In our opinion, it is necessary to understand it as an aggregate of all identified and owned date, used in computers, systems and networks. The identified information is information fixed in the machine carrier with essential properties allowing to identify it.

The given norm of the Criminal Code, naturally, does not contain concrete technical requirements. It refers to departmental instructions and the rules establishing the operating procedure and which should be set specially by the authorized person and be brought to users. Application of the specified Article to the Internet is impossible; its effect applies only to local networks of organizations.

An investigatory relation should be established between the fact of violation of operation rules of automated computers and the fact of caused essential harm. It should be completely proved, that consequences come exactly from violations of operation rules.

Determining of essential harm provided for by the Article 361 is an evaluating process. The harm is determined by court in each concrete case, in view of all circumstances, however it is obvious, that essential harm should be less significant, rather than essential consequences.

A criminal realizes that he is breaking operation rules; he foresees an opportunity and inevitability of illegal influence on information and causing essential harm or meaningly wishes causing such harm. Such action is punished by deprivation of the right to occupy certain positions or by engaging in certain work for the term up to five years or correctional work for the term up to two years.

Part 1 of the Article 363 of the Criminal Code is complicated for interpretation of the contents. Grammatical, logical and system structural analysis of all the Article allows to say that illegal copying of computer information and essential infringement of operation of automated computers, systems and networks are not forms of crime provided for by this Article, and make up only a set of possible consequences which can arise as a result of its commitment. Part 2 of the Article 363 has a blanket reference to described in the Part 1 illegal action.

One more feature of crime is provided for by the Article 363 of the Criminal Code. Only a special subject accounts for its commitment, it is the person responsible for operation of automated computers, systems and networks.

TECHNIQUES TO PENETRATE SYSTEMS OR OBTAIN SYSTEM INFORMATION

This involves using unsuspecting and gullible users to provide information. The hacker uses his verbal skills to deceive victims into disclosing information they ought not to divulge, or convinces victims to commit acts that facilitate the hacker's scheme. Often posing as an employee or someone hired by the organisation, the hacker easily deceives real employees into revealing information.

In order to research his scheme, he may avail himself of documents in the company bins or site rubbish receptacles, such as internal telephone directories and correspondence. The hacker may assume a number of different guises to accomplish this deception. He may pose as a new or temporary worker and ask information systems employees for a password so that he can begin work. He may also pose as someone in a position of authority and intimidate employees into revealing confidential information.

Sometimes overt deception is not required. In large corporations, hackers can take advantage of anonymity among employees. By donning office attire, they can blend into the crowd and thus peruse the premises, perhaps gaining a password written down at an employee's desk in the process.

War-Diallers

War-diallers are programs written by hackers to automate the hacking process. The program can be configured to call a series of telephone numbers to determine if any of the numbers are connected to a computer. These programs can also be configured to a dial a range of numbers to modems or fax machines A hacker can program a war-dialler to dial hundreds of numbers in random patterns in an attempt to avoid detection. The war-dialler can recognize when a computer answers because of the unique tone of the answering modem. When the war-dialler finds a valid number of a computer, the program saves this information in a separate file.

Trojan Horse

A Trojan Horse is the covert placement of instructions inside a valid program or replacement of a valid program with a 'doctored' one, that causes the computer to perform unauthorised functions but usually still allow the program to perform its intended purpose. This is probably the most common method used in computer-based frauds and sabotage.

Trap Doors

When developing large programs, programmers insert instructions for additional code and intermediate output capabilities. The design of computer operating systems attempts to prevent this from happening. Therefore, programmers insert instructions that allow them to circumvent these controls. Hackers take advantage of these trap doors. There are often 'harmless' Trojans in software called 'Easter Eggs'. These are programs within the real program—usually that have nothing to do with the real host software. They can be games, lists of developers, pictures or any other sort of file. A list of these is maintained at www.eeggs.com.

Salami Techniques

Salami techniques involve the theft of small amounts of assets from a large number of sources without noticeably reducing the whole. In a banking system, the amount of interest to be credited to an account is rounded off. Instead of rounding off the number, that fraction of it is credited to a special account owned by the perpetrator. Typically this is used when sequential processing occurs and each account is processed with the fractions added to the special account. This got its name from the slicing of small amounts from the accounts like a salami sausage. The original perpetrator was only caught because the Bank held a competition for the first and last alphabetical account holder in the bank (i.e. a name beginning with 'aa' and a name beginning with 'zz'. The programmer had used the last account to be processed for the storage of the salami additions and the account name stated 'zz'. This account was chosen and then the owner could not be found so it was investigated and the fraud came to light.

Logic Bombs

A logic bomb is a computer program executed at a specific time period or when a specific event occurs. For example, a programmer can write a program to instruct the computer to delete all personnel and payroll files if his name were ever removed from the file.

Data Diddling

Data diddling is the changing of data before or during entry into the computer system. Examples include forging or counterfeiting documents used for data entry and exchanging valid disks and tapes with modified replacements.

Scavenging

Scavenging is the obtaining of information left around a computer system, in the computer room rubbish bins, etc. Bin diving (called 'Dumpster Diving' in the US) also involves obtaining sensitive information from an organisation's rubbish receptacles and bins. This also refers to scavenging from areas of hard disks that are not in use by files but are currently 'file slack' or 'unallocated clusters'

Data Leakage

Data leakage is the removing of information by smuggling it out as part of a printed document, encoding the information to look like something different, and removing it from the facility.

Piggybacking/Impersonation

Physical access is one method used in piggybacking/ impersonation. Examples include following someone in through a door with a badge reader, electronically using another's user identification and password to gain computer access, and tapping into the terminal link of a user to cause the computer to believe that both terminals are the same person.

Simulation and Modelling

Simulation and modelling is a computer manipulation

technique using the computer as a tool or instrument to plan or control a criminal act.

Wire Tapping

Wire tapping into a computer's communications links to read the information being transmitted between computers, or between computers and terminals, is another technique used by hackers. This is often called 'system hijacking'.

Network Weaving

This technique, more commonly known as "looping," involves using numerous networks in an attempt to avoid detection. For example, a hacker might dial into Company A's PBX system to obtain an outside line that can be used to dial into Company B's network. This typically happen if DISA (Dial Inwards, System Access) is enabled with no protection. If Company B can track the origin of the hacker's call, it will lead them to Company A, not to the hacker.

The above is a relatively simple example. Hackers have been known to "loop" through 15 or 20 different networks before arriving at their final destination. Network weaving can make it extremely difficult for an investigator to trace the point of origin for a specific telephone call or data transmission. A Windows utility called Traceroute can map the route that you take to get to a final destination, identifying any 'hops' on the way

Altering the Way a System Generates Passwords

Not all passwords are supplied by users. Some are generated by a computer system or password generators. For example, many Internet Service Providers (ISPs) and corporates give first-time users a randomly generated password (and sometimes a random user name as well), which gets the person online.

Then the user changes the log-on information to their own preference. By learning how a certain system's randomizer works or how the IT Department assign new user IDs and passwords, the hacker can imitate the generation of valid passwords, or alter how the system operates.

A good example of how manipulating a randomizer works is as follows. Dennis Ritchie, who helped develop UNIX technology, reported how a hacker attacked one company's system. Computer officials at the company had their system generate passwords, each eight characters long, mixing letters and digits. In a brute force attack, it should have taken 112 years to crack the nearly 3 trillion possibilities.

However, the randomizer on the company system could only take 32,768 seeds for passwords. The hacker used his own machine to generate and test each of those combinations, using, according to Ritchie, "a total of only about one minute of machine time." In less time than the average commercial break runs on television, the hacker breached a seemingly impenetrable system.

Buffer Overflow Exploits

Buffer overflow exploits are a significant problem in computer security today. In all application programs, there are buffers that hold data. These buffers have a fixed size. If an attacker sends too much data into one of these buffers, the buffer overflows. The server then executes the data that "overflowed" as a program. This program may do any number of things, from sending passwords to Russia to altering system files, installing backdoors, etc., depending on what data the attacker sent to the buffer.

Privilege Escalation Exploits

Privilege escalation exploits grant administrator or root-level access to users who previously did not have such access. For example, an account exists on many servers called "Guest." This account, by default, has a default or no password. Anyone can log-on to the server using this "Guest" account and then by using readily available hacking software to gain administrator-level access to the system. These exploits are very useful, since they allow anyone who has any level of access to a system to easily elevate their privilege level and perform any activities they desire.

5

Crime and the Internet

CYBER CRIME THROUGH INTERNET FRAUD

The best source of information concerning the growing incidence of fraud committed on the Internet is the Internet Fraud Complaint Center (IFCC), a partnership between the National White Collar Crime Center (NW3C) and the Federal Bureau of Investigation (FBI).

The following findings are taken from the IFCC's 2001 Internet Fraud Report:

- From January 1, 2001 – December 31, 2001 the IFCC's website received 49,711 complaints. This total includes many different fraud types and non-fraudulent complaints, such as computer intrusions, SPAM/unsolicited email, and child pornography. During this same time period, the IFCC referred 16,775 complaints of fraud, the majority of which was committed over the Internet or similar online service. The total dollar loss from all referred cases of fraud was $17.8 million, with a median dollar loss of $435 per complaint.

- Internet auction fraud was by far the most reported offense, comprising 42.8% of referred complaints. Non-deliverable merchandise and payment account for 20.3% of complaints, and Nigerian Letter fraud made up 15.5% of complaints. Credit/debit Card fraud and Confidence fraud (such as home improvement scams and multi-level marketing) round out the top five categories of complaints referred to law enforcement during the year. Among those individuals who reported a dollar loss, the highest median dollar losses were found among Nigerian Letter Scam ($5,575), Identity Theft ($3,000), and Investment fraud ($1,000) complainants.

- – The Nigerian Letter Scam is defined as a correspondence outlining an opportunity to receive non-existent government funds from alleged dignitaries that is designed to collect advance fees from the victims. This sometimes requires payoff money to bribe government officials. While other countries may be mentioned, the correspondence typically indicates "The Government of Nigeria" as the nation of origin. This scam has run since the early 1980's and is also referred to as "419 Fraud" after the relevant section of the Criminal Code of Nigeria, as well as "Advance Fee Fraud." Because of the scam, the country of Nigeria ranks 2nd for total complaints reported at the IFCC on businesses by country.

- Nearly 76% of alleged fraud perpetrators are individuals (as opposed to businesses), 81% are male, and half reside in one of the following states: California, Florida, New York, Texas, and Illinois. While most are from the United States, perpetrators have a representation in Canada, Nigeria, Romania and the United Kingdom.

- The amount loss by complainants tends to be related to a number of factors. Business victims tend to lose more than individuals and males tend to lose more than females. This may be a function of both online purchasing differences by gender, and the type of fraud the individual finds themselves involved in. While there isn't a strong relationship between age and loss, proportion of individuals losing at least $5,000 is higher for those 60 years and older than it is for any other age category.

- Electronic mail (E-mail) and web pages are the two primary mechanisms by which the fraudulent contact took place. Nearly 70% of complainants reported they had e-mail contact with the perpetrator.

The primary federal statute used to prosecute Internet fraud is 18 U.S.C. § 1343, which provides that: Whoever, having devised or intending to devise any scheme or artifice to defraud, or for obtaining money or property by means of false or fraudulent pretenses, representations, or promises, transmits or causes to be transmitted by means of wire, radio, or television communication in interstate or foreign commerce, any writings, signs, signals, pictures, or sounds for the purpose of executing such scheme or artifice, shall be fined under this title or imprisoned not more than five years, or both. If the violation affects a financial institution, such person shall be fined not more than $1,000,000 or imprisoned not more than 30 years, or both.

The following essay by Jonathan Rusch, Special Counsel for Fraud Prevention in the Fraud Section of the Criminal Division at the U.S. Department of Justice, describes in more detail the types of fraud frequently perpetrated through the Internet and the Justice Department's efforts – relying on section 1343 and other statutes – to stop them.

Fraud Involving Online Auctions

Online auction fraud typically involves several recurring approaches. The most common approach appears to be the offering of some valuable item, such as computers, high-priced watches, or collectible items, through a known online auction site. The individuals who are informed that they are successful bidders send their money to the seller, but never receive the promised merchandise. In a variation of this approach, the criminals send counterfeit merchandise in place of the promised merchandise. A third approach involves the criminal contacting losing bidders in a particular online auction, informing them that additional units of the item on which they bid have become available, and taking the bidders' money without delivering the items.

Consumers interested in a particular auction sometimes want to learn if other buyers have had favorable experiences with the purported seller in that auction. Major auction sites like eBay and Amazon.com allow legitimate customers to provide feedback on their experiences with particular sellers. Criminals, however, can also use false e-mail identities to provide "shill feedback" — false favorable information about themselves — to make it appear that they are satisfied customers and to give consumers a false sense of security about that auction.

In a recent prosecution, United States v. Denlinger, No. 00CR573IEG (S.D. Cal. filed Feb. 28, 2000), the defendant used online auction sites to offer Beanie Babies for sale, but failed to deliver the products after receiving the victim's money. He used various "screen names" (or aliases) in sending e-mails to prospective victims, and provided them with screen names and e-mail addresses of persons he falsely described as "references." In fact, those screen names were assigned to the defendant, so that when victims e-mailed the "references," the defendant responded with messages that gave victims false and favorable information about his own reliability and trustworthiness as a seller. The defendant also used two techniques to prevent victims from contacting him directly: he gave victims a pager number and falsely told them it was his home telephone number; and he asked them to send their payments to various commercial mail receiving agencies, which he falsely told them was his home address. His scheme defrauded more than 200 victims of nearly $50,000. (The defendant, after pleading guilty to mail and wire fraud, was sentenced to twelve months imprisonment and $46,701 in restitution.)

Fraud Involving Online Retail Sales

One category of fraud that overlaps with auction fraud is fraud in online retail sales of goods and services. The IFCC reports that so-called "nondeliverable" merchandise accounts for 22 percent of all referred complaints. One approach to retail fraud has involved placing banner advertisements on an auction site that offers the same types of goods being auctioned. Prospective buyers who click on the banner advertisement are taken to a different Website that is not part of the auction site, and that offers none of the protections that leading auction Websites have adopted for their members. Another approach involves using unsolicited commercial e-mail ("spam") to lure prospective victims to a Website which purports to sell items of the same type that are available through well-known online auction sites.

In retail sales of services, some criminals have taken advantage of the complexities of the Internet's operations to compel or mislead consumers into visiting their Websites. In United States v. Kashpureff, 98CR0218 (E.D.N.Y. filed March 19, 1998), the defendant operated a Website, AlterNIC, that competed with the InterNIC Website for domain name registration. He wrote and placed software on that Internet that caused persons who wanted to visit the InterNIC Website to be involuntarily redirected to his Website. Ultimately, he pleaded guilty to a violation of the computer fraud statute, 18 U.S.C. § 1030.

In United States v. Lee, No. 99-00560 SOM (D. Haw. filed Dec. 9, 1999), the defendant knew that the Hawaii Marathon Association operated a Website with the Uniform Resource Locator (URL) "www.hawaiimarathon.org" to provide information about the Marathon and enable runners to register online.

Although he had no affiliation with the real Hawaii Marathon, he copied the authorized Marathon Website, and created his own Website with the confusingly similar name, "www.hawaiimarathon.com." Runners who came to his Website thinking that it was the real Hawaii Marathon site were charged a $165 registration fee — $100 more than the real site charged for entry. The defendant also operated another Website where he sold Viagra over the Internet without a prescription. (The defendant later pleaded guilty to wire fraud and unlawful sale of Viagra, and in February 2001 was given a split sentence of ten months imprisonment.)

Investment Fraud

Another major category of online fraud is investment fraud. The Securities and Exchange Commission (SEC) has reported that it receives between 200 and 300 online complaints each day about possible securities fraud online. While the major types of online securities fraud generally parallel traditional securities fraud schemes, market manipulation schemes are a frequent focus of enforcement actions.

"Pump-and-Dump." The most widely publicized form of online market manipulation is the so-called "pump and dump" scheme. In a "pump and dump," criminals identify one or more companies whose stock is thinly traded or not traded at all, then adopt various means to persuade individual online investors to buy that company's stock. These means can include posting favorable, but false and misleading, representations on financial message boards or Websites, and making undisclosed payments to people who are ostensibly independent but who will recommend that stock. Once the price has increased sufficiently, the participants in the scheme — who may be company insiders, outsiders, or both, sell their stock, and the stock price eventually declines sharply, leaving uninformed investors with substantial financial losses. While an outsider who merely expresses his opinions about the worth or likely increase or decrease of a particular stock may not be committing criminal fraud, outsiders or insiders whose conduct extends beyond mere advocacy to manipulation of markets for their personal profit by giving the public false and misleading information may violate securities fraud statutes and other criminal statutes.

In one pump-and-dump case, United States v. Aziz-Golshani, No. 00-007-GAF (C.D. Cal. filed Jan. 4, 2000), two defendants manipulated the stock of a bankrupt company, NEI Webworld, Inc. They posted messages on several financial message boards, falsely stating that NEI was going to be taken over by a California company, and, with the help of a third individual, bought 130,000 shares of NEI before their manipulations resulted in a dramatic price increase. In an attempt to conceal their identities, the two defendants and their confederates used computers at the UCLA Biomedical Library to post the false reports. An SEC amended complaint charged that the defendants and another individual had also engaged in similar manipulative conduct concerning the securities of eleven other issuers in 1999. (In January, 2001, both defendants were sentenced to fifteen months and ten months imprisonment, respectively).

"Cybersmear." The converse of the "pump and dump" is the "cybersmear." A "cybersmear" scheme is organized in the same basic manner as a "pump-and- dump," with one important difference: the object is to induce a decline in the stock's price, to permit the criminals to realize profits by short-selling. To accomplish a sufficiently rapid decline in the stock's price, the criminal must resort to blatant lies and misrepresentations likely to trigger a substantial sell off by other investors.

In United States v. Moldofsky, No. S100CR388 (RPP) (S.D.N.Y. convicted March 8, 2001), the defendant, a day trader, on the evening of March 22, 2000, and the morning of the next day, posted a message nearly twenty times what was designed to look like a Lucent press release announcing that Lucent would not meet its quarterly earnings projections. For most of those postings, he used an alias designed to resemble a screen name used by a frequent commentator on the Lucent message board who had historically expressed positive views of Lucent stock. He also posted additional messages, using other screen names that commented on the release or on the message poster's conduct. On March 23, Lucent's stock price dropped more than 3.7 percent before Lucent issued a statement disavowing the false press release, but rose by 8 percent within ten minutes of Lucent's disavowal.

In United States v. Jakob, No. CR-00-1002-DT (C.D. Cal. indictment filed Sept. 28, 2000; pleaded guilty Dec. 29, 2000), the defendant engaged in even more elaborate fraudulent conduct to effect a "cybersmear." After he tried to short-sell stock in Emulex, but found that the market was bidding up the price, he wrote a press release falsely reporting that Emulex was under investigation by the SEC, that Emulex's Chief Executive Officer was resigning, and that Emulex was reporting a loss in its latest earnings report. He then caused his former employer, a company that distributed online press releases, to send it to major news organizations, which reported the false statements as fact. When Emulex stock rapidly declined, the defendant covered his short-sale position by buying Emulex stock and realizing nearly $55,000 in profits. He also bought more Emulex stock at lower prices, and sold when the stock had recovered most of its value.

One notable feature of online market manipulation schemes is the speed with which the scheme's participants can induce dramatic, though short-term, fluctuations in stock prices, and can realize substantial profits by correctly timing their purchases and sales. In Aziz-Golshani, during the week of November 9, 1999, the defendants bought their NEI stock at prices ranging from 9 cents to 13 cents per share.

On November 15, 1999, NEI stock opened at 9:00 a.m. Eastern time at $8 per share, and within 45 minutes had risen to $15 5/16 per share.

Less than a half-hour later, NEI stock had dropped to approximately 25 cents per share. By selling when the stock price was still high, the defendants realized profits of more than $360,000. In Jakob, once the false press release was distributed, Emulex's stock price dropped in less than one hour from more than $110 per share to approximately $43 per share, and the trading volume of Emulex stock increased significantly as individual traders sold off the stock at notably lower prices. The defendant realized nearly $55,000 in profits from his short sale, and additional profits of nearly $187,000 as the stock price rebounded.

PRIVACY THROUGH INTERNET

An electronic communications network that connects computer networks and organizational computer facilities around the world, the Internet has led to significant changes within our society. An infinite amount of information can be easily obtained and through the development of technology, has become more accessible.

The introduction of the Internet into our daily activities has transitioned our society into a technology dependent era. The Internet has become an increasingly popular source for gathering information and a frequent form of communication.

Privacy focuses on the control over information about oneself, and is argued vital for human dignity and intimacy. The Internet increased the availability of personal information that can be tracked, recorded, and accessed. The personal invasion of privacy due to Internet monitoring has become more of an ethical concern and looking at aspects from the business world we can better determine how the evolution of the Internet has shaped our lives.

Thesis : Issue of Privacy

The issue of privacy and ones right to privacy while at work or on the Internet has become increasingly an important issue companys deal with everyday. Companies have to spend time and money to write policies to cover these issues to protect themselves as well as the well being of their employees.

They need to monitor their employees to ensure productivity and to make sure they are not doing anything illegal at work that could hurt the company. How far these companies can go to protect these things is what makes such an interesting issue. A person has a right to privacy and what they do on their break or outside of the office should be their business, but more and more companies are tapping into this to monitor them. A company can only go as far as to monitor them while they are working or doing work related activities anything outside of this realm in their private lives and emails should not be exploited.

Utilitarianism

Ethics has become a major concern within our society, especially within the business world. It is important to conduct business in an appropriate manner, monitoring productivity, and profit, while maintaining employee satisfaction.

There are two fundamental ideas that underlie utilitarianism; first, that the results of our actions are the key to their moral evaluation, and second, that the one should assess and compare those results in terms of the happiness or unhappiness they cause "or, more broadly, in terms of their impact on peoples wellbeing." It is important to install morals into all aspects of business, including competitors, customers and employees. It is important to keep a sense of well being in order to provide a trustworthy service.

Utilitarianisms guiding impulse is simple and transparent, and many people have found it attractive: human well-being or happiness is what really matters and, accordingly the promotion of well being is what morality is, or ought to be, all about." From a utilitarian perspective employees should be provided with a well being that satisfies each ones personal goals.

The Right of Privacy

The right of privacy has become a controversial issue. While there is no fundamental law or amendment that states ones right to privacy; however it has been implied by the Supreme Court in the United States Amendments and is considered ethically correct in our society. There is no specific law that governs ones right to privacy and this has resulted in a fine line between what is deemed acceptable and what information can be revealed to the public. This has resulted in various court cases in which citizens have tried to determine their own right to privacy. There have been numerous cases over the past century where the Supreme Court has had to determine whether a citizens privacy rights have been violated. This dates back to May 25, 1891 in the Union Pacific Railway Co. v. Botsfold, where it was decided that the plaintiff did not have to submit to physical examination as „no right is held more sacred, or is more carefully guarded, by the common law, than the right of every individual to the possession and control of his own person, free from all restraint or interference of others".

The Evolution of the Internet in the Workplace

The evolution of the Internet has shaped the way that companies conduct business. This has led to a dramatic change within the workplace and the responsibilities of employees. It is an employers responsibility to monitor employees and assess the quality and quantity of work that is being achieved. In the past, employers have done this by monitoring punch cards, productivity reports, profits and consumer satisfaction. The increase in technology and development of computers and the Internet has changed the security and supervision of daily business activities. Companies have a variety of reasons to maintain surveillance within the workplace. There are concerns for employees well being, competitors obstruction, and the productivity and profits of the business. These concerns are all relevant; however, the use of technology has made it easier for employers to snoop on their employees.

Employers have the ability to intercept electronic communication and access the information that has been stored on the companys computers. The easy access that employers have to this information raises the question of whether employers can ethically monitor employees. It has become Employees are expected to conduct business productively and to complete their job under the expectations that they were hired for. The Internet has made it easier for employees to be distracted from their tasks. Personal emailing and browsing the Internet has become a major concern within corporations, leading to the increase in electronic monitoring.

Right of Employers to Keep Work Place Efficient

Employers use electronic monitoring for two basic functions: providing feedback and implementing control. Providing feedback is an essential aspect in conducting business. Employees are monitored in order to provide performance-related feedback and suggestions for improvement, such as with recording a receptionists typing speed or accuracy of data entry clerks. This form of monitoring is understandable and an efficient way to conduct business. The type of monitoring that implements control is more harming to the business environment and calls into question the ethics of the company. The competitiveness of industries in todays business society has led to an increase in security and the need to monitor efficiency within the workplace. This has increased the level of acceptance of employee monitoring, especially through electronic measures. The increase of use of the Internet and its ease, has led to a dependency of many businesses using this form of a communication for all their business transactions. The security that each business requires, also involves the monitoring of their employees online activity in order to ensure there are no security breaches. This form of monitoring is vital in order to maintain the success of the business; however there is a fine line between monitoring electronic activity for the security of the business and monitoring to spy on employees.

Right of Employees Privacy

It is customary for every business to install a code of ethics, setting the standards for employee behavior, standard of practice and it can also be used as a benchmark of evaluation. "The need for special ethical principles in a scientific society is the same as the need for ethical principles in society as a whole. They are mutually beneficial. They help make our relationships mutually pleasant and productive. A professional society is a voluntary, cooperative organization, and those who must conform to its rules are also those who benefit from the conformity of others. Each has a stake in maintaining general compliance.

" It is important for both employers and employees to follow these ethical guidelines. Employers create codes in order to provide standards to which employees should obey; however employers also have to maintain an ethical stance, ensuring the well being and utilitarian rights of their employees. Employees are often unaware of the control that their supervisors have and the intrusion that this can have on their personal life. In the historic case Smyth vs. The Pillsbury Company, Smyth sent inappropriate emails from his home computer to the Pillsbury system. At a later date the company intercepted these email messages and terminated Smyths employment based upon their content. There had been a prior promise of confidentiality within the company; however, this did not protect Smyths rights to privacy.

Employees should be able to work in a trusting environment where they are respected. The Fourth Amendment states the public has the constitutional right to privacy. This is a fundamental right that is upheld within the United States; however, the increase in technology and the ability to observe others has weakened this imperative right. "The computers eye is unblinking and ever present. Sophisticated software allows every minute of every day to be recorded and evaluated". The introduction of the Internet to the workplace has made it easier for employers to observe what employees are doing at every moment. It is an employees utilitarian ethical right to receive privacy and to be treated in a manner that will result in happiness for the entire staff. They have the ethical right to dutiful respect and the right of common good, which contributes most to the achievement of quality of life. It is under these ethics that employees should be made aware of the surveillance within their workplace and the duties that are expected of them.

Right of Employers to Keep the Workplace Safe

The Internet has led to an increase in pornography, racist jokes, and inappropriate forms of electronic communication. The government has condoned the use of electronic monitoring to ensure the safety of employees and uphold civil rights. Under Title VII of the Civil Rights Act, an employers inefficient monitoring of the Internet and email use and abuse may allow racial offensive or sexually explicit material to pervade the work environment and create or contribute to a hostile environment.

Employers are expected to monitor their employees activities online to ensure civil rights are not violated and that employees receive the fundamental rights they are entitled to. This has been an effective form of detection within the workplace. In Strauss vs. Microsoft Corporation, the court held that among other remarks several jokes and parodies of a sexual nature emailed by a supervisor to employees were administered and relevant evidence of sexual harassment. The government has approved online regulation however no standards have been introduced that respect the well being of the employees or considers the effects that these actions cause. The ethical values of employees have been discarded.

THE ALREADY BIG THING ON THE INTERNET: SPYING ON USERS

In 1993, the dawn of the Internet age, the liberating anonymity of the online world was captured in a well-known New Yorker cartoon. One dog, sitting at a computer, tells another: "On the Internet, nobody knows you're a dog." Fifteen years later, that anonymity is gone.

It's not paranoia: they really are spying on you. Technology companies have long used "cookies," little bits of tracking software slipped onto your computer, and other means, to record the Web sites you visit, the ads you click on, even the words you enter in search engines — information that some hold onto forever. They're not telling you they're doing it, and they're not asking permission. Internet service providers are now getting into the act. Because they control your connection, they can keep track of everything you do online, and there have been reports that I.S.P.'s may have started to sell the information they collect.

The driving force behind this prying is commerce. The big growth area in online advertising right now is "behavioral targeting." Web sites can charge a premium if they are able to tell the maker of an expensive sports car that its ads will appear on Web pages clicked on by upper-income, middle-aged men.

The information, however, gets a lot more specific than age and gender — and more sensitive. Tech companies can keep track of when a particular Internet user looks up Alcoholics Anonymous meetings, visits adult Web sites, buys cancer drugs online or participates in anti-government discussion groups.

Serving up ads based on behavioral targeting can itself be an invasion of privacy, especially when the information used is personal. ("Hmm... I wonder why I always get those drug-rehab ads when I surf the Internet on Jane's laptop?")

The bigger issue is the digital dossiers that tech companies can compile. Some companies have promised to keep data confidential, or to obscure it so it cannot be traced back to individuals. But it's hard to know what a particular company's policy is, and there are too many to keep track of. And privacy policies can be changed at any time.

There is also no guarantee that the information will stay with the company that collected it. It can be sold to employers or insurance companies, which have financial motives for wanting to know if their workers and policyholders are alcoholics or have AIDS.

It could also end up with the government, which needs only to serve a subpoena to get it (and these days that formality might be ignored).

If George Orwell had lived in the Internet age, he could have painted a grim picture of how Web monitoring could be used to promote authoritarianism. There is no need for neighborhood informants and paper dossiers if the government can see citizens' every Web site visit, e-mail and text message.

The public has been slow to express outrage — not, as tech companies like to claim, because they don't care about privacy, but simply because few people know all that is going on. That is changing. "A lot of people are creeped-out by this," says Ari Schwartz, a vice president of the Center for Democracy and Technology. He says the government is under increasing pressure to act.

The Federal Trade Commission has proposed self-regulatory guidelines for companies that do behavioral targeting. Anything that highlights the problem is good, but self-regulation is not enough. One idea starting to gain traction in Congress is a do-not-track list, similar to the federal do-not-call list, which would allow Internet users to opt out of being spied on. That would be a clear improvement over the status quo, but the operating principle should be "opt in" — companies should not be allowed to track Internet activities unless they get the user's expressed consent.

The founders wrote the Fourth Amendment — guaranteeing protection against illegal search and seizure — at a time when people were most concerned about protecting the privacy of their homes and bodies. The amendment, and more recent federal laws, have been extended to cover telephone communications. Now work has to be done to give Internet activities the same level of privacy protection.

INTERNET CRIME THROUGH PAYMENT CARD FRAUD

One of the fastest-growing categories of Internet fraud is payment card (i.e., credit card and debit card) fraud. One Internet research firm, Meridien Research, predicted in January 2001 that online payment-card fraud worldwide will increase from $1.6 billion in 2000 to $15.5 billion by 2005.

Online credit card fraud causes substantial problems for online merchants. Initially, many online merchants were defrauded when people, using others' credit card numbers, ordered merchandise and had it shipped to foreign locations that were clearly different from the addresses of the true credit card holders. Under the policies that major credit card issuers established, merchants must bear the losses for online purchases, which qualify as "card- not-present" transactions. As a number of merchants took defensive measures, such as installing software designed to flag possibly fraudulent online transactions, some criminals changed their methods to request shipment of the goods they ordered with others' credit card numbers to United States addresses. Confederates then sell or ship those goods to another location.

To commit online payment-card fraud, criminals need access to valid payment-card numbers. One means of acquiring them is the unlawful accessing of e-commerce Websites. Within the past year, several computer intrusions that made possible the downloading of tens of thousands, if not millions, of credit card numbers — such as the exposure of more than 3 million credit cards at Egghead.com — have received worldwide attention in the media.

A number of Internet credit card schemes involve computer hacking as the means of accessing the numbers. For example, in United States v. Bosanac, No. 99CR3387IEG (S.D. Cal. filed Dec. 7, 1999), the defendant was involved in a computer hacking scheme that used home computers for electronic access to several of the largest United States telephone systems and for downloading thousands of calling card numbers (access codes).

The defendant, who pleaded guilty to possession of unauthorized access devices and computer fraud, used his personal computer to access a telephone system computer and to download and transfer thousands of access codes relating to company calling card numbers. In taking these codes, the defendant used a computer program he had created to automate the downloading, and instructed his coconspirators on how to use the program. The defendant admitted that the loss suffered by the company as a result of his criminal conduct was $955,965. He was sentenced to eighteen months' imprisonment and $10,000 in restitution.

Identity Theft and Fraud

Online payment-card fraud is closely related to the problem of identity theft and fraud. The Federal Trade Commission (FTC) reports that its Consumer Sentinel Website, which provides law enforcement with access to more than 300,000 complaints about all types of consumer fraud, has received more complaints about identity theft and fraud than any other category of consumer fraud. While identity theft can be committed in furtherance of many types of crime, a number of recent federal prosecutions have combined identity theft and Internet fraud.

In United States v. Christian, No. 00-03-SLR (D. Del. filed Aug. 3, 2000), two defendants obtained the names and Social Security numbers of 325 high-ranking United States military officers from a public Website, then used those names and identities to apply for instant credit at a leading computer company and to obtain credit cards through two banks. They fenced the items they bought under the victims' names, and accepted orders from others for additional merchandise. The two defendants, after pleading guilty to conspiracy to commit bank fraud were sentenced to thirty-three and forty-one months imprisonment and restitution of more than $100,000 each.

Similarly, in United States v. Wahl, No. CR00-285P (W.D. Wash. sentenced Oct. 16, 2000), the defendant obtained the date of birth and Social Security number of the victim (who shared the defendant's first and last name and middle initial). He then used the victim's identifying information to apply online for credit cards with three companies and to apply online for a $15,000 automobile loan. He actually used the proceeds of the automobile loan to invest in his own business. (The defendant, after pleading guilty to identity theft, was sentenced to seven months' imprisonment and nearly $27,000 in restitution).

Business Opportunity Fraud

Business opportunity or "work-at-home" schemes are also making their way onto the Internet. In United States v. Shklowskiy (C.D. Cal. sentenced June 9, 2000), the defendants used the Internet to harvest e-mail addresses and send more than 50 million unsolicited e-mails ("spam") to offer people a "work-at-home" opportunity that promised tremendous returns in exchange for a $35 "processing fee." Approximately 12,405 individual victims sent money to what they thought were various businesses, but in fact, were postal mailboxes. As part of the scheme, the defendants forged the e-mail headers in their "spam" to make it appear that the e-mails were coming from an Internet service provider, BigBear.Net. As a result of the header forgery, when approximately 100,000 recipients of the spam responded with complaints by e-mail, the unexpected large volume of e-mails caused BigBear.Net's computer file servers to crash or cause disruptions in their service to customers. BigBear.Net had to hire three temporary workers for nearly six months to respond to the large numbers of complaints. (Ultimately, two defendants, after pleading guilty to conspiracy to commit mail and wire fraud, were sentenced to twenty seven months' imprisonment and restitution of $104,000 to fraud victims, including BigBear.Net).

The Response to Internet Fraud

As the case examples above indicate, more and more United States Attorneys' Offices are pursuing significant cases of Internet fraud. The cases being prosecuted tend to show that the criminal statutes that apply to other types of white collar crime — conspiracy, mail and wire fraud, credit card fraud, securities fraud, money laundering, and identity theft — are equally applicable to various forms of Internet fraud. In addition, a variety of existing sentencing guidelines enable federal prosecutors to seek higher sentences in appropriate cases of Internet fraud. These include enhancements for mass-marketing (USSG § 2F1.1(b)(3)), identity theft (USSG § 2F1.1(b)(5)(C)), conducting a substantial part of a scheme from outside the United States (USSG § 2F1.1(b)(6)(B)), large numbers of vulnerable victims (USSG § 3A1.1(b)(2)(B)), and use of a special skill (USSG 3B1.3; compare United States v. Petersen, 98 F.3d 502, 506-08 (9th Cir. 1996), with United States v. Godman, 223 F.3d 320, 322 (6th Cir. 2000)).

COMPUTER CRIME : HACKING

Computer crime often involves illegally accessing and damaging computers. Illegally accessing and damaging computers runs the gamut from the mischievous to the malicious. This section first addresses hacktivism, a relatively benign form of illegal access and damage to computers undertaken for a political purpose.

Hacktivism includes web defacement, web sit-ins, and denial-of-service attacks. The discussion then shifts to more malicious denial-of-service attacks; worms and viruses, which propagate destructively through the Internet; and finally systems hacking.

Hacktivism

As Palestinian rioters clashed with Israeli forces in the fall of 2000, Arab and Israeli hackers took to cyberspace to participate in the action. According to the Middle East Intelligence Bulletin, the cyberwar began in October, shortly after the Lebanese Shi'ite Hezbollah movement abducted three Israeli soldiers.

Pro-Israeli hackers responded by crippling the guerrilla movement's website, which had been displaying videos of Palestinians killed in recent clashes and which had called on Palestinians to kill as many Israelis as possible.

Pro-Palestinian hackers retaliated, shutting down the main Israeli government website and the Israeli Foreign Ministry website. From there the cyberwar escalated. An Israeli hacker planted the Star of David and some Hebrew text on one of Hezbollah's mirror sites, while pro-Palestinian hackers attacked additional Israeli sites, including those of the Bank of Israel and the Tel Aviv Stock Exchange. Hackers from as far away as North and South America joined the fray, sabotaging over 100 websites and disrupting Internet service in the Middle East and elsewhere.

The Palestinian-Israeli cyberwar illustrates a growing trend. Cyberspace is increasingly used as a digital battleground for rebels, freedom fighters, terrorists, and others who employ hacking tools to protest and participate in broader conflicts. The term "hacktivism," a fusion of hacking with activism, is often used to describe this activity.

Hacktivists see cyberspace as a means for non-state actors to enter arenas of conflict, and to do so across international borders. They believe that nation-states are not the only actors with the authority to engage in war and aggression. And unlike nation-states, hacker warriors are not constrained by the "law of war" or the Charter of the United Nations. They often initiate the use of aggression and needlessly attack civilian systems.

Hacktivism is a relatively recent phenomenon. One early incident took place in October 1989, when anti-nuclear hackers released a computer worm into the US National Aeronautics and Space Administration (NASA) SPAN network. The worm carried the message, "Worms Against Nuclear Killers....Your System Has Been Officially [sic] WANKed....You talk of times of peace for all, and then prepare for war." At the time of the attack, anti-nuclear protesters were trying (unsuccessfully) to stop the launch of the shuttle that carried the plutonium-fueled Galileo probe on its initial leg to Jupiter. The source of the attack was never identified, but some evidence suggested that it might have come from hackers in Australia.

In recent years, hacktivism has become a common occurrence worldwide. It accounts for a substantial fraction of all cyberspace attacks, which are also motivated by fun, curiosity, profit, and personal revenge. Hacktivism is likely to become even more popular as the Internet continues to grow and spread throughout the world. It is easy to carry out and offers many advantages over physical forms of protest and attack.

The Attraction to Hacktivism

For activists, hacktivism has several attractive features, not the least of which is global visibility. By altering the content on popular websites, hacktivists can spread their messages and names to large audiences. Even after the sites are restored, mirrors of the hacked pages are archived on sites such as Attrition.org, where they can be viewed by anyone at any time and from anywhere. Also, the news media are fascinated by cyberattacks and are quick to report them. Once the news stories hit the Internet, they spread quickly around the globe, drawing attention to the hackers as well as to the broader conflict.

Activists are also attracted to the low costs of hacktivism. There are few expenses beyond those of a computer and an Internet connection. Hacking tools can be downloaded for free from numerous websites all over the world. It costs nothing to use them and many require little or no expertise. Moreover, hacktivism has the benefit of being unconstrained by geography and distance.

Unlike street protesters, hackers do not have to be physically present to fight a digital war. In a "sit-in" on the website of the Mexican Embassy in the United Kingdom, the Electronic Disturbance Theater (EDT) gathered over 18,000 participants from 46 countries. Hacktivists could join the battle simply by visiting the EDT's website.

Hacktivism is thus well-suited to "swarming," a strategy in which hackers attack a given target from many directions at once. Because the Internet is global, it is relatively easy to assemble a large group of digital warriors in a coordinated attack. The United Kingdom-based Electrohippies Collective estimated that 452,000 people participated in their sit-in on the website of the World Trade Organization (WTO). The cyberattack was conducted in conjunction with street protests during WTO's Seattle meetings in late 1999.

Another attraction of hacktivism is the ability to operate anonymously on the Internet. Cyberwarriors can participate in attacks with little risk of being identified, let alone prosecuted. Further, participating in a cyberbattle is not life-threatening or even dangerous: hacktivists cannot be gunned down in cyberspace.

Many hacktivists, however, reject anonymity. They prefer that their actions be open and attributable. EDT and Electrohippies espouse this philosophy. Their events are announced in advance and the main players use their real names.

Web Defacement and Hijacking

Web defacement is perhaps the most common form of attack. Attrition.org, which collects mirrors and statistics of hacked websites, recorded over 5,000 defacements in the year 2000 alone, up from about 3,700 in 1999. Although the majority of these may have been motivated more by thrills and bragging rights than by some higher cause, many were also casualties of a digital battle.

Web hacks were common during the Kosovo conflict in 1999. The US hacking group called Team Spl0it broke into government sites and posted statements such as, "Tell your governments to stop the war." The Kosovo Hackers Group, a coalition of European and Albanian hackers, replaced at least five sites with black and red "Free Kosovo" banners. In the wake of the accidental bombing of China's Belgrade embassy by the North Atlantic Treaty Organization (NATO), angry Chinese citizens allegedly hacked several US government sites. The slogan "Down with Barbarians" was placed in Chinese on the web page of the US Embassy in Beijing, while the US Department of Interior website showed images of the three journalists killed during the bombing and crowds protesting the attack in Beijing. The US Department of Energy's home page read:

"Protest USA's Nazi action!...We are Chinese hackers who take no cares about politics. But we can not stand by seeing our Chinese reporters been killed which you might have know [sic]....NATO led by USA must take absolute responsibility....We won't stop attacking until the war stops!"

Web defacements were also popular in a cyberwar that erupted between hackers in China and Taiwan in August 1999. Chinese hackers defaced several Taiwanese and government websites with pro-China messages saying Taiwan was and always would be an inseparable part of China. "Only one China exists and only one China is needed," read a message posted on the website of Taiwan's highest watchdog agency. Taiwanese hackers retaliated and planted a red and blue Taiwanese national flag and an anti-Communist slogan, "Reconquer, Reconquer, Reconquer the Mainland," on a Chinese high-tech Internet site. The cyberwar followed an angry exchange between China and Taiwan in response to Taiwanese President Lee Teng-hui's statement that China must deal with Taiwan on a "state-to-state" basis.

Many of the attacks during the Palestinian-Israeli cyberwar were web defacements. The hacking group GForce Pakistan, which joined the pro-Palestinian forces, posted heart-wrenching images of badly mutilated children on numerous Israeli websites. The Borah Torah site also contained the message, "Jews, Israelis, you have crossed your limits, is that what Torah teaches? To kill small innocent children in that manner? You Jews must die!" along with a warning of additional attacks.

Hacktivists have also hijacked websites by tampering with the Domain Name Service so that the site's domain name resolves to the IP address of some other site. When users point their browsers to the target site, they are redirected to the alternative site.

In what might have been one of the largest mass website takeovers, the anti-nuclear Milw0rm hackers joined with the Ashtray Lumberjacks hackers in an attack that affected more than 300 websites in July 1998. According to reports, the hackers broke into the British Internet service provider (ISP) EasySpace, which hosted the sites. They altered the ISP's database so that users attempting to access the sites were redirected to a Milw0rm site, where they were greeted by a message protesting the nuclear arms race. The message concluded with "Use your power to keep the world in a state of PEACE and put a stop to this nuclear bullshit."

Web Sit-ins

Web sit-ins are another popular form of attack. Thousands of Internet users simultaneously visit a target website and attempt to generate sufficient traffic to disrupt normal service. A group calling itself Strano Network conducted what was probably the first such demonstration as a protest against the French government's policies on nuclear and social issues. On December 21, 1995, they launched a one-hour Net'Strike attack against the websites operated by various government agencies. At the appointed hour, participants from all over the world pointed their browsers to the government websites. According to reports, at least some of the sites were effectively knocked out for the period.

In 1998, EDT took the concept a step further and automated the attacks. They organized a series of sit-ins, first against Mexican President Ernesto Zedillo's website and later against US President Bill Clinton's White House website, the Pentagon, the US Army School of the Americas, the Frankfurt Stock Exchange, and the Mexican Stock Exchange. The purpose was to demonstrate solidarity with the Mexican Zapatistas. According to EDT's Brett Stalbaum, the Pentagon was chosen because "we believe that the US military trained the soldiers carrying out the human rights abuses." For a similar reason, the US Army School of the Americas was selected. The Frankfurt Stock Exchange was targeted, Stalbaum said, "Because it represented capitalism's role in globalization utilizing the techniques of genocide and ethnic cleansing, which is at the root of the Chiapas' problems. The people of Chiapas should play a key role in determining their own fate, instead of having it pushed on them through their forced relocation....which is currently financed by Western capital."

To facilitate the strikes, the organizers set up special websites with automated software. All that was required of would-be participants was to visit one of the FloodNet sites. When they did, their browser would download the software (a Java Applet), which would access the target site every few seconds. In addition, the software let protesters leave a personal statement on the targeted server's error log. For example, if they pointed their browsers to a non-existent file such as "human_rights" on the target server, the server would log the message, "human_rights not found on this server."

When the Pentagon's server sensed the attack from the FloodNet servers, it launched a counter-offensive against the users' browsers, redirecting them to a page with an Applet program called "HostileApplet." Once there, the new applet was downloaded to their browsers, where it endlessly tied up their machines trying to reload a document until the machines were rebooted. The Frankfurt Stock Exchange reported that they were aware of the protest but believed it had not affected their services. Overall, EDT considered the attacks a success. "Our interest is to help the people of Chiapas to keep receiving the international recognition that they need to keep them alive," said Stalbaum.

Since the time of the strikes, FloodNet and similar software have been used in numerous sit-ins sponsored by EDT, the Electrohippies, and others. There were reports of FloodNet activity during the Palestinian-Israeli cyberwar. Pro-Israel hackers created a website called Wizel.com, which offered FloodNet software and other tools before it was shut down. Pro-Arab hackers put up similar sites.

The Electrohippies have been criticized for denying their targets' right to speech when conducting a sit-in. Their response has been that a sit-in is acceptable if it substitutes the deficit of speech by one group with a broad debate on policy issues and if the event used to justify the sit-in provides a focus for the debate. The Electrohippies also demand broad support for their actions. An operation protesting genetically modified foods was aborted when the majority of visitors to their site did not vote for the operation.

Denial-of-Service Attacks

Whereas a web sit-in requires participation by tens of thousands of people to have even a slight impact, the so-called denial-of-service (DoS) and distributed denial-of-service (DDoS) tools allow lone cyberwarriors to shut down websites and e-mail servers. With a DoS attack, a hacker uses a software tool that bombards a server with network messages. The messages either crash the server or disrupt service so badly that legitimate traffic slows to a crawl. DDoS is similar except that the hacker first penetrates numerous Internet servers (called "zombies") and installs software on them to conduct the attack. The hacker then uses a tool that directs the zombies to attack the target all at once.

During the Kosovo conflict, Belgrade hackers were credited with DoS attacks against NATO servers. They bombarded NATO's web server with "ping" commands, which test whether a server is running and connected to the Internet. The attacks caused line saturation of the targeted servers.

Similar attacks took place during the Palestinian-Israeli cyberwar. Pro-Palestinian hackers used DoS tools to attack Netvision, Israel's largest ISP. While initial attacks crippled the ISP, Netvision succeeded in fending off later assaults by strengthening its security.

6

The Role of Intelligence in the Cyber Arena

INTRODUCTION

As in any form of security, intelligence is a key component of tactical and strategic decision-making. Effective cyber intelligence will enhance our ability to assess the effects of cyber attacks, mitigate risks associated with the threat, and streamline cyber security into an efficient and cost-effective process based on well informed decisions.

The Role of Intelligence

The role of intelligence in any capacity is to collect, analyse, and produce information to provide complete, accurate, timely, and relevant threat assessments to inform decision makers who act on the information. It is usually most effective when it is disseminated at the lowest possible classification level for the maximum number of relevant users facing these threats. In performing this mission, the intelligence agencies seek to penetrate actual or potential threat targets consistent with national strategic, operational, and tactical priorities. These agencies then seek to produce intelligence on adversary or threat capabilities and intentions in a manner that "connects" with the maximum number of relevant customers.

Intelligence and threat analysis does not exist for its own purposes. When threat details are suppressed or ignored, national security incurs significant consequences. It is important to sustain a high level of performance in the dynamic cyber arena. This environment is where threats develop rapidly and are fuelled by new concepts for the use of pervasive IT. new waves of innovative capabilities seem to break over users in tsunami fashion, be it the coming cloud architectures or the continuing revolution in personal devices connected to the networks. given this relentless and constantly unfolding environment, intelligence might be successful in keeping pace with technological innovation. Conversely, it might be slow, or even wrong in its assessments of the threat dynamic. It is therefore important to evaluate public and private cyber intelligence activities that support these security missions in a strategic manner.

The Cyber Intelligence Community

This unique, currently *ad hoc*, community is made up of government, telecommunication and Internet providers, CERTs, and other formal information security entities, specialty companies, and vendors. The members of this community engage in a myriad of activities that could be the potential victim of a cyber threat. This "Cyber Intelligence Community" is currently an informal coalition of the willing that collects and analyses unclassified and classified cyber intelligence data and trends. There is no formal mechanism across industry and government cyber intelligence entities that successfully collects, processes, and analyses all identifiable key cyber threat behaviour and reports it at an unclassified or reasonable classification level to all appropriate customers.

An effective connection between intelligence provider and the customer means that the customer has understood and internalized the intelligence resulting in action to work the intelligence and mitigate the threat. Good intelligence professionals relentlessly pursue interactions with customers to ensure that: the data is collected, analysed, and conveyed; the intelligence serves customers' purposes; and some action is being taken (or deliberately not taken). This cycle can be referred to as a constant process of story-finding, story-telling, story-updating, story-listening, and story-heeding. A concept to institutionalize this *ad hoc* community is currently missing.

Investing in Cyber Intelligence Tradecraft

A substantial and continuing investment in cyber intelligence should be a strategic imperative in the information age. It is also imperative to use that intelligence to safe guard our ability to maintain security. We must ensure that stable domestic and international economies are not jeopardized by possible conflict with rival powers, rogue states, failing or failed states, modern terrorists and thieves, and WMD proliferators.

All formal and informal intelligence disciplines contribute to these imperatives, including Signals Intelligence (SIGINT), Human Intelligence (HUMINT), Open Source Intelligence (OSINT), Geospatial and Measurement Intelligence (GEOINT), and the volumes of unclassified network data and behaviour being watched by global CERTs. Continuous liaison among all related parties is critical so that sharing is seamless. This ensures an evolving, improved level of insight and reporting to an increasingly secure and highly performing cyber environment for all.

This evolving cyber intelligence tradecraft requires deep and powerful technical and analytic expertise at all levels. Such technical talent and related capabilities remain ill-defined and in short supply across government and industry. An institution that has made some headway in this regard is the Information Assurance Directorate (IAD) at the National Security Agency. IAD is the front line of the defensive cyber mission. It commands substantial resources, high performing talent, strong processes, and informed outreach. It also works hand in hand with military, public, and private partners to ensure that our cyber capabilities and intellectual property are defended and that our defence is informing offence and vice versa. IAD is a good start, but we must emulate their good practices and innovativeness in defining professional attributes, associated education, and training goals for the unique career fields associated with the cyber realm.

CAPABILITIES OF CYBER INTELLIGENCE

Individual cyber intelligence capabilities have been applied for decades, some since the earliest days of IT system design. Beyond the inflection point of a unified, comprehensive approach, there have been significant advancements in the overall discipline. Given the importance of cyber intelligence in today's environment, business executives should join their IT colleagues in understanding how this discipline is evolving. Here's a look at four critical topics:

Cyber Security

Many cyber security efforts were geared to detecting and protecting against intrusions of the perimeter. As threats shifted to inside the trust zone (*e.g.*, employees who inadvertently enable security breaches), new tools and techniques were needed. Identity and access management solutions were siloed systems—with isolated entitlements, activity logging, and controls. Pattern detection of higher-order threats was extremely difficult because these solutions had limited access to the context of external events. Technology solutions were manually operated, which the business perceived as a nuisance and often circumvented. The chief security officer (CSO) or chief information security officer (CISO), if they existed at all, were typically technologists with deep domain knowledge, but without a seat in the boardroom.

Today, cyber security is increasingly framed as a combination of architecture, practices, and processes—with equal focus on internal and external threats. Highly integrated tool sets and investments in cyber analytics have helped connect dots and identify previously undetectable exposures. Automated identity management tools are incorporated into day-to-day tasks, including smart cards, biometrics, fingerprint, and handprint scanners. The CSO role has become commonplace, requiring a mix of technology and leadership skills and gaining a seat at the boardroom table.

Cyber Forensics

In the past, incident investigations would conclude once a root-cause analysis was completed. These self-contained analyses were rarely used to augment existing controls or update policies. At best, a script was created to improve response in case a breach recurred.

Cyber forensics now looks beyond the host to the network layer, determining the source (inside or outside the organization) of the malware. This determination is correlated with other internal and known external threats using cyber analytics, in an attempt to identify future vulnerabilities. Forensics results are part of a closed-loop cycle in cyber intelligence, improving directly affected and associated controls.

Cyber Analytics

In the past, cyber analytics was a reactive approach based on situational awareness and descriptive analysis. It provided an understanding of the value of business analytics, but without the models to apply the patterns.

These days, this discipline is an established tradecraft of analytics, reinforced by the realization that threats and opportunities are often hidden in plain sight. Cyber analytics is predictive, prescriptive, and a part of a closed-loop cycle of continuous refinement based on other cyber intelligence activities.

Cyber Logistics

Supplier security reviews were typically limited to deal signings and cursory annual audits. Notably in manufacturing, companies relied on several ever-changing sub-contractors and small hardware providers, each with its own risk profile, which created potential weaknesses upstream in the supply chain. Personnel checks occurred only during the hiring or contracting process, with clearance processing handled by largely unknown third parties.

Today, cyber logistics includes extensive analysis to identify, assess, and mitigate risks posed by vendors subject to foreign ownership, control or influence, or other significant concerns prior to a purchase or the awarding of a contract. It entails the continuous assessment of suppliers, including organization structures and corporate activity as well as ongoing confirmation of the integrity of goods.

Cyber intelligence strategies include provisions for personnel security such as verifying the legitimacy of background investigation agencies, proactive foreign travel risk advisory, and automated reinvestigations of executives and privileged roles.

New Approach to IT Security

Intelligence expert Terry Roberts says cyber intelligence, a new approach to IT security, could make significant gains in the coming year. "The good thing is, this isn't really rocket science," says the chair of the Intelligence and National Security Alliance's Cyber Council. Pilot projects are underway to determine if methods employed by the 17 federal intelligence agencies could be adapted to safeguard non-classified but sensitive information in the private sector. To succeed, Roberts says, the government and private sector must collaborate and share information. "In a year or two, we could actually have the private-public partnership established, with the beginnings of an unclassified cyber-intelligence approach," Roberts says in an interview with Information Security Media Group (select one of the Podcast Options at right to listen).

Roberts edited the alliance's just-issued paper, Cyber Intelligence: Setting the Landscape for an Emerging Discipline, which discusses how the current cyberthreat landscape requires a new way to share intelligence in unclassified cyberspace.

"It's important to understand that when we use the word *intelligence* that we're really talking about knowledge, not just information, and we're not necessarily talking about something that has to be classified," Roberts says. "When we're talking about intelligence as an approach for the cyber arena, it's really about pulling together all the information that we know, processing it, analysing it and providing unclassified, situational awareness and situations of warning to both government and industry."

In the interview, Roberts discusses the:

- Difficulties of industry to adapt the highly sophisticated approach the federal intelligence agencies employ to share cyber intelligence. "What we are not doing really is applying those intelligence techniques and tradecraft to the unclassified arena," she says. "Think about it this way: 90 percent of infrastructure in the cyber arena is owned by industry, and 90 percent of the information or data of cyber activity is in the unclassified arena. But we're not focusing on that realm in a comprehensive, consistent manner that we can provide unclassified cyber intelligence to all of industry."

- Multidisciplinary skills that cyber intelligence requires. "In the beginning nuclear age, you brought in people with the technical body of knowledge, then your brought people with a body of knowledge on that particular adversary, the culture, the leadership, and you brought it all together so you would have a 360 view," she says. We haven't been doing that in the (private-sector) cyber realm.

"Actually, in cyber intelligence, you need analytics types of folks, you need people who understand the network environment, that operational background; you need people with technical background who understand the particulars of an attack vector or a fraud approach or sabotage approach that's being used. And, those folks together, need to be looking at the data, analysing it and coming up with so what, the impact of what they're seeing today and what that means for the future."

THE "OPEN SOURCE" INTELLIGENCE INDUSTRY

The US military defines 'Open Source Intelligence' (OSINT) as "relevant information derived from the systematic collection, processing and analysis of publicly available information in response to intelligence requirements". "Open source" is "any person or group that provides the information without the expectation of privacy", while "publicly available information" includes that which is "available on request to a member of the general public; lawfully seen or heard by any observer; or made available at a meeting open to the general public". 'Open source' intelligence is thus defined by virtue of what it is not: "confidential", "private" or otherwise "intended for or restricted to a particular person, group or organization". But this distinction is undermined in practice by the categorisation of 'weblogs', internet 'chat-rooms' and social-networking sites as "public speaking forums".

Prior to the IT revolution, OSINT gatherers were primarily concerned with the left wing press and the situation in foreign countries. Intelligence was obtained by reading the papers, debriefing businessmen and tourists, and collaborating with academics and scholars. Indeed, OSINT specialists have bemoaned the substantial decline in the number of foreign correspondents working for major newspapers (a consequence of declining print media revenues). This loss has been off-set, however, by the wealth of information now available on the world-wide-web, which has seen OSINT transformed into a desk-based activity requiring nothing more than an internet connection, a web browser and a telephone. As the RAND Corporation has observed: "the proliferation of [online] media and research outlets mean that much of a state's intelligence requirements can today be satisfied by comprehensive monitoring of open sources". The CIA has even been quoted as saying that "80% of its intelligence comes from Google". From a security perspective there is nothing inherently problematic about the use of OSINT. On the contrary, the security services would be negligent if they didn't utilise information in the public domain to inform their work; everyone else engaged in public policy matters does the same thing.

However, from a civil liberties perspective, the process of appropriating personal information for the purpose of security classification is inherently problematic, since it is often based on wholly flawed assumptions about who or what poses a 'threat'. The mere act of recording that someone spoke out publicly against the War, attended a demonstration, or is friends with a known 'security risk', brings with it a significant possibility that this information will be used prejudicially against them at some point in the future. This in turn calls into question the democratic legitimacy of surveillance and intelligence gathering, a legitimacy that rests on questions of who is doing the watching, how, and why?

OSINT and the Police

In an address to the Eurointel '99 conference, a spokesman for New Scotland Yard's (NSY) OSINT described open sources as "any form or source of information available to us either as a paying customer or for free". Such information may be used for tactical or strategic purposes. "Tactical" information is that which is needed urgently, whereas "strategic" information "can be collected through long-term research as part of an ongoing project", around topics such as organised crime, money laundering, terrorism and drugs. According to NSY:

Much of this is surprisingly easily using some very simple tools and officers are astonished when they come to us with nothing more than a name and we return address lists, family names and addresses, companies and directorships, financial details and associates.

The police OSINT specialists also use 'people finder' sites that "can employ directories, public records, telephone records, lists, e-mail finders, homepage finders etc".

In reality we use on-line sources as the first string to our bow, but we frequently dip into our list of real people—experts in their particular field whenever we reach a dead-end or want that little bit more.

Tellingly, all of Scotland Yard's "online transactions are done covertly" using "undercover companies, pseudonyms and covert companies in the same way [as] with any other covert operation". "This helps to prevent anyone seeing that the police have been looking", they explain. It also raises fundamental questions of accountability [unlike the intelligence services, the police are supposed to be accountable for their investigative techniques], regulation [to what extent do police intelligence gatherers respect the laws and principles of privacy and data protection] and democratic control [what oversight mechanisms exist?]. The Yard's spokesman was candid about viewing data protection as an unreasonable 'barrier' to his work:

Other challenges came, and continue to come, from the Data Protection Registrar. We must comply with the law but it seems that time after time we face an uphill struggle in the use of legitimate data collection which is so valuable in the fight against sophisticated and well organised criminals and those of a generally evil disposition. Even as we speak there is contention and confusion amongst a number of on-line service providers, Equifax and Experian [credit rating and financial intelligence companies], to name but two, over exactly how DP legislation is to be interpreted.

Privatising OSINT

In recent year, Dr. Andrew Rathmell of RAND Europe called for the "privatisation of intelligence", arguing that there was "little reason to think that [OSINT collection] can better be done by in-house experts than by established private sector research institutes and companies". As in other areas of security and defence, it was argued that outsourcing could "relieve budgetary pressures". "In order to benefit from the ongoing information and intelligence revolutions", suggested RAND, "all European states could benefit from closer European collaboration, both between governments and with the private sector". Dr. Rathmell also observed that: Not only are open sources now more widely available, but the information revolution is now blurring the boundaries between open and covert sources in regard to the formerly sacrosanct technical collection means.

The OSINT industry has grown rapidly over the past decade as a trend that began in the USA has quickly taken hold in Europe. Equifax and Experian, are 'data aggregators', organisations that are able to create an increasingly high-resolution picture of an individuals' activities by drawing together data from a variety of sources.

As the American Civil Liberties Union (ACLU) has explained: "These companies, which include Acxiom, Choicepoint, Lexis-Nexis and many others, are largely invisible to the average person, but make up an enormous, multi-billion-dollar industry". Whereas privacy statutes constrain governments' ability to collect information on citizens who are not the targets of actual police investigations, "law enforcement agencies are increasingly circumventing that requirement by simply purchasing information that has been collected by data aggregators", say ACLU.

European data aggregators include World-Check, a commercial organisation that offers "risk intelligence" to reduce "customer exposure to potential threats posed by the organisations and people they do business with". World-Check is the sort of place you go to check if an individual or entity appears on any of the 'terrorism lists' drawn-up by the UK, EU, USA or UN (among many others).

The organisation claims to have a client base of "over 4,500 organisations", with a "renewal rate in excess of 97%". According to World-Check's website, its research department "methodically profiles individuals and entities deemed worthy of enhanced scrutiny"; its "highly structured database" is "derived from thousands of reliable public sources". Another service offered by World-Check is an online "Passport-Check" that "verifies the authenticity of 'machine readable' (MRZ) passports from more than 180 countries" as proof of due diligence". An annual subscription allows for "unlimited access, look-ups, printouts and suspicious name reporting".

OSINT Theory and Practice

With information and communications technology offering up so much potential 'open source intelligence', scientists and computer programmers have teamed up to automate the process of collecting and analysing this data. The University of Southern Denmark, for example, has established an institute for applied mathematics in counter terrorism, the "Counterterrorism Research Lab" (CTR Lab), which conducts research and development around: advanced mathematical models, novel techniques and algorithms, and useful software tools to assist analysts in harvesting, filtering, storing, managing, analysing, structuring, mining, interpreting, and visualizing terrorist information.

Its products include the iMiner ("terrorism knowledge base and analysis tools"), CrimeFighter (a "toolbox for counterterrorism") and EWaS, (an "early warning system" and "terrorism investigation portal"). The CTR Lab has also organised international conferences on themes like "Counterterrorism and OSINT", "Advances in Social Networks Analysis and Mining" and "OSINT and Web Mining". As the EU's Joint Research Centre observes:

The phenomenal growth in Blog publishing has given rise to a new research area called opinion mining. Blogs are particularly easy to monitor as most are available as RSS feeds. Blog aggregators like Technorati and Blogger allow users to search across multiple Blogs for postings. Active monitoring of Blogs applies information extraction techniques to tag postings by people mentioned, sentiment or tonality or similar... Ostensibly, governments use this technology to help them understand public opinion, in much the same way as they use 'focus groups'. Of course, the very same technology can also be used to identify groups and individuals expressing 'radical' or 'extremist' views.

In the USA, the Mercyhurst College offers degrees in "Intelligence Analysis", promising its graduates jobs with the CIA and the US Army, amongst others. In July 2010, Mercyhurst organised a "Global Intelligence Forum" in Dungarvan, Ireland, with panels on medicine, law, finance, technology, journalism, national security, law enforcement, and business intelligence.

Kings' College in London now offers an OSINT diploma, covering "both theoretical and practical aspects of OSINT, including OSINT collection and analysis methodologies". It advises that 6 "Students taking this module should consider applying for the traineeship scheme with the EU Institute for the Protection and Security of the Citizen" (IPSC, part of the EU Joint Research Centre).

From the private sector, Jane's Strategic Advisory Services (the consultancy division of defence specialist Jane's), also offers an OSINT collection and analysis training service. The course covers "overarching methods, best practices, considerations, challenges and tools available to open source intelligence analysts". Tutors include Nico Prucha, whose expertise includes "on-line jihadist movements and ideologies", "using blogs and social networking tools for intelligence collection", "navigating and assessing forums and the 'Deep Web'", "key word analysis", "sentiment analysis" and "on-line recruitment and radicalization patterns".

Crossing the Boundaries

The information revolution is, in the words of the RAND Corporation, "blurring the boundaries between open and covert sources in regard to the formerly sacrosanct technical collection means". On the one hand, OSINT tools can be used to 'mine' publicly available (and privately held) datasets to conduct de facto surveillance on named groups and individuals. On the other, the very same 'community' of scientists, programmers and hackers, has developed a whole range of so-called 'spyware' applications that enable to users to conduct covert and intrusive surveillance. Products include 'phishing' applications, used to acquire sensitive information such as usernames and passwords, and a variety of 'keystroke loggers', used to surreptitiously record computer users activities.

Meanwhile, the illegal interception of GSM (mobile) telecommunications is "cheap, easy, and getting easier" and, as Google demonstrated recently, the hacking of unsecured wireless networks is straightforward. Although the EU has criminalised the unauthorised use of spyware, hacking and interception techniques, this has done nothing to stem their development.

Moreover, some EU law enforcement are in clearly using them, having repeatedly demanded so-called 'lawful access' powers, allowing them to legally access suspects' computer hard drives through the Internet, and without the knowledge of those affected. The crux of the matter is that both the police and the private investigator are steadily accumulating the capacity (if not the lawful powers) to conduct the kind of covert and intrusive surveillance that was once the preserve of GCHQ and the secret intelligence services.

INTELLIGENCE FOR CYBER-SPACE

Although many of the intelligence methodologies and principles remain the same, new ways of thinking appropriate to the cyber-domain are essential. The lack of borders in cyber-space is a critical difference from the more familiar domains of intelligence. Indeed, geography and political borders often aided traditional military intelligence analysis-it is a simple thing to develop threat scenarios if the potential enemy can only use certain terrain or sea lines of communication and then, only at certain times of the year-while simple factors of physics such as time and distance also provided opportunities for warning. Within the Internet, however, these limiting factors are absent, (although other limiting factors, such as geometry of network connectivity, might exist in a form useful to be incorporated into intelligence analysis), contributing to what can appear to be "instantaneous threats".

Assessment of cyber-space threats requires not only a merger of old methodologies and new modes of thinking but also analysts willing and able to approach the art of threat assessment and warning from new perspectives. Only with a distinctive blend of the traditional and the new will it be possible to obtain real understanding of threats and vulnerabilities, to differentiate among types of intrusions and to forecast or anticipate specific incidents or clusters of incidents in ways that lengthen warning time. Enhancing the ability to identify perpetrators is also highly desirable: removing the cloak of anonymity would make perpetrators more concerned about the potential costs and risks of their actions and could have an important deterrent effect. In short, there are several fundamental questions at the heart of the intelligence process. They consist of variations on the who, what, when, where, why and how questions that are familiar parts of most research and analysis.

Security Challenging

Efforts to identify intruders are critical both to the assessment of the challenge and the nature of the response. Potential intruders run the gamut from young hobbyists engaged in the equivalent of joy riding to terrorist organizations and nations that are intent on maximizing damage to the target. The problem of identification is particularly difficult in a domain where maintaining anonymity is easy and there are sometimes time lapses between the intruder action, the intrusion itself, and the actual disruptive effects. Moreover, the consequences are not always commensurate with the objectives, in some cases falling short of what the intruders hoped to achieve, and in others going well beyond what they had envisaged.

There is a broad spectrum of potential intruders on the Internet and an almost equal number of motives for intrusions against organizations. Not surprisingly, this includes perpetrators conducting operations against other perpetrators. As enticing as this prospect is, it does not mitigate the effects of such internecine rivalry. New and more sophisticated tools are often the result of such interplay. This sort of jousting can also provide valuable insights to analysts once it is recognized, but does not simplify the analytic task and puts an incredible strain on limited analytic/ warning resources. With the continuing proliferation of sophisticated computer technologies into the mainstream population, attribution for an intrusion becomes more difficult by the day.

The dynamism of the intruder population is itself a problem. On the one hand, success breeds imitation and the sophistication of readily available tools means that even those with limited skills can become intruders.

On the one hand, there is a certain degree of attrition in the intruder community. Indeed, there are many reasons why intruders might cease their activity, including increased maturity, a need to find gainful employment, and a perception of the rewards of working to increase network security rather than attack it. The implication, of course, is that the mix of agents threatening network security is changing as the nature of the Internet changes.

The vast majority of the intrusions are probably being conducted by nuisance hackers or "ankle-biters" who have limited objectives and are usually satisfied with the actual penetration of the system or conduct relatively harmless cyber-vandalism such as the defacement or alteration of web-sites. While aggravating to the target, no significant or lasting damage occurs. The more serious problem occurs when an intrusion is carried out by a more sophisticated intruder (either an individual or a group) whose objective is better defined and involves malicious intent. Motives for these sorts of intrusions are also as varied as the persons carrying them out. They range from greed to defined military strategy and doctrine, and all that falls in between.

Four of the more dangerous, and less well defined categories of intruder are governments conducting operations against other sovereign states, the organized terrorist group, insurgency or revolutionary groups, and organized crime. All these entities are beginning to appreciate the potential power, anonymity, and effectiveness of the Internet. There are myriad examples of governments instituting programmes for Computer Network Warfare. In the case of Russia, policy-makers consider the security of their information infrastructure so critical that–rhetorically at least-they equate an attack against it with a strategic nuclear strike (and have promised an appropriate response). As a result of the realization of the criticality of information infrastructures, computer warfare is now a part of the formal Russian Military Strategy and Doctrine. The same is true of organized terrorist groups. In fact, "most of the 30 top terrorist organizations identified by the U.S. government have web pages and use e-mail, and are "fairly well developed" at using the Internet."[Casciano] In many cases, dependence on technology is viewed as an Achilles Heel to be exploited by terrorist organizations.

Within the U.S., many of the more militant indigenous groups have discovered the power of the Internet and have well designed and effective Web sites. Indeed, militia and supremacist groups have had significant increases in membership since developing their Web pages. It is a natural progression from using the Internet for propaganda and recruiting to exploiting its potential as a weapon. There is also growing evidence that some of the active insurgency groups around the world are discovering the potential of the computer. It is just a matter of time until they discover the effect of a computer-generated attack against the infrastructure of the government they are fighting. Once that realization is made, cyber-attacks will likely become a weapon of choice for organizations intent on overthrowing an existing government. Disturbingly, Aum Shinrikyo, the group responsible for the Sarin gas attack on the Japanese subway, has increasingly been involved in the Japanese software industry!

Organized crime probably was the first of the sophisticated intruder threats to realize the power and value of the computer. In 1995, it was discovered that the Cali cartel had sophisticated state-of-the-art equipment for electronic eavesdropping, while smaller drug trafficking organizations in Colombia are using the Internet to pressure the Colombian government to change the policy of extraditing traffickers to the United States. Furthermore, the use of computers by organized crime organizations to garner illicit profits is well documented. However, some criminal efforts have gone beyond simple siphoning of funds and money laundering. Extortion of money from financial institutions by threatening to destroy or modify their computer databases is also evident. It is probable that at least some of these extortion operations are conducted by transnational criminal groups. Some of the extortion efforts go wrong–as did the effort to extort Bloomberg. In other cases, however, large payoffs are almost certainly made to the extortionist. It seems likely, therefore, that larger and potentially more dangerous operations should be anticipated.

The obvious challenge is to develop a capacity to identify and track the activities of these potential intruders with the goal of being able to provide predictive analysis and warning of intrusions. Some of the traditional intelligence techniques should apply to these threats, but new methodologies and the ability to contemplate new and complex concepts have to be developed concurrently.

This will become even more important (and difficult) as perpetrators of increasing sophistication operate on the Internet. As motivations vary, so will the efforts of the individuals behind malicious operations to either conceal or reveal their responsibility. All of this complicates efforts to track responsible parties determine attribution.

Nations and transnational criminal organizations, by their nature, will be diligent in their efforts to maintain anonymity. In some of these cases, identifying the intended victim may give valuable insight into tracking the intruder. Sometimes the target of an intrusion allows the analyst to rule out certain possible perpetrators.

A multi-million dollar extortion plot against a major financial institution is probably not the work of a 13-year-old hacker working out of his bedroom. At the same time, however, many victims, especially within government or sensitive industries such as banking or insurance, often complicate the effort to track intruders because of their reluctance to report the incident. In other cases, such as politically motivated attacks, the perpetrators may want their identity known, but not their location. As such operations become more sophisticated, tracking the attack back to its point of origin will be a major challenge to the intelligence analysts involved. What is clear from all of this is that tracking intruders and gaining attribution is much more than just a technical challenge.

One difficulty, of course, is that there are legal constraints on intelligence collection, especially by the military and the national security establishment. Traditionally the focus of intelligence has been on foreign threats, and there are restrictions on intelligence activities directed against individuals or groups that are domestic in nature. Insofar as these groups are the focus of government attention, it is from the law enforcement community. This points to yet another problem: that of coordination and information sharing between the traditional national security agencies and the law enforcement community. Generally law enforcement focuses on individual cases and wants evidence that stands up in court; intelligence agencies in contrast are concerned with protecting the sources of their information so that they can continue to use them. The problem with cyber-threats is that they fall in the gray area where crime and national security merge into one another.

THE NATURE AND LEVELS OF INTELLIGENCE ANALYSIS

Intelligence analysis requires many of the same analytical methods and techniques, irrespective of domain. From this perspective, intelligence analysis for Internet security is no different from the intelligence task in any other area of national and international security. The commonality is the concern with those who want to inflict harm and the vulnerabilities they can exploit to do this. Threats can come from many sources: the military activities of hostile nations; inimical economic strategies pursued by adversarial or even allied states; the activities of terrorist groups intent on inflicting harm on society in order to achieve political objectives; transnational criminal organizations pursuing the acquisition of large profits through illegal activities, violence, and corruption; and groups (including any of those just mentioned) and individuals with the ability and desire to distort, disrupt, degrade or destroy information and communications systems. Whatever their source, threats are inextricably linked to vulnerabilities. Indeed, absolute security could only be achieved if there were no vulnerabilities to be exploited. It is crucial, therefore, not only to identify vulnerabilities but also to understand how hostile groups or individuals might exploit them. Strictly speaking, real security threats only come from those with a combination of hostile intent (i.e. a desire to do us harm) and the capacity to inflict harm (i.e. exploit vulnerabilities in ways that transform intent into reality).

In the realm of cyber-space, vulnerabilities are inescapable. There are many reasons for this, ranging from the inherent weaknesses in complex systems to specific problems in the creation of software code. Even if protective security measures were an integral part of information systems rather than being subsequently grafted onto them, problems would remain. Some vulnerabilities stem from the underlying protocols used to communicate on the Internet, which were formulated when the Internet was a relatively small community of trusted systems, with connectivity determined by government contract. Other vulnerabilities stem from development practices, which may ignore validation of input (or even length checking) and avoid controlling the environment in which programs execute. Finally, vulnerabilities stem from the rapidly evolving use of software, in which programs meant for a limited purpose are applied in ways not anticipated by their developers. The intruder community is constantly seeking to find interesting (and, from their point of view, profitable) ways to discover and exploit vulnerabilities. This behavior tends to be quite trend-driven. A newly discovered interesting vulnerability exploit in an application will spawn both intensive interest in other vulnerabilities in that application and an intensive search for similar vulnerabilities in other applications. This results in waves of discovered vulnerabilities that impact both specific vendors and the community in general. At the same time, the recognition that there are measurable trends in vulnerability exploitation are at least a temporary advantage to intelligence analysis efforts. From a tactical perspective, the recognition of a trend in intrusion tools and their applications may well allow for at least short-term predictive analysis and the potential for limited warning.

One of the greatest challenges to system owners and administrator is determining how much security is enough. Managing risks inherent in information systems is problem that changes as fast as new technologies are brought online. Intelligence analysis of the threats to information systems should, by definition, be a major component of the risk management process. Without application, intelligence analysis efforts are merely an intellectual exercise and have no value. It is only when the results of that analysis, the assessments derived from the analytic process, are provided to operators that they begin to have value.

Obtaining prior knowledge of both threats and vulnerabilities – as well as sensitivity to possible opportunities to exploit the vulnerabilities - is essential. Intelligence analysis, of course, operates at different levels, ranging from the specific to the general, and from short-term incidents and operations to long term patterns and challenges. Each form or level of analysis is crucial, and complements and supplements the others. Nevertheless, it is important to distinguish them from one another and to be clear at which level the activities are taking place. It is also important to recognize that the most critical insights will be obtained from fusion efforts that combine these different levels. The several complementary levels of intelligence analysis are strategic analysis, tactical analysis and operational analysis. In practice, these categories shade into each other and are not always sharply differentiated, and differing definitions for these terms exist in the intelligence community. Nevertheless, they offer a useful framework within which intelligence tasks and requirements can initially be delineated.

Strategic Intelligence Analysis

Strategic analysis is perhaps the most important form of intelligence. It provides a framework within which other forms of intelligence collection and analysis take place, offers an overall assessment from the top down rather than from the bottom up, and helps to provide a basis for policy formulation, strategic planning, and resource allocation. Its weakness is its focus on macro-level issues rather than the more detailed levels of analysis. On the Internet, such analysis is even more problematic, due to the rapidly evolving nature of Internet usage. Prior to 1994, for example, Internet commerce was illegal. Today it is a multi-billion dollar economic force. New methods of organizational and economic cooperation are constantly evolving, with greater or less security. Maintaining continuity on this constantly shifting environment is one of the greatest challenges to conducting effective strategic analysis of cyber-threats. Furthermore, for many consumers, strategic intelligence is irrelevant to day-to-day tasks and needs. At the end of the day, however, the importance of strategic intelligence analysis is undeniable. Such an effort helps to discern and make sense of trends, to identify and extract patterns that would otherwise not be visible, and to provide an overall picture of the evolving threat environment and the level of damage that might be occurred in certain specified contingencies.

Analytical initiatives that would fall under the rubric of strategic intelligence analysis include:

- *Overall threat assessments.* These include in the analysis the vulnerabilities of critical missions (including levels of dependence), the kind of disruption and damage that could be caused to the implementation of these missions, the kinds of weapons/instruments that could be used to cause such disruptions, and the likelihood of such attacks and intrusions taking place

- *Sector threat assessments.* Such analyses focus on vulnerabilities and threats either in particular areas such as national infrastructure, or in particular sectors of the economy such as banking or e-commerce. In effect, a strategic analysis of this kind has to take account of changes in what can be a very dynamic environment.

- *Trend Analysis to highlight changing threats and vulnerabilities.* These might include base-line assessments so as to better recognize departures from the baseline. Alternatively, they might focus on future threats and vulnerabilities in an effort to determine in what ways the problem is evolving – and what can be done to anticipate and contain future challenges. The way in which e-commerce has become a major issue suggests that the pace of change in the cyber-space environment is posing novel challenges that can best be understood through strategic intelligence analysis that is very forward looking. Indeed, trend analysis is likely to be most effective when it is linked with careful attention to drivers, i.e. fundamental trends in the political, economic, social and technological sectors that will shape the future threat and vulnerability environment of the future.

- *Potential Damage Assessments.* Because of the macro-level view taken by strategic analysis, it also offers the best approach for assessing potential cascade effects of intrusions. The specific target of a an intrusion might be a regional electric power grid, but the effects of a failure to that system can cascade to include telecommunications, public emergency services, water systems, etc. The potential for such wide-spread effects will be recognized most readily as a result of in-depth strategic analysis – which in turn would offer opportunities to develop both defensive and mitigation strategies. Crisis management, contingency planning, mitigation strategies, and disaster management would all be enhanced by strategic analysis of potential damage assessment. Indeed, the capacity for effective and rapid reconstitution might depend on such analysis.

- *Categorizing and differentiating attacks and attackers.* Intrusions in cyber-space can emanate from individuals, whether insiders or outsiders; from hacker groups intent on displaying their skills and capabilities; activist groups using direct action on the Internet to publicize their political cause; terrorist organizations using intrusions to create massive disruption or other forms of large-scale harm, and seeking to obtain widespread publicity and create a climate of fear; transnational criminal organizations responding to law enforcement pressure with cyber-retaliation, and states using attacks on, or through, information systems as a form of asymmetric warfare. One of the most important tasks of intelligence analysis for the Internet is to discover ways of differentiating among intrusions from these various sources. This will be especially true as groups or individuals develop intrusion strategies that mimic other forms and thereby lessen their chances of identification or, in the case of nation states, provide plausible deniability of their actions. From the perspective of strategic intelligence analysis, this is critical in efforts to determine appropriate responses that might go beyond simply defensive or mitigation strategies. How specific attacks are categorized, of course, will also be an issue at the tactical and operational level. But the differentiating and categorization methodologies, initially at least, are a matter for strategic analysis.

• *Identification of Anomalies.* Searching for anomalies that provide indicators of emerging threats and problems is an important task of strategic intelligence analysis (albeit one that both feeds into and relies on tactical and operational efforts). Anomalies in this context can be understood as developments or events that do not fit typical or known patterns. The detection of anomalies or novel patterns can be a major element in anticipating new methods of intrusion, new targets, or even new classes of intruders. It is a macro-level task that requires careful and systematic "environmental scanning" as well as the coalescing of tactical and operational intelligence reports that identify and highlight specific aberrations from the norm.

• *Analysis of Future Net Environments.* The greatest constant about the Internet is change. Strategic intelligence analysis must take that into account and attempt to provide assessments of potential future environments on the Net and the potential impact of malicious activity within those environments. Given the dramatic changes in technology within the recent past, and seeing the rapid pace with which innovation continues to grow, it seems a reasonable assumption that the Internet (in one form or another) will become more and more integrated into the fabric of society. As this occurs, intrusions or attacks will have far more wide-ranging consequences. Considerations of social as well as political and economic impacts will have to be factored into intelligence assessments.

It is clear from this discussion that not only does strategic intelligence analysis provide a framework for tactical and operational assessments, but that work done at these levels in turn helps to shape the strategic intelligence focus.

As for the strategic assessments themselves they should be useful for consumers, providing forecasting estimates that help to reduce uncertainties in ways that feed into policy processes, providing a basis for more informed decision-making and more effective resource allocation.

As strategic analytic methodologies mature, they will also offer the basis for predictive or anticipatory assessments that can serve to provide warning of potential hostile operations. In effect, strategic intelligence assessments provide a basis for the development of high-level policy and strategy and for strategic responses to vulnerabilities, whether actual or potential.

Tactical Intelligence Analysis

Tactical analysis is a necessary and important complement to work done at the strategic level. It is the natural linking element between macro-level analysis and the micro-level focus on individual cases.

Among the kinds of studies that come under the level of tactical analysis would be:

- Cluster and pattern analysis designed to discern temporal patterns, the use of particular intrusion methods, commonalities of targets, and attempts to build profiles of perpetrators, whether hackers or insiders.

- Stimulus-response analysis designed to identify potential actions that could be taken by intruders in response to specific known or predicted events. This analysis could be used both proactively in development of warnings or reactively in lending significance to otherwise-unrecognized activity.

- Network environmental analysis methods will have to be developed. It is probable that in-depth analysis of the Internet will reveal patterns similar to those in the physical world. Net weather is already being discussed, and network terrain is a viable concept. Unlike physical environments, however, the Internet environment will probably be subject to much more rapid shifting. That places this sort of analytic effort squarely in the realm of Tactical Analysis.

In physical space, geography helps to differentiate tactical from strategic, but on the Internet this component is lacking, an absence that makes the distinction between strategic and tactical somewhat more tenuous than in other domains.

At the same time, the strategic and tactical levels are mutually reinforcing: although strategic intelligence analysis provides the framework for tactical assessments, these assessments in turn help to feed strategic analysis. With a highly dynamic inter-relationship among the various levels of analysis, each level is strengthened by and strengthens the others.

Operational Intelligence Analysis

Operational intelligence analysis overlaps with investigation and is often single-case oriented. It involves technological assessments of the methods used for an intrusion, specific investigations of intruders, and the like.

An important component of operational analysis is identifying the particular vulnerability or vulnerabilities that have been exploited and providing guidance on how it or they can be minimized or eliminated.

Another component of operational analysis will be the potential ability to provide attribution during, or shortly after an intrusion. The data collected during an incident, combined with the profiling efforts provided at the tactical level could lead to attribution. While there are significant policy and legal questions associated with such a capability, its importance to the overall analytical process cannot be overstated.

Most of the existing analysis of network intrusions has been capability analysis, dealing principally with information privacy, integrity and availability. Selected methodologies to address organizational missions in a network context exist [Ellison99], but have not been widely applied. Intent and effect analysis has not been systematically pursued. In addition to supporting attribution, operational analysis should lead to sparking defensive coordinated efforts. What is needed is to connect these efforts into some form of cohesive goal that can promote a measurably effective response to on-line threats.

TRADITIONAL APPROACHES IN CYBER INTELLIGENCE

Cyber intelligence and their applicability to Internet security, it is tempting to suggest that cyber-space has so many unique characteristics that none of the traditional approaches is relevant. Such a temptation should be avoided. There are important parallels with, and critical lessons to be learned from, experience in other domains.

One of the most notable parallels is between cyber intelligence and business intelligence, particularly in product monitoring. In the case of intelligence for the Internet, it is the development and diffusion of tools for intrusion and disruption that need to be monitored.

Yet, such efforts are not that different from monitoring the development and marketing of new products in the business world. Consequently, some of the methods and techniques developed in the world of competitive intelligence might be particularly helpful as one component of intelligence collection and analysis in relation to cyber-space threats.

The most serious and useful model for intelligence analysis of information threats, however, is probably intelligence methodologies in the area of national security intelligence, and specifically, counter-terrorism. The terrorism threat has several characteristics that are also apply to cyber-threats. The parallels include the diversity of the actors involved, the reliance of at least some of them on networks, the broad range of motivations, the anonymity of the perpetrators of terrorist incidents, (something that has become more pronounced in recent years as the traditional practice of claiming responsibility giving way to the cloak of silence) and the enormous array of potential targets and weapons. Terrorists can choose from a set of options that obviously include firearms and conventional explosives but could conceivably involve WMD capabilities. Not surprisingly, one of the major concerns of intelligence analysis in this domain is with predicting and either preventing or pre-empting terrorism incidents. The utility of early warning is hard to exaggerate as such warning facilitates preventive and defensive measures as well as damage mitigation efforts.

Whether the emphasis is on a single threat or multiple threats, however, crucial aspects of the intelligence task remain the same. Although the focus of the collection and analysis effort might shift, the intelligence process itself involves the same cycle of activities: focus on the mission, collection of sources and information, collation and management of the collected intelligence, analysis and assessment resulting in an intelligence product, and the dissemination of this product to the customer. The intelligence cycle remains constant whatever the target of the efforts. Similarly, good intelligence not only moves from data streams to data fusion but also from fused data to knowledge, and from knowledge to forecasting or prediction. And whatever the domain of activity, whether business intelligence, military intelligence, or cyber intelligence, there is always a requirement to overcome pathologies and obstacles that can undermine the analytical process and dilute or distort finished intelligence products.

In terms of collection methods, however, a critical addition needs to be made. As well as traditional reliance on Comint, Humint, and Sigint, it might be necessary to develop a separate category of Cyberint. In effect, Cyberint would require a blending of Sigint, Humint, and Comint methodologies to be effective. Each of those traditional intelligence disciplines brings components that are critical for analysis of on-line threats. The Humint aspect would provide for the monitoring and profiling of potential threat groups. It could take the form of simple monitoring of intruder chat rooms and web sites or in-depth profiling of identified individuals or groups. It will require that analysts are able to identify which players, whether individuals or groups, have the technical expertise to carry out their intended operations. Consequently, much effort will need to be focused on existing use of the Net and identified intrusions to establish a baseline of data from which to proceed.

The Sigint perspective is useful from the point of analysing intruder tools and specific system vulnerabilities. This is not to say that an analytic organization would necessarily intercept and collect data being transmitted across targeted systems. There are too many questions of legality and ethics to anticipate that sort of effort. However, studying identified tools and how they have been implemented does call for the utilization of existing Sigint methodologies to provide value added assessments. Similarly, one of the basic tenets of Comint analysis is to establish a communications activity baseline–this readily applies to various information and communication systems. Establishing baseline information on the normal data flow for a given system would make it easier and quicker to identify anomalies that could be indicative of probes or attempts at intrusion. As with the overall intelligence process, each of these recognized intelligence disciplines provide individual parts of a greater whole. They are the tools through which fusion intelligence of both current and future cyber-threats can be obtained. It goes without saying that collecting this sort of data will require a major cooperative effort between the analytic organization and past, as well as potential future, victims. In sum, cyberint would not supercede other collection methods but is likely to prove a crucial addition that would help to focus the intelligence effort and contribute significantly to the successful analysis of cyber-threats and intrusions.

7

Cyber Crime and Punishment

OVERVIEW

The growing danger from crimes committed against computers, or against information on computers, is beginning to claim attention in national capitals. In most countries around the world, however, existing laws are likely to be unenforceable against such crimes. This lack of legal protection means that businesses and governments must rely solely on technical measures to protect themselves from those who would steal, deny access to, or destroy valuable information.

Self-protection, while essential, is not sufficient to make cyberspace a safe place to conduct business. The rule of law must also be enforced. Countries where legal protections are inadequate will become increasingly less able to compete in the new economy. As cyber crime increasingly breaches national borders, nations perceived as havens run the risk of having their electronic messages blocked by the network. National governments should examine their current statutes to determine whether they are sufficient to combat the kinds of crimes discussed in this report. Where gaps exist, governments should draw on best practices from other countries and work closely with industry to enact enforceable legal protections against these new crimes.

This report analyzes the state of the law in 52 countries. It finds that only ten of these nations have amended their laws to cover more than half of the kinds of crimes that need to be addressed. While many of the others have initiatives underway, it is clear that a great deal of additional work is needed before organizations and individuals can be confident that cyber criminals will think twice before attacking valued systems and information.

What's Different About Cyber Crime?

Undeterred by the prospect of arrest or prosecution, cyber criminals around the world blurk on the Net as an omnipresent menace to the financial health of businesses, to the trust of their customers, and as an emerging threat to nations' security. Headlines of cyber attacks command our attention with increasing frequency. According to the Computer Emergency Response Team Coordination Center (CERT/CC), the number of reported incidences of security breaches in the first three quarters of 2000 has risen by 54 percent over the total number of reported incidences in 1999. Moreover, countless instances of illegal access and damage around the world remain unreported, as victims fear the exposure of vulnerabilities, the potential for copycat crimes, and the loss of public confidence.

Cyber crimes—harmful acts committed from or against a computer or network—differ from most terrestrial crimes in four ways. They are easy to learn how to commit; they require few resources relative to the potential damage caused; they can be committed in a jurisdiction without being physically present in it; and they are often not clearly illegal. As this report shows, the laws of most countries do not clearly prohibit cyber crimes. Existing terrestrial laws against physical acts of trespass or breaking and entering often do not cover their "virtual" counterparts. Web pages such as the e-commerce sites recently hit by widespread, distributed denial of service attacks may not be covered by outdated laws as protected forms of property. New kinds of crimes can fall between the cracks, as the Philippines learned when it attempted to prosecute the perpetrator of the May 2000 Love Bug virus, which caused billions of dollars of damage worldwide.

Effective law enforcement is complicated by the transnational nature of cyberspace. Mechanisms of cooperation across national borders to solve and prosecute crimes are complex and slow. Cyber criminals can defy the conventional jurisdictional realms of sovereign nations, originating an attack from almost any computer in the world, passing it across multiple national boundaries, or designing attacks that appear to be originating from foreign sources. Such techniques dramatically increase both the technical and legal complexities of investigating and prosecuting cyber crimes.

Six weeks after the Love Bug attack, the Philippines outlawed most computer crimes as part of a comprehensive e-commerce statute. In order to prevent a repeat of the catastrophe that prompted this action, however, the future of the networked world demands a more proactive approach, whereby governments, industry, and the public work together to devise enforceable laws that will effectively deter all but the most determined cyber criminals.

THE VAST RANGE OF CYBER CRIMES

Hacking

It is the most common type of Cyber crime being committed across the world. Hacking has been defined in section 66 of The Information Technology Act, 2000 as follows "whoever with the intent to cause or knowing that he is likely to cause wrongful loss or damage to the public or any person destroys or deletes or alters any information residing in a computer resource or diminishes its value or utility or affects it injuriously by any means commits hacking".

Punishment for hacking under the above mentioned section is imprisonment for three years or fine which may extend Upto two lakh rupees or both. A Hacker is a person who breaks in or trespasses a computer system. Hackers are of different types ranging from code hackers to crackers to cyber punks to freaks. Some hackers just enjoy cracking systems and gaining access to them as an ordinary pastime; they do not desire to commit any further crime. Whether this itself would constitute a crime is a matter of fact. At most such a crime could be equated with criminal trespass.

Security Related Crimes

With the growth of the internet, network security has become a major concern. Private confidential information has become available to the public. Confidential information can reside in two states on the network. It can reside on the physical stored media, such as hard drive or memory or it can reside in the transit across the physical network wire in the form of packets. These two information states provide opportunities for attacks from users on the internal network, as well as users on the Internet.

Network Packet Sniffers

Network computers communicate serially where large information pieces are broken into smaller ones. The information stream would be broken into smaller pieces even if networks communicated in parallel.

These smaller pieces are called network packets. Since these network packets are not encrypted they can be processed and understood by any application that can pick them off the network and process them. A network protocol specifies how packets are identified and labeled which enables a computer to determine whether a packet is intended for it.

The specifications for network protocols such as TCP/IP are widely published. A third party can easily interpret the network packets and develop a packet sniffer. A packet sniffer is a software application that uses a network adapter card in a promiscuous mode (a mode in which the network adapter card sends all packets received by the physical network wire to an application for processing) to capture all network packets that are sent !across a local network. A packet sniffer can provide its users with meaningful and often sensitive information such as user account names and passwords.

IP Spoofing

An IP attack occurs when an attacker outside the network pretends to be a trusted computer either by using an IP address that is within its range or by using an external IP address that you trust and to which you wish to provide access to specified resources on your network. Normally, an IP spoofing attack is limited to the injection of data or commands into an existing stream of data passed between client and server application or a peer to peer network connection.

Password Attacks

Password attacks can be implemented using several different methods like the brute force attacks, Trojan horse programmes. IP spoofing can yield user accounts and passwords. Password attacks usually refer to repeated attempts to identify a user password or account. These repeated attempts are called brute force attacks. Distribution of sensitive internal information to external sources: At the core of these security breaches is the distribution of sensitive information to competitors or others who use it to the owners' disadvantage. While an outside intruder can use password and IP spoofing attacks to copy information, an internal user could place sensitive information on an external computer or share a drive on the network with other users

Man-in-the-middle-attacks

This attack requires that the attacker have access to network packets that come across the networks. The possible use of such attack are theft of information, hijacking an ongoing session to gain access to your internal network resources, traffic analysis to drive information about one's own network and its users, denial of service, corruption of transmitted data, and introduction of new information into network sessions.

POOR INFORMATION SECURITY REDUCES THE COMPETITIVENESS OF NATIONS

In our August 2000 report, Risk E-Business: Seizing the Opportunity of Global EReadiness, McConnell International rated mid-level economies' capacity to participate in the digital economy. In considering nations' information security, the report evaluated public trust in the security of information processed and stored on networks in each country. In this context, information security included: an assessment of the strength of legal protections and progress in protecting intellectual property rights, especially for software; the extent of efforts to protect electronic privacy; and the strength and effectiveness of the legal framework to authorize digital signatures. The E-Readiness report also examined the existence of legal frameworks to prosecute cyber criminals, for a predictable environment of strong deterrence for computer crime is critical to the effective protection of valuable information and networks.

Although several countries, particularly in Europe and Asia, were found to have addressed a number of these broader information security factors, few countries were able to demonstrate that adequate legal measures had been taken to ensure that perpetrators of cyber crime would be held accountable for their actions. Overall, nearly half of the countries included in the E-Readiness study were rated as needing substantial improvement in information security.

In addition, only a small fraction of countries needing substantial improvement indicated that progress was currently underway. Outdated laws and regulations, and weak enforcement mechanisms for protecting networked information, create an inhospitable environment in which to conduct e-business within a country and across national boundaries. Inadequate legal protection of digital information can create barriers to its exchange and stunt the growth of e-commerce. As ebusiness expands globally, the need for strong and consistent means to protect networked information will grow.

The Cyber Crime Laws of Nations

Based on its findings in the E-Readiness study, and in the wake of the Philippines inability to prosecute the student responsible for the "I Love You" virus, McConnell International surveyed its global network of information technology policy officials to determine the state of cyber security laws around the world. Countries were asked to provide laws that would be used to prosecute criminal acts involving both private and public sector computers.

Over fifty national governments4 responded with recent pieces of legislation, copies of updated statutes, draft legislation, or statements that no concrete course of action has been planned to respond to a cyber attack on the public or private sector. Countries were provided the opportunity to review the presentation of the results in draft, and this report reflects their comments.

Countries that provided legislation were evaluated to determine whether their criminal statutes had been extended into cyberspace to cover ten different types of cyber crime in four categories: data-related crimes, including interception, modification, and theft; network-related crimes, including interference and sabotage; crimes of access, including hacking and virus distribution; and associated computer-related crimes, including aiding and abetting cyber criminals, computer fraud, and computer forgery.

Thirty-three of the countries surveyed have not yet updated their laws to address any type of cyber crime. Of the remaining countries, nine have enacted legislation to address five or fewer types of cyber crime, and ten have updated their laws to prosecute against six or more of the ten types of cyber crime.

Law is Only Part of the Answer

Extending the rule of law into cyberspace is a critical step to create a trustworthy environment for people and businesses. Because that extension remains a work in progress, organizations today must first and foremost defend their own systems and information from attack, be it from outsiders or from within. They may rely only secondarily on the deterrence that effective law enforcement can provide.

To provide this self-protection, organizations should focus on implementing cyber security plans addressing people, process, and technology issues. Organizations need to commit the resources to educate employees on security practices, develop thorough plans for the handling of sensitive data, records and transactions, and incorporate robust security technology--such as firewalls, anti-virus software, intrusion detection tools, and authentication services-- throughout the organizations' computer systems.

These system protection tools--the software and hardware for defending information systems--are complex and expensive to operate. To avoid hassles and expense, system manufacturers and system operators routinely leave security features "turned off," needlessly increasing the vulnerability of the information on the systems. Bugs and security holes with known fixes are routinely left uncorrected. Further, no agreed-upon standards exist to benchmark the quality of the tools, and no accepted methodology exists for organizations to determine how much investment in security is enough.

The inability to quantify the costs and benefits of information security investments leave security managers at a disadvantage when competing for organizational resources. Much work remains to improve management and technical solutions for information protection. Industry-wide efforts are underway to address prevention, response, and cooperation.

Around the world, various industries have been establishing information sharing and analysis centers (ISACs) to share real-time information related to threats, vulnerabilities, attacks, and countermeasures.

A recent Global Information Security Summit sponsored by the World Information Technology and Services Alliance (www.witsa.org) brought together industry, governments, and multilateral organizations across economic sectors to share information and build partnerships.

Post-summit working groups are now developing cooperative approaches to addressing the most critical information security problems. The results of that work will be taken up at a second summit in Belfast in May 2001. That summit will also provide an opportunity to revisit the progress of nations in updating their laws to cover cyber crimes.

CONCLUSIONS

1. Reliance on terrestrial laws is an untested approach. Despite the progress being made in many countries, most countries still rely on standard terrestrial law to prosecute cyber crimes. The majority of countries are relying on archaic statutes that predate the birth of cyberspace and have not yet been tested in court.

2. Weak penalties limit deterrence. The weak penalties in most updated criminal statutes provide limited deterrence for crimes that can have large-scale economic and social effects.

3. Self-protection remains the first line of defense. The general weakness of statutes increases the importance of private sector efforts to develop and adopt strong and efficient technical solutions and management practices for information security.

4. A global patchwork of laws creates little certainty. Little consensus exists among countries regarding exactly which crimes need to be legislated against. Unless crimes are defined in a similar manner across jurisdictions, coordinated efforts by law enforcement officials to combat cyber crime will be complicated.

5. A model approach is needed. Most countries, particularly those in the developing world, are seeking a model to follow. These countries recognize the importance of outlawing malicious computer-related acts in a timely manner in order to promote a secure environment for ecommerce. But few have the legal and technical resources necessary to address the complexities of adapting terrestrial criminal statutes to cyberspace. A coordinated, public-private partnership to produce a model approach can help eliminate the potential danger from the inadvertent creation of cyber crime havens.

Recommendations

The weak state of global legal protections against cyber crime suggests three kinds of action.

Firms should secure their networked information.

Laws to enforce property rights work only when property owners take reasonable steps to protect their property in the first place. As one observer has noted, if homeowners failed to buy locks for their front doors, should towns solve the problem by passing more laws or hiring more police? Even where laws are adequate, firms dependent on the network must make their own information and systems secure. And where enforceable laws are months or years away, as in most countries, this responsibility is even more significant.

Governments should assure that their laws apply to cyber crimes.

National governments remain the dominant authority for regulating criminal behavior in most places in the world. One nation already has struggled from, and ultimately improved, its legal authority after a confrontation with the unique challenges presented by cyber crime. It is crucial that other nations profit from this lesson, and examine their current laws to discern whether they are composed in a technologically neutral manner that would not exclude the prosecution of cyber criminals. In many cases, nations will find that current laws ought to be updated. Enactment of enforceable computer crime laws that also respect the rights of individuals are an essential next step in the battle against this emerging threat.

Firms, governments, and civil society should work cooperatively to strengthen legal frameworks for cyber security.

To be prosecuted across a border, an act must be a crime in each jurisdiction. Thus, while local legal traditions must be respected, nations must define cyber crimes in a similar manner. An important effort to craft a model approach is underway in the Council of Europe, comprising 41 countries.

The Council is crafting an international Convention on Cyber Crime. The Convention addresses illegal access, illegal interception, data interference, system interference, computer-related forgery, computer-related fraud, and the aiding and abetting of these crimes. It also addresses investigational matters related to jurisdiction, extradition, the interception of communications, and the production and preservation of data. Finally, it promotes cooperation among law enforcement officials across national borders.

Late in its process, the Council began to consider the views of affected industry and civil society. This process is making the Council's product more realistic, practical, efficient, balanced, and respectful of due process that protects individual rights.

At this point, most observers support provisions to improve law enforcement cooperation across borders. However, industry, through the World Information Technology and Services Alliance, argues that the requirements on service providers to monitor communications and to provide assistance to investigators, as outlined in the Draft Convention, would be unduly burdensome and expensive. Another provision considered objectionable could criminalize the creation and use of intrusive software, or hacking programs, which are designed for legitimate security testing purposes.

This action could stifle the advances in technology vital to keep up with evolving cyber threats. Privacy and human rights advocates object to the Draft Convention's lack of procedural safeguards and due process to protect the rights of individuals, and to the possibility that the ensuing national laws would effectively place restrictions on privacy, anonymity, and encryption.

The Council plans to release a final draft of the Convention in December 2000. In 2001, a political process involving national governments will determine the scope and coverage of the final Convention.

Because of cyber crime's international potential, all countries, and all companies, are affected. Interested parties, including national governments from outside Europe, and businesses and non-governmental organizations from around the world, should participate vigorously in a consensus process to develop measures that support effective international law enforcement and foster continued growth and innovation.

8

Cyber Security

CYBER SECURITY STRATEGY

The Federal Government aims at making a substantial contribution to a secure cyberspace, thus maintaining and promoting economic and social prosperity in Germany. Cyber security in Germany must be ensured at a level commensurate with the importance and protection required by interlinked information infrastructures, without hampering the opportunities and the utilization of the cyberspace. In this context the level of cyber security reached is the sum of all national and international measures taken to protect the availability of information and communications technology and the integrity, authenticity and confidentiality of data in cyberspace.

Cyber security must be based on a comprehensive approach. This requires even more intensive information sharing and coordination. The Cyber Security Strategy mainly focuses on civilian approaches and measures. They are complemented by measures taken by the Bundeswehr to protect its capabilities and measures based on mandates to make cyber security a part of Germany's preventive security strategy. Given the global nature of information and communications technology, international coordination and appropriate networks focusing on foreign and security policy aspects are indispensable. This includes cooperation not only in the United Nations, but also in the EU, the Council of Europe, NATO, the G8, the OSCE and other multinational organizations. The aim is to ensure the coherence and capabilities of the international community to protect cyberspace.

Protection of Critical Information Infrastructures

The protection of critical information infrastructures is the main priority of cyber security. They are a central component of nearly all critical infrastructures and become increasingly important. The public and the private sector must create an enhanced strategic and organizational basis for closer coordination based on intensified information sharing. To this end, cooperation established by the CIP implementation plan is systematically extended, and legal commitments to enhance the binding nature of the CIP implementation plan are examined. With the participation of the National Cyber Security Council (cf. objective 5), the integration of additional sectors is examined and the introduction of new relevant technologies is considered to a greater extent. Whether and where protective measures have to be made mandatory and whether and where additional powers are required in case of specific threats have to be clarified, too. Furthermore we will examine the necessity of harmonizing rules to maintain critical infrastructures during IT crises.

Strengthening IT Security in the Public Administration

The public administration will further enhance the protection of its IT systems. State authorities have to serve as role models for data security. We will create a common, uniform and secure network infrastructure in the federal administration ("federal networks") as a basis for electronic audio and data communication. We will continue to press ahead with the implementation plan for the federal administration.

Should the IT security situation get worse, this plan may be aligned accordingly. Effective IT security requires powerful structures in all federal authorities. For this reason resources must be deployed appropriately at central and local level. To facilitate implementation through uniform action by authorities, joint investments into the Federal Government's IT security will be made regularly in line with budgetary possibilities. Operational cooperation with the federal Länder, particularly with regard to CERTs (computer emergency response teams), will be further intensified by the IT planning council.

National Cyber Response Centre

To optimize operational cooperation between all state authorities and improve the coordination of protection and response measures for IT incidents we will set up a National Cyber Response Centre.

It will report to the Federal Office for Information Security (BSI) and cooperate directly with the Federal Office for the Protection of the Constitution (BfV) and the Federal Office of Civil Protection and Disaster Assistance (BBK).

Cooperation in the National Cyber Response Centre will strictly observe the statutory tasks and powers of all authorities involved on the basis of cooperation agreements. The Federal Criminal Police Office (BKA), the Federal Police (BPOL), the Customs Criminological Office (ZKA), the Federal Intelligence Service (BND), the Bundeswehr and authorities supervising critical infrastructure operators all participate in this centre within the framework of their statutory tasks and powers.

Quick and close information sharing on weaknesses of IT products, vulnerabilities, forms of attacks and profiles of perpetrators enables the National Cyber Response Centre to analyse IT incidents and give consolidated recommendations for action. The interests of the private sector to protect itself against crime and espionage in cyberspace should also be adequately taken into account. At the same time respective responsibilities must be observed. Every stakeholder takes the necessary measures in its remit on the basis of the jointly developed national cyber security assessment and coordinates them with the competent authorities as well as partners from industry and academia. Since security preparedness is best achieved by early warning and prevention, the Cyber Response Centre will submit recommendations to the National Cyber Security Council both on a regular basis and for specific incidents. If the cyber security situation reaches the level of an imminent or already occurred crisis, the National Cyber Response Centre will directly inform the crisis management staff headed by the responsible State Secretary at the Federal Ministry of the Interior.

CYBER SECURITY: A PROBLEM OF NATIONAL IMPORTANCE

Trusting Systems in a Dangerous World

The Nation's information technology (IT) infrastructure, still evolving from U.S., technological innovations such as the personal computer and the Internet, today is a vast fabric of computers – from supercomputers to handheld devices – and interconnected networks enabling high-speed communications, information access, advanced computation, transactions, and automated processes relied upon in every sector of society. Because much of this infrastructure connects one way or another to the Internet, it embodies the Internet's original structural attributes of openness, inventiveness, and the assumption of goodwill.

These signature attributes have made the U.S., IT infrastructure an irresistible target for vandals and criminals worldwide. The PITAC believes that terrorists will inevitably follow suit, taking advantage of vulnerabilities including some that the Nation has not yet clearly recognised or addressed. The computers that manage critical U.S., facilities, infrastructures, and essential services can be targeted to set off system wide failures, and these computers frequently are accessible from virtually anywhere in the world via the Internet.

The Information Technology Infrastructure is 'Critical'

Most Americans see and use the components of the IT infrastructure – mainly desktop computers connected to the Internet – that enable e-mail, instant messaging, exchange and downloading of sound and images, online shopping, information searches, interactive games, and even telephony.

Americans also work with the information technologies that drive day-to-day operations in industry and government and are relied upon by organisations large and small for a range of functions including design, manufacturing, inventory, sales, payroll, information storage and retrieval, education and training, and research and development. In fact, economists credit successful applications of information technologies throughout the economy for the spectacular gains in U.S., productivity over the last decade. Less visible, and certainly less well understood, is the fact that these technologies – computers, mass storage devices, high-speed networks and network components such as routers and switches, systems and applications software, embedded and wireless devices, and the Internet itself – are now also essential to virtually all of the Nation's critical infrastructures. Computing systems control the management of power plants, dams, the North American power grid, air traffic control systems, food and energy distribution, and the financial system, to name only some.

The reliance of these sensitive physical installations and processes on the IT infrastructure makes that infrastructure itself critical and in the national interest to safeguard. The electric power generation industry, for example, relies on a range of IT systems and capabilities.

As in other industries, power companies implement business management systems for administrative and information services. But the power industry uses much more information technology. It relies on supervisory control and data acquisition (SCADA) systems to collect information about system operation, help regulate and control power generation, optimise power production, respond to changing power demands and system parameters, control distribution, and coordinate among the various generation and storage facilities within a power company system. Increasingly, SCADA systems are also used to integrate electric companies into regional or national power grids to optimise power production, minimize production and distribution costs, and provide backup services. This requires a private network that often includes links to the Internet. A cyber attack that disables key Internet nodes could disrupt the power network's communications. And if an entity within the private network is compromised, an attacker could gain direct control of the SCADA systems and their data and operation.

Today, the Internet also is used to manage essential services provided by business and government, such as electronic financial transactions, law enforcement dispatch and support, emergency response and community alerts, and military communications.

Banks, for example, rely on extensive distributed Internet and information services, both for customer interaction and in interbank operations. To assure reliability and security of its most sensitive systems, the banking industry, like the power industry, uses private networks and is vulnerable to cyber attacks that cripple Internet nodes and/or result in unauthorised access to data and services. Such shared Internet links, for example, enabled the "Slammer" worm to disable a major bank's ATM system and an airline's computer system, even though they were not directly connected to the Internet.

During a national emergency, it is imperative that the Nation's communications infrastructure be available for emergency response coordination. Today, that vital infrastructure is vulnerable to a variety of denial of service attacks, including the release of simple viruses and worms that can disrupt Internet communications as well as more sophisticated attacks in which modems from compromised servers are used to flood key parts of the telephone network.

The latter example demonstrates how vulnerability in one system (e.g., the Internet) can be exploited to attack a totally separate system (e.g., the telephone network). These examples illustrate how computing and computer communications have become integral to virtually every domain of activity in the U.S., today. Those systems are interconnected and interdependent in highly complex ways, which are often surprisingly fragile.

Ubiquitous Interconnectivity = Widespread Vulnerability

The Internet – now a global network of networks linking more than 300 million computers worldwide – was designed in a spirit of trust. Neither the protocols for neither network communication nor the software governing computing systems (nodes) connected to the network were architected to operate in an environment in which they are under attack. Indeed, the protocols used by the Internet today are derived from the protocols that were developed in the 1960s for the Federal government's experimental ARPANET. Only a few researchers used ARPANET and they were trusted to do no harm. The civilian networks, such as NSFNET, that developed from ARPANET into the Internet likewise did not incorporate security technologies at the system software or network protocol levels.

Ubiquitous interconnectedness – first exhibited by the Internet and further extended in local area networks, wide area networks, and wireless and hybrid networks – has generated whole new industries, rejuvenated productivity in older ones, and opened new avenues for discourse and education and an unprecedented era of collaborative science and engineering discovery worldwide. That is indeed good news. The bad news is that ubiquitous interconnectivity provides the primary conduit for exploiting vulnerabilities on a widespread basis. Despite efforts in recent years to add security components to computing systems, networks, and software, the acts of a hostile party – whether a terrorist, an adversary nation, organised crime, or a mischievous hacker – can propagate far and wide, with damaging effects on a national or international scale.

For example:

- In the past several years, worms such as Code Red, which defaces World Wide Web sites and/or launches distributed denial of service (DDoS) attacks, and Slammer, which severely degraded the Bank of America's ATM network in January 2003, have caused damage estimated in the billions of dollars.

- The Department of Defence responded to the Code Red worm by disconnecting its unclassified network (NIPRnet) from the Internet to protect it from infection. This protective measure disabled the Army Corps of Engineers' control of the locks on the Mississippi River, since, the NIPRnet was used to transmit commands to the locks through the Internet.

- By using a laptop computer and radio transmitter, a former contractor for an overseas wastewater system was able to assume command of hundreds of control systems that manage sewage and drinking water. Over a period of two months, hundreds of thousands of gallons of putrid sludge were intentionally released from the wastewater system.

- Many businesses are now being attacked by cyber extortionists who demand payment in return for not attacking the businesses' Web presence. Seventeen percent of the 100 companies surveyed in a 2004 poll by Carnegie Mellon University-*Information Week* reported being the target of some form of cyber extortion.
- Identity theft is a rapidly increasing problem for Internet users. One of the simplest methods of stealing a user's identity is known as "phishing," a technique that uses fake e-mail messages and fraudulent Web sites to fool recipients into divulging personal financial data. Consumers Union estimates that 1 per cent of U.S., households fell victim to such attacks at a cost of $400 million in the first half of 2004.

HISTORY OF NETWORK SECURITY

Recent interest in security was fuelled by the crime committed by Kevin Mitnick. Kevin Mitnick committed the largest computer-related crime in U.S. history. The losses were eighty million dollars in U.S. intellectual property and source code from a variety of companies. Since then, information security came into the spotlight. Public networks are being relied upon to deliver financial and personal information. Due to the evolution of information that is made available through the Internet, information security is also required to evolve. Due to Kevin Mitnick's offence, companies are emphasizing security for the intellectual property. Internet has been a driving force for data security improvement.

Internet protocols in the past were not developed to secure themselves. Within the TCP/IP communication stack, security protocols are not implemented. This leaves the Internet open to attacks. Modern developments in the internet architecture have made communication more secure.

Brief History of Internet

The birth of the Internet takes place in 1969 when Advanced Research Projects Agency Network (ARPANET) is commissioned by the department of defence (DOD) for research in networking.

The ARPANET is a success from the very beginning. Although originally designed to allow scientists to share data and access remote computers, e-mail quickly becomes the most popular application. The ARPANET becomes a high-speed digital post office as people use it to collaborate on research projects and discuss topics of various interests. The InterNetworking Working Group becomes the first of several standards-setting entities to govern the growing network. Vinton Cerf is elected the first chairman of the INWG, and later becomes known as a "Father of the Internet."

In the 1980s, Bob Kahn and Vinton Cerf are key members of a team that create TCP/IP, the common language of all Internet computers. For the first time the loose collection of networks which made up the ARPANET is seen as an "Internet", and the Internet as we know it today is born. The mid-80s marks a boom in the personal computer and super-minicomputer industries. The combination of inexpensive desktop machines and powerful, network-ready servers allows many companies to join the Internet for the first time. Corporations begin to use the Internet to communicate with each other and with their customers.

In the 1990s, the Internet began to become available to the public. The World Wide Web was born. Netscape and Microsoft were both competing on developing a browser for the Internet. Internet continues to grow and surfing the internet has become equivalent to TV viewing for many users.

Security Timeline

Several key events contributed to the birth and evolution of computer and network security. The timeline can be started as far back as the 1930s. Polish cryptographers created an enigma machine in 1918 that converted plain messages to encrypted text. In 1930, Alan Turing, a brilliant mathematician broke the code for the Enigma. Securing communications was essential in World War II.

In the 1960s, the term "hacker" is coined by a couple of Massachusetts Institute of Technology (MIT) students. The Department of Defense began the ARPANET, which gains popularity as a conduit for the electronic exchange of data and information. This paves the way for the creation of the carrier network known today as the Internet. During the 1970s, the Telnet protocol was developed. This opened the door for public use of data networks that were originally restricted to government contractors and academic researchers.

During the 1980s, the hackers and crimes relating to computers were beginning to emerge. The 414 gang are raided by authorities after a nine-day cracking spree where they break into top-secret systems. The Computer Fraud and Abuse Act of 1986 was created because of Ian Murphy's crime of stealing information from military computers. A graduate student, Robert Morris, was convicted for unleashing the Morris Worm to over 6,000 vulnerable computers connected to the Internet. Based on concerns that the Morris Worm ordeal could be replicated, the Computer Emergency Response Team (CERT) was created to alert computer users of network security issues.

In the 1990s, Internet became public and the security concerns increased tremendously. Approximately 950 million people use the internet today worldwide. On any day, there are approximately 225 major incidences of a security breach. These security breaches could also result in monetary losses of a large degree. Investment in proper security should be a priority for large organizations as well as common users.

CYBER PROTECTION/CYBER SECURITY LIABILITY

The dawn of the internet provided many new avenues for doing business, and the protection of computer data has become a main concern in today's working environment.

"Cyber Liability," as it is called, encompasses a gamut of new risks for businesses that not only conduct business over the internet, but that also may store private confidential information subject to several federal laws.

To provide some insurance protection for these new risks, most insurance companies have developed cyber security liability policies which cover both first party "the insured" and third party liabilities which can arise because of attacks by outside parties or because of losing of sensitive data due to mistakes on the part of the insured.

Up until a few years ago, these policies were available under most property and general liability policies. However, since 2005 the loss of intangible property has been excluded under standard property policies; likewise, bodily injury or property damage, previously covered under the general liability policy, is also excluded if it emanates from a cyber breach or error.

Some examples of the claims that have occurred are as follows:

Theft of Digital Assets

A regional retailer contracted with a third party service provider. A burglar stole two laptops from the service provider containing the data of over 800,000 clients of the retailer. Under applicable notification laws, the retailer-not the service provider-was required to notify affected individuals. The total expenses incurred for crisis management notification of customers cost nearly $5 million.

In a second example a home health care organization had backup data, laptops and disks containing social security numbers, clinical and demographic information. In a small number of cases, patient financial data was stolen. In total, over 365,000 patient records were exposed. The organization settled with the State Attorney General and provided patients with free credit monitoring, credit restoration to patients that were victims of identity fraud, and reimbursement to patients for direct losses that resulted from the data breach.

Human Error

An employee of a private high school mistakenly distributed via e-mail the names, social security numbers, birth dates and medical information of students and faculty creating a privacy breach. Overall, 1,250 individuals' information was compromised.

Malicious Code

A juvenile released a computer worm that caused a launch of denial of service attack against a regional computing consulting and application outsourcing firm. The infection caused an 18 hour shut down of the entity's computer systems. The computer firm incurred extensive cost and expenses to repair and restore their systems, as well as business income expenses which totaled approximately $875,000.

The cyber liability policy is sufficiently flexible so that a business can buy either third party or first party coverages, or both. Here is an example of how the language in a carrier's insurance policy protects first party assets:

Loss of Digital Assets

"We will indemnify you for loss you incur, in excess of the deductible, as a result of damage, alteration, corruption, distortion, theft, misuse, or destruction of your digital assets directly caused by a covered cause of loss". In this case, digital assets mean electronic data and computer programmes that exist in a computer system. Please note that digital assets do not include computer hardware. In addition to this, protection can be provided for the business income loss that may result from any direct first party claims.

Here is an example of the coverage grants available for third party protection under a typical insurance carrier's policy:

Network Security and Privacy Liability Coverage

The insurance company "will pay on your behalf those amounts, in excess of the applicable deductible, which you are legally obligated as damages on claim expenses arising from your acts, errors or omissions or from acts, errors or omissions for others for whom you are legally responsible, including outsourcers, or vendors provided such acts, errors or omissions follow a security breach or privacy breach". An example of this claim is the loss of a laptop containing sensitive information, which results in the public disclosure of a person's private information. Also, this insuring agreement would cover unauthorized access into your computer system, a denial of service attack against your computer system, or an infection of your computer system by malicious code.

There are a number of other coverage protection grants available on most policies, which The Fedeli Group, after an assessment of your risks, can review with you. Please contact The Fedeli Group team to arrange for this type of risk assessment and possible valuable insurance protection.

CYBER SECURITY AND CYBER CRIME

Cyber security plays an important role in the ongoing development of information technology, as well as Internet services. Enhancing cyber security and protecting critical information infrastructures are essential to each nation's security and economic well-being.

Making the Internet safer (and protecting Internet users) has become integral to the development of new services as well as governmental policy. Deterring cyber crime is an integral component of a national cyber security and critical information infrastructure protection strategy. In particular, this includes the adoption of appropriate legislation against the misuse of ICTs for criminal or other purposes and activities intended to affect the integrity of national critical infrastructures. At the national level, this is a shared responsibility requiring coordinated action related to the prevention, preparation, response, and recovery from incidents on the part of government authorities, the private sector and citizens. At the regional and international level, this entails cooperation and coordination with relevant partners.

The formulation and implementation of a national framework and strategy for cyber security thus requires a comprehensive approach. Cyber security strategies – for example, the development of technical protection systems or the education of users to prevent them from becoming victims of cyber crime – can help to reduce the risk of cyber crime. The development and support of cyber security strategies are a vital element in the fight against cyber crime. The legal, technical and institutional challenges posed by the issue of cyber security are global and far-reaching, and can only be addressed through a coherent strategy taking into account the role of different stakeholders and existing initiatives, within a framework of international cooperation.

In this regard, the World Summit on the Information Society (WSIS) recognised the real and significant risks posed by inadequate cyber security and the proliferation of cyber crime. Paragraphs 108-110 of the WSIS *Tunis Agenda for the Information Society* set out a plan for multi-stakeholder implementation at the international level of the WSIS *Geneva Plan of Action* describing the multi-stakeholder implementation process according to eleven action lines and allocating responsibilities for facilitating implementation of the different action lines. At the WSIS, world leaders and governments designated ITU to facilitate the implementation of WSIS Action Line C5, dedicated to building confidence and security in the use of ICTs.

In this regard, the ITU Secretary-General launched the Global Cyber security Agenda (GCA) on 17 May 2007, alongside partners from governments, industry, regional and international organizations, academic and research institutions. The GCA is a global framework for dialogue and international cooperation to coordinate the international response to the growing challenges to cyber security and to enhance confidence and security in the Information Society. It builds on existing work, initiatives and partnerships with the objective of proposing global strategies to address today's challenges related to building confidence and security in the use of ICTs. Within ITU, the Global Cyber security Agenda complements existing ITU work programmes by facilitating the implementation of the three ITU Sectors' cyber security activities, within a framework of international cooperation.

The GCA main strategic goals, built on five work areas:

1. Legal Measures;
2. Technical and Procedural Measures;
3. Organizational Structures;
4. Capacity Building; and
5. International Cooperation.

The fight against cyber crime needs a comprehensive approach. Given that technical measures alone cannot prevent any crime, it is critical that law enforcement agencies are allowed to investigate and prosecute cyber crime effectively. Among the GCA work areas, "Legal measures" focuses on how to address the legislative challenges posed by criminal activities committed over ICT networks in an internationally compatible manner.

"Technical and Procedural Measures" focuses on key measures to promote adoption of enhanced approaches to improve security and risk management in cyberspace, including accreditation schemes, protocols and standards. "Organizational Structures" focuses on the prevention, detection, response to and crisis management of cyberattacks, including the protection of critical information infrastructure systems.

"Capacity Building" focuses on elaborating strategies for capacity-building mechanisms to raise awareness, transfer knowhow and boost cyber security on the national policy agenda. Finally, "International cooperation" focuses on international cooperation, dialogue and coordination in dealing with cyber-threats. The development of adequate legislation and within this approach the development of a cyber crime-related legal framework is an essential part of a cyber security strategy. This requires first of all the necessary substantive criminal law provisions to criminalise acts such as computer fraud, illegal access, data interference, copyright violations and child pornography. The fact that provisions exist in the criminal code that are applicable to similar acts committed outside the network does not mean that they can be applied to acts committed over the Internet as well.

Therefore, a thorough analysis of current national laws is vital to identify any possible gaps. Apart from substantive criminal law provisions, the law enforcement agencies need the necessary tools and instruments to investigate cyber crime. Such investigations themselves present a number of challenges. Perpetrators can act from nearly any location in the world and take measures to mask their identity. The tools and instruments needed to investigate cyber crime can be quite different from those used to investigate ordinary crimes.

THE FUTURE OF CYBER SECURITY

The product of human ingenuity and innovation, cyberspace now delivers a range of critical services to more citizens around the world than ever before. Yet, the online world as we know it stands at the threshold of unprecedented change. Being invited to speak at the EastWest Institute's Worldwide Security Conference in Brussels this week provided an opportunity to examine the needs faced by the global security community as we prepare to meet the needs of the Internet's next billion users.

The International Telecommunication Union (ITU) reported that the number of Internet users reached the two billion threshold in March of this year and according to a Boston Consulting Group report, another billion are expected to come online in the next four years, bringing the total number of Internet users worldwide to about three billion by 2015.

Planning to ensure that our online world—cyberspace—is trustworthy, resilient and secure as we move into this uncertain future, policy leaders need to consider the fundamental changes that are occurring in cyberspace, and the policy issues that these changes will likely present and that will need to be addressed.

Looking towards the future of three billion users, four factors will fundamentally change the future of cyberspace security: people, devices, data, and cloud services.

The Global Online Population Expands

The emergence of the next billion Internet users will impact security in two ways.

Most important will be the impact of the demographic characteristics of these users. Consider that the next billion users will (1) be younger, (2) spend more time online, (3) be more mobile, (4) see the world through social media and apps, and (5) make greater use of natural interfaces.

These five factors could hasten the onset of totally digital lifestyles making connectivity seemingly as essential as oxygen. The next billion could also help foster new innovation in the development and application of technology.

Separately, however, this emerging user population also represents a greatly expanded "target rich" environment for cybercriminals that want to exploit their data, social networks, and devices via botnets or other means.

Internet of Things to Immersive Computing

These new users will require new devices. According to The Boston Consulting Group, the number of Internet-connected devices is predicted to exceed 15 billion—twice the world's population–by 2015, and to soar to 50 billion devices by 2020. "Devices" of course refers to more than smart phones, netbooks and tablets. It also systems such as smart grids, intelligent transportation, healthcare monitoring, smart manufacturing, and environmental sensors.

The advent of powerful wireless devices that both run infrastructure and deliver infrastructure services, including providing access to cloud services, means that cybercriminals and other threat actors need not merely target traditional, and increasingly protected, commercial software and consumer applications to execute attacks with significant consequences. Attackers may well target the embedded software, firmware and hardware in these devices to attack the infrastructure or seize control of the devices and turn them into sensors that can report status, collect personally identifiable information, or conduct other espionage.

Data: Rapid Increases in Understanding

The striking growth in the number of users and devices will also produce an exponential growth in the amount of data that is being generated, stored, analysed and transformed into innovation and knowledge. Analysing large data sets—so-called big data—will become a key basis of competition, underpinning new waves of productivity growth, innovation, and consumer surplus, according to research by MGI and McKinsey's Business Technology Office. However, such data sets also represent attractive targets for organized cyber criminals and other threat actors. From a security standpoint, safeguarding these huge data sets, protecting privacy and integrity, will require concerted global effort requiring collaboration among governments, the private sector, and users.

Cloud Computing: The Information Society Enabler

With an exponentially growing community of increasingly

mobile users, cloud computing will commensurately grow in importance. It will fundamentally change how businesses operate, how every manner of services are delivered, and even how lives are lived.

On the positive side, the security best practices implemented by an effective cloud provider may rival or surpass the measures that cloud customers might themselves be able to provide, resulting in enhanced security. Yet there are global issues that will need to be addressed in terms of transparency and jurisdiction to enable cloud services that are both secure and scalable to service the needs of this expanded user community across multiple countries.

Reducing the Cyber-attack Surface

Reducing the cyber-attack surface can be achieved by industry and government working inpartnership to make the ICT infrastructure less susceptible to attack and compromise.

One important way to achieve this is through concerted action to address risks in the supply chain for information and communications technology products and services. Vendors and service providers need to build and maintain world-class approaches to secure software and hardware development methodologies.

Microsoft began this journey over 10 years ago and has openly shared its Security Development Lifecycle. The nonprofit alliance SAFECode provides a platform for companies to share, both within the software development community and more broadly, information on secure software development techniques that have proven to be effective as well as those that have not. Industry needs to do more.

For their part, governments need to understand the nature of ICT supply chain risk more clearly and work collaboratively with one another and with vendors to develop a common risk management framework rooted in core principles that both address supply chain integrity concerns and preserve the fruits of global free trade. Such a system should be risk-based, transparent, flexible, and should recognize the realities of reciprocal treatment in the global economic environment.

Improving Internet Health

Improving Internet health requires a global, collaborative approach to protecting people from the potential dangers of the Internet. Despite the best efforts at education and protection, many consumer computers host malware and may be part of a "botnet," unbeknownst to their legitimate owners. There is currently no concerted mechanism to shield users from or help them mitigate these risks. Such infected computers do not simply expose their owners' valuable information and data; they place others at risk too. This threat to greater society makes it is essential that the technology ecosystem take collective action to combat it.

Work has been underway in industry circles to build cooperation among various stakeholder groups including ISPs, software vendors, and others; to leverage investments made in key regions of the world; and to create a future roadmap for an Internet health system. The active discussions of cyber security policy and legislation now underway in many nations afford a ripe opportunity to promote this Internet health model. As part of this discussion, it is important to focus on building a socially acceptable model. While the security benefits may be clear, it is important to achieve those benefits in a way that does not erode privacy or otherwise raise concern.

CYBER SECURITY LIABILITY

The dawn of the internet provided many new avenues for doing business, and the protection of computer data has become a main concern in today's working environment.

"Cyber Liability," as it is called, encompasses a gamut of new risks for businesses that not only conduct business over the internet, but that also may store private confidential information subject to several federal laws.

To provide some insurance protection for these new risks, most insurance companies have developed cyber security liability policies which cover both first party "the insured" and third party liabilities which can arise because of attacks by outside parties or because of losing of sensitive data due to mistakes on the part of the insured.

Up until a few years ago, these policies were available under most property and general liability policies. However, since 2005 the loss of intangible property has been excluded under standard property policies; likewise, bodily injury or property damage, previously covered under the general liability policy, is also excluded if it emanates from a cyber breach or error.

Some examples of the claims that have occurred are as follows:

Theft of Digital Assets

A regional retailer contracted with a third party service provider. A burglar stole two laptops from the service provider containing the data of over 800,000 clients of the retailer. Under applicable notification laws, the retailer-not the service provider-was required to notify affected individuals. The total expenses incurred for crisis management notification of customers cost nearly $5 million.

In a second example a home health care organization had backup data, laptops and disks containing social security numbers, clinical and demographic information. In a small number of cases, patient financial data was stolen. In total, over 365,000 patient records were exposed. The organization settled with the State Attorney General and provided patients with free credit monitoring, credit restoration to patients that were victims of identity fraud, and reimbursement to patients for direct losses that resulted from the data breach.

Human Error

An employee of a private high school mistakenly distributed via e-mail the names, social security numbers, birth dates and medical information of students and faculty creating a privacy breach. Overall, 1,250 individuals' information was compromised.

Malicious Code

A juvenile released a computer worm that caused a launch of denial of service attack against a regional computing consulting and application outsourcing firm. The infection caused an 18 hour shut down of the entity's computer systems. The computer firm incurred extensive cost and expenses to repair and restore their systems, as well as business income expenses which totaled approximately $875,000. The cyber liability policy is sufficiently flexible so that a business can buy either third party or first party coverages, or both. Here is an example of how the language in a carrier's insurance policy protects first party assets:

Loss of Digital Assets

"We will indemnify you for loss you incur, in excess of the deductible, as a result of damage, alteration, corruption, distortion, theft, misuse, or destruction of your digital assets directly caused by a covered cause of loss". In this case, digital assets mean electronic data and computer programmes that exist in a computer system. Please note that digital assets do not include computer hardware. In addition to this, protection can be provided for the business income loss that may result from any direct first party claims. Here is an example of the coverage grants available for third party protection under a typical insurance carrier's policy:

Network Security and Privacy Liability Coverage

The insurance company "will pay on your behalf those amounts, in excess of the applicable deductible, which you are legally obligated as damages on claim expenses arising from your acts, errors or omissions or from acts, errors or omissions for others for whom you are legally responsible, including outsourcers, or vendors provided such acts, errors or omissions follow a security breach or privacy breach". An example of this claim is the loss of a laptop containing sensitive information, which results in the public disclosure of a person's private information. Also, this insuring agreement would cover unauthorized access into your computer system, a denial of service attack against your computer system, or an infection of your computer system by malicious code. There are a number of other coverage protection grants available on most policies, which The Fedeli Group, after an assessment of your risks, can review with you. Please contact The Fedeli Group team to arrange for this type of risk assessment and possible valuable insurance protection.

9

Cyber Terrorism

CYBER TERRORISM: MASS DESTRUCTION OR MASS DISRUPTION?

Just days after the September 11 terrorist attacks the U.S. Federal Bureau of Investigation began warning the public that the potential for future attacks exist, and among the threats was that of cyber terrorism. The concept is not a new one, such attacks have been taking place between Palestinian and Israeli groups, and between U.S. and Chinese sources, in response to political conflicts. And now, in light of new terrorism and cyber exclusions in insurance policies, commercial insurance buyers are wondering how to protect themselves from the potential threat of today's "hacktivists" becoming tomorrow's cyber terrorists, and weapons of mass disruption turning into weapons of mass destruction.

February 2002 - Al-Qaida, (the notorious terrorist group formed by Osama bin Laden, has not engaged in computer-based attacks in the past. However, in the wake of the World Trade Center (WTC) attacks, bin Laden has suggested that Al-Qaida has the expertise to use computer technology as a weapon, reports Canada's Office of Critical Infrastructure Protection and Emergency Preparedness (OCIPEP).

In response to reports from the FBI about the potential threat of cyber attacks in the wake of September 11, OCIPEP began issuing such advisories, and notes that "retaliatory cyber attacks" against coalition countries, primarily in the form of website defacements had already begun. In late November, the Canadian government helped draft the Council of Europe's Convention on

Cybercrime, an international effort to deal with issues of terrorist financing, money laundering and cyber terrorism.

The September 11 terrorist attacks changed perceptions of the world's security infrastructure, and the insurance industry's understanding of risk. What had once been inconceivable was now reality and so began the process of imagining the unimaginable in terms of catastrophic risks. Cyber terrorism, a heretofore unconsidered threat, was suddenly put on the world stage amongst a host of new potential threats.

Digital Pearl Harbor

When the U.S. government's new cyber terrorism expert, Richard Clarke, suggested the possibility of a "digital Pearl Harbor", he was greeted with skepticism. The concept of one, large-scale attack on the Internet seems far-reaching, despite the claims of Al Qaida and other Muslim extremist groups who claim to, or are known to, use the Internet as a tool. *That said, there is ample evidence that politically motivated hack attacks are on the rise, notes DK Matai, chairman and CEO of the mi2g intelligence unit, which deals in cyber security.*

Tensions between the U.S. and China following the accidental bombing of the Chinese Embassy in Belgrade led to a cyber conflict. In the U.S., key government sites, including the Energy Department, the Interior Department and even the White House were targeted.

The Chinese domain, ".cn", and that of Taiwan, ".tw", became the two most defaced domains behind ".com" last year. India (.in) and Pakistan (.pk) saw similar increases in the number of web site defacements due to political tensions (see Charts 1 and 2).

Following NATO air attacks on Serbia in 1999, hackers began to tap into U.S. defense computers and those of other defense related businesses.

And, since September 11, several high profile U.S. government sites have been defaced, some bearing the Saudi flag and threatening messages aimed at the U.S. The groups involved, sometimes called "cyber mujihadeens", have hit sites including the U.S. Army Waterways Experiment Station and the National Institute of Health's Human Genome Project.

Striking at.ca: Canada is not immune to the cyber threat, experts say. *Matai points out that the ".ca" domain experienced a similar increase in defacements last year, with 215 hits, up from 59 in 2000 and 52 in 1999. He notes that many Canadian sites bear the ".com" domain, as well as ".org" and ".net", also popular targets. Hits are similarly not aimed solely at government sites, he adds. "Admittedly there is some bias of attacks towards high profile sites such as whitehouse.gov or fbi.gov, however more and more attacks are on commercial web sites."*

"The 11 September attack had an even deeper ripple effect: the temporary disruption of the entire U.S. financial and transportation infrastructure," notes the OCIPEP report. "If the terrorists did not fully anticipate these aftershocks, they can see them clearly now. This raises the possibility that those responsible may shift their sights away from primarily symbolic targets, such as heavily populated buildings or sports stadiums, toward critical infrastructures."

There are about 10,000 "serious grade crackers" using original code attack systems, as opposed to what Matai calls "script-kiddies", or hackers who rely on ready-made tools. "In terms of defacement attacks on large corporations, attackers penetrate the systems as multi-level attacks using subterfuge and social engineering," he explains. Criticisms of lax electronic security are still being heard, despite the growing awareness created by large-scale attacks such as the "I Love You" and "Melissa" viruses, and worms like "Nimda" and "Code Red". Criticisms of lax electronic security are still being heard, despite the growing awareness created by large-scale attacks such as the "I Love You" and "Melissa" viruses, and worms like "Nimda" and "Code Red".

"My own opinion is that the potential is there [for cyber terrorists to attack], everyone's networks are so poorly protected, but no one has taken advantage of it," says Chuck Wilmink, director of the Canadian Center for Information Technology Security (CCITS).

A study by the U.S.-based Computer Security Institute reports that 85% of companies admit to having their networks breached in 2000, and 64% acknowledge significant financial losses due to those breaches. A recent report by the U.S. Congress gave two-thirds of American's federal agencies failing grades in cyber security, including the departments of Defense, Justice, Energy and Treasury.

Similarly, in Canada, a 1999 Senate report pointed to the potential for a major cyber attack in Canada, and admitted that the FBI has characterized Canada as a "hacker haven".

Perhaps fortunately, Canada is more often a base for hackers to attack other countries, rather than a target itself.

"Canadian hackers have traditionally tended to attack outside of Canada as opposed to within," says Matai. He notes that Canada's quieter political demeanor means that it is less often viewed as a target. ".ca Canadian sites are less vulnerable than .com or .uk because Canada is not seen to be so aggressive on the world stage."

"I really don't think we've ever considered Canada to be at the same threat level (as the U.S.)," says Max London, manager of public affairs for OCIPEP. However, OCIPEP has issued the FBI warnings post-September 11, giving companies advance warning in the event of a cyber attack. Ultimately, London explains, corporations are responsible for their own security systems.

He notes that OCIPEP is aware of "hacktivist" activity in Canada, specifically "around some of the larger meetings", such as the G-8 Summit or World Trade Organization meetings. However, these are a far cry from the threat by a foreign government or terrorist organization that might harm Canada's critical infrastructure, including systems that support communications, transportation and services such as health care and finance.

With the "increasing dependence and increasing interconnectivity" of such systems comes a greater risk, however. In the past, OCIPEP has been involved in public awareness campaigns around threats including the "Code Red" worm, which was viewed as "a very real threat to the Internet", and has worked with the U.S. National Infrastructure Protection Center (NIPC), an FBI operation, to disseminate information. The NPIC issued warnings in mid-October of a potential cyber threat aimed at the U.S. power grid, and yet another aimed at online financial sites.

Insurer Reaction

Canada's insurers have been jumping into the terrorism risk fray since September 11, trying to understand what exposures they might face in the future. Just as no one predicted the events that represent the largest insurance loss in history, there is fear of what other unforeseen risks may lie ahead.

As insurers met through the Insurance Bureau of Canada's (IBC) terrorism task force to discuss the new risk horizon, cyber threats were one possibility on the table, says Anne MacKenzie, assistant vice president, claims technical, at the Dominion of Canada General Insurance Company and a member of the task force. She adds, however, that they did not top the list of concerns for several reasons, including the notion that terrorists generally tend towards visible, high profile acts. "It's usually physical acts of terrorism," she says. "Terrorists like to put the population at fear." OCIPEP also notes that terrorists have traditionally relied on "bombs over bytes" as the weapon of choice.

Cyber terrorism has not dominated discussion of electronic risks, adds Jennifer Soper, assistant vice president, technology, at St. Paul Canada. Most of the talk seems centered around the major viruses that have plagued companies. This is partly because many companies do not see themselves as targets for such acts. "When you're not in the Fortune 500 or brand name companies, you can get an 'it can't happen to me', almost false sense of security."

She adds that companies often do not discuss the nature of attacks, and still have a "keep it in the closet" attitude about cyber security breaches. The benefit is that this policy of silence denies attackers the desired result of publicity. However, terrorists may soon find that cyber attacks will gain them the same kind of notoriety as physical attacks, MacKenzie adds. "Nothing would scare people more than to learn that terrorists had hacked into government sites".

Exclusions, Exclusions

Commercial insurance buyers are no doubt facing a tough market in the post-September 11 era, although the situation was already beginning to grow bleak prior to the terrorist attacks.

Reinsurers had already stated their intention to introduce cyber exclusions into their treaties, leaving insurers to follow suit.

However, insurers assert that cyber or "data" coverage was never really part of commercial general liability (CGL) policies. In light of the potential for differing interpretations (such as the U.S. case of Ingram v. Micro, where it was found that business interruption due to computer failure should be included in CGL policies), more specific wording was added to most policies.

"The data exclusion was just a clarification to make sure consumers knew what they were buying, there never was coverage for data," explains MacKenzie. This clarification is apparent in most policies as of yearend 2001, adds Dominion president George Cooke. "Our view is that the wordings don't do anything the old wordings didn't do, they're just clearer."

However, the wordings have left many companies scrambling for coverage, Soper says. "What is available is not widely available." Companies will either have to negotiate coverage as a limited buy-back option in existing policies, or hunt it down as a separate policy from another carrier. "In terms of coverage, if there is anything going on it is on a customer-by-customer level. It has to be." Given the difficulty in quantifying cyber risks, there is no "one size fits all" policy.

Cooke says he is concerned with the lack of cyber coverage available, but acknowledges that insurers simply are not in a position to offer it. "It's a situation that troubles me. But we can't buy coverage [in the reinsurance market], so it's impossible for us to offer it."

September 11 did not help the situation either. He predicts that notwithstanding the terrorist attacks, cyber coverage would have been a top issue for insurers, but given the shift in priorities, insurers were unable to come up with private market capital solutions in advance of yearend commercial policy renewals. "September 11 kind of eclipsed concerns over whether we should be developing new products to deal with cyber risks," says MacKenzie. However, she adds, "we will want to revisit it" in the future.

Overriding Concern

Regardless of new cyber covers, with the current terrorism exclusions being written, any act deemed as "cyber terrorism" would not be covered, as the terrorism exclusion would be overriding. In the wake of September 11, with reinsurers refusing to cover terrorism in their treaties, insurers were forced to either introduce similar exclusions in their policies or to negotiate a deal with the government, which would act as excess of loss reinsurer through a "terrorism pool" arrangement.

By yearend, no such pool had been devised, despite lengthy discussions between IBC representatives and the government. "The nature of the discussions evolved as the market evolved," says Cooke, who is also chair of the IBC. "The decision was taken to wait. It was probably a smart decision."

The U.S. government's inability to come to a solution prior to breaking at the end of the year was among the contributing factors. Cooke recognizes that it was "politically difficult" for the Canadian government to come forward with a solution before the U.S., given the fact that the situation was not of the same scale here. This situation may change as the U.S. House reconvenes in late January. "People have said that the government wasn't prepared to act, but I don't buy that," he adds. "Minister Peterson and the staff in Finance were seriously engaged in discussions and are prepared to act if the need arises."

The need for a solution may not be quite as pressing as originally thought, with renewals moving along despite the lack of a solution, and the fact that many commercial policies on target risks have not yet reached renewal.

However, Cooke still feels a solution is needed. The government has consulted with other associations, most notably the Canadian Bankers Association (CBA), who claim that there is no need for the coverage. "I think they're wrong," Cooke says, but their resistance makes it difficult for insurers to press for a solution. He is most displeased with the view that insurers are looking for a "bail out". "We are not doing an 'Air Canada' here. We're more than prepared to take our pains for our past sins." But without reinsurance coverage in place, it is not economically feasible for insurers to offer the coverage.

The terrorism task force was "driven by the sudden recognition that there was now infinite risk and infinite exposure and that wasn't economically sustainable," says MacKenzie. "It [terrorism coverage] isn't anything we could write even if we wanted to."

With no cap on the exposure, insurers would be leaving themselves open to unquantifiable risks, a situation that extends into the domain of cyber terrorism.

"Putting a box around the exposure" or quantifying the risk is especially difficult with cyber risks, says Soper.. "The 'net is worldwide. It is difficult to know where it (an attack) is going to come from, and how it's going to come."

She adds, "It's hard when you're an industry that likes to put dollars and cents to things. There's just no history. You can't go into the archives and pluck out something and say 'this is going to work for me today'." September 11 was a "humbling" experience for the industry, says MacKenzie, and as the industry learns more about that event, "we realize we don't know about all the risks". Prior to September 11 "there was a sense that we could talk about 100-year events and worst case scenarios...everyone's trying to come up with scenarios, however, the end of the conversation always comes to the same conclusion, we just can't imagine."

Web Site Defacement s, 2001 (increase over 2000)

Location	Domain	Number Incidents	Percentage Increase
Canada	.ca	215	265
China	.cn	1298	1326
Taiwan	.tw	1355	1178
Israel	.il	413	220
India	.in	250	205
pakistan	.pk	72	300
UK government	.gov.uk	43	378
UK organisations	.org.uk	25	400
UK companies	.co.uk	385	181
US government	.gov.com	248	37
US military	.mil.com	n/a	128

TERRORISTS IN CYBERSPACE

Terrorists have moved into cyberspace to facilitate traditional forms of terrorism such as bombings. They use the Internet to communicate, coordinate events, and advance their agenda. While such activity does not constitute cyberterrorism in the strict sense, it does show that terrorists have some competency using the new information technologies.

By 1996, the headquarters of terrorist financier Osama bin Laden in Afghanistan was equipped with computers and communications equipment. Egyptian "Afghan" computer experts were said to have helped devise a communication network that used the Web, e-mail, and electronic bulletin boards. Hamas activists have been said to use chat rooms and e-mail to plan operations and coordinate activities, making it difficult for Israeli security officials to trace their messages and decode their contents. The Revolutionary Armed Forces of Columbia (FARC) uses e-mail to field inquiries from the press.

The Web is especially popular as a medium for reaching a global audience. For example, after the Peruvian terrorist group Tupac Amaru stormed the Japanese Ambassador's residence in Lima on December 17, 1996 and took 400 diplomatic, political, and military officials as hostage, sympathizers in the United States and Canada put up solidarity Web sites. One site included detailed drawings of the residence and planned assault.

In February 1998, Hizbullah was operating three Web sites: one for the central press office (www.hizbollah.org), another to describe its attacks on Israeli targets (www.moqawama.org), and the third for news and information (www.almanar.com.lb).

That month, Clark Staten, executive director of the Emergency Response & Research Institute (ERRI) in Chicago, testified before a U.S. Senate subcommittee that "even small terrorist groups are now using the Internet to broadcast their message and misdirect/ misinform the general population in multiple nations simultaneously." He gave the subcommittee copies of both domestic and international messages containing anti-American and anti-Israeli propaganda and threats, including a widely distributed extremist call for "jihad" (holy war) against America and Great Britain.

In June 1998, *U.S. News & World Report* noted that 12 of the 30 groups on the U.S. State Department=s list of terrorist organizations are on the Web. Now, it appears that virtually every terrorist group is on the Web. Forcing them off the Web is impossible, because they can set up their sites in countries with free-speech laws. The government of Sri Lanka, for example, banned the separatist Liberation Tigers of Tamil Eelam, but they have not even attempted to take down their London-based Web site.

Even in democracies, however, there are limits to what terrorists can post on the Net. After a group of anti-abortionists put up a Web site terrorizing doctors who performed abortions, a federal jury ordered the pages be taken down and damages of more than $100 million paid. The Nuremberg Files site had listed the names of about 200 abortion providers under the heading of "baby butchers."

Readers were invited to send in such personal details as the doctors' home addresses, license plate numbers, and the names of their children. Three doctors whose names appeared on the list were killed, and after each, the doctor's name was promptly crossed out. Doctors named on the site testified that they lived in constant fear and used disguises, bodyguards, and bulletproof vests. In ordering the site down, the federal jury said the site and "wanted" posters amounted to death threats against the doctors.

Many terrorists are using encryption to conceal their communications and stored files, compounding the difficulties of providing effective counter-terrorism. Hamas, for example, reportedly has used encrypted Internet communications to transmit maps, pictures, and other details pertaining to terrorist attacks. Ramsey Yousef, a member of the international terrorist group responsible for bombing the World Trade Center in 1994 and a Manila Air airliner in late 1995, encrypted files on his laptop computer. The files, which U.S. government officials decrypted, contained information pertaining to further plans to blow up eleven U.S.-owned commercial airliners in the Far East. The Aum Shinrikyo cult, which gassed the Tokyo subway in March 1995, killing 12 people and injuring 6,000 more, also used encryption to protect their computerized records, which included plans and intentions to deploy weapons of mass destruction in Japan and the United States.

Cyberspace Attacks

Cyberspace is constantly under assault. Cyber spies, thieves, saboteurs, and thrill seekers break into computer systems, steal personal data and trade secrets, vandalize Web sites, disrupt service, sabotage data and systems, launch computer viruses and worms, conduct fraudulent transactions, and harass individuals and companies. These attacks are facilitated with increasingly powerful and easy-to-use software tools, which are readily available for free from thousands of Web sites on the Internet.

Many of the attacks are serious and costly. The ILOVEYOU virus and variants, for example, was estimated to have hit tens of millions of users worldwide and cost billions of dollars in damage. Denial-of-service attacks against Yahoo, CNN, eBay, and other e-commerce Web sites were estimated to have caused over a billion in losses. They also shook the confidence of business and individuals in e-commerce. Governments are particularly concerned with terrorist and state-sponsored attacks against the critical infrastructures that constitute their national life support systems. The Clinton Administration defined eight: telecommunications, banking and finance, electrical power, oil and gas distribution and storage, water supply, transportation, emergency services, and government services.

There have been numerous attacks against these infrastructures. Hackers have invaded the public phone networks, compromising nearly every category of activity, including switching and operations, administration, maintenance, and provisioning (OAM&P). They have crashed or disrupted signal transfer points, traffic switches, OAM&P systems, and other network elements. They have planted "time bomb" programs designed to shut down major switching hubs, disrupted emergency 911 services throughout the eastern seaboard, and boasted that they have the capability to bring down all switches in Manhattan. They have installed wiretaps, rerouted phone calls, changed the greetings on voice mail systems, taken over voice mailboxes, and made free long-distance calls at their victims= expense — sticking some victims with phone bills in the hundreds of thousands of dollars. When they can=t crack the technology, they use "social engineering" to con employees into giving them access.

In March 1997, one teenage hacker penetrated and disabled a telephone company computer that serviced the Worcester Airport in Massachusetts. As a result, telephone service to the Federal Aviation Administration control tower, the airport fire department, airport security, the weather service, and various private airfreight companies was cut off for six hours. Later in the day, the juvenile disabled another telephone company computer, this time causing an outage in the Rutland area. The lost service caused financial damages and threatened public health and public safety. On a separate occasion, the hacker allegedly broke into a pharmacist=s computer and accessed files containing prescriptions.

Banks and financial systems are a popular target of cyber criminals. The usual motive is money, and perpetrators have stolen or attempted to steal tens of millions of dollars. In one case of sabotage, a computer operator at Reuters in Hong Kong tampered with the dealing room systems of five of the company=s bank clients. In November 1996, he programmed the systems to delete key operating system files after a delay long enough to allow him to leave the building. When the "time bombs" exploded, the systems crashed. They were partially restored by the next morning, but it took another day before they were fully operational. However, the banks said the tampering did not significantly affect trading and that neither they nor their clients experienced losses.

In another act of sabotage against a critical infrastructure, a fired employee of Chevron's emergency alert network disabled the firm=s alert system by hacking into computers in New York and San Jose, California, and reconfiguring them so they=d crash. The vandalism was not discovered until an emergency arose at the Chevron refinery in Richmond, California, and the system could not be used to notify the adjacent community of a noxious release. During the 10-hour period in 1992 when the system was down, thousands of people in 22 states and 6 unspecified areas of Canada were put at risk.

An overflow of raw sewage on the Sunshine Coast of Australia in June was linked to a 49-year-old Brisbane man, who allegedly penetrated the Maroochy Shire Council's computer system and used radio transmissions to create the overflows. The man faced 370 charges that included stealing, computer hacking, and use radio communications equipment without authority.

Government computers, particularly Department of Defense computers, are a regular target of attack. Detected attacks against unclassified DoD computers rose from 780 in 1997 to 5,844 in 1998 and 22,144 in 1999.

The most damaging and costly attacks have been conducted for reasons other than the pursuit of terrorism. As the above cases illustrate, they have been motivated by greed, thrills, ego, revenge, and a variety of other non-ideological factors. They are properly classifified as cybercrimes, but not cyberterrorism

Politically and Socially Motivated Cyberattacks

Terrorism is normally associated with attacks conducted in furtherance of political and social objectives. Numerous cyberattacks have been so motivated. For example, in 1998, ethnic Tamil guerrillas swamped Sri Lankan embassies with 800 e-mails a day over a two-week period. The messages read "We are the Internet Black Tigers and we=re doing this to disrupt your communications." Intelligence authorities characterized it as the first known attack by terrorists against a country=s computer systems.

Also in 1998, Spanish protestors bombarded the Institute for Global Communications (IGC) with thousands of bogus e-mail messages. E-mail was tied up and undeliverable to the San Francisco based ISP=s users, and support lines were tied up with people who couldn=t get their mail. The protestors also spammed IGC staff and member accounts, clogged their Web page with bogus credit card orders, and threatened to employ the same tactics against organizations using IGC services. They demanded that IGC stop hosting the Webs site for the *Euskal Herria Journal*, a New

York-based publication supporting Basque independence. Protestors said IGC supported terrorism because a section on the Web pages contained materials on the terrorist group Fatherland and Liberty, or ETA, which claimed responsibility for assassinations of Spanish political and security officials, and attacks on military installations. IGC finally relented and pulled the site because of the "mail bombings."

During the Kosovo conflict in 1999, NATO computers were blasted with e-mail bombs and hit with denial-of-service attacks by hacktivists protesting the NATO bombings. In addition, businesses, public organizations, and academic institutes received highly politicized virus-laden e-mails from a range of Eastern European countries, according to reports. Web defacements were also common. After the Chinese Embassy was accidentally bombed in Belgrade, Chinese hacktivists posted messages such as "We won=t stop attacking until the war stops!" on U.S. government Web sites.

Since December 1997, the Electronic Disturbance Theater (EDT), a New York City based activist group, has been conducting Web sit-ins against various sites in support of the Mexican Zapatistas. At a designated time, thousands of protestors point their browsers to a target site using software that floods the target with rapid and repeated download requests. EDT=s software has also been used by animal rights groups against organizations said to abuse animals. Electrohippies, another group of hacktivists, conducted Web sit-ins against the WTO when they met in Seattle in late 1999. These sit-ins all require mass participation to have much effect, and thus are more suited to use by activists than by relatively small groups of terrorists operating in secrecy.

Future Prospects

In August 1999, the Center for the Study of Terrorism and Irregular Warfare at the Naval Postgraduate School in Monterey, California, issued a report titled "Cyberterror: Prospects and Implications." Their objective was to articulate the demand side of terrorism. Specifically, they assessed the prospects of terrorist organizations pursuing cyberterrorism. They concluded that the barrier to entry for anything beyond annoying hacks is quite high, and that terrorists generally lack the wherewithal and human capital needed to mount a meaningful operation. Cyberterrorism, they argued, was a thing of the future, although it might be pursued as an ancillary tool.

The Monterey team defined three levels of cyberterror capability. First is simple-unstructured: the capability to conduct basic hacks against individual systems using tools created by someone else. The organization possesses little target analysis, command and control, or learning capability.

Second is advanced-structured: the capability to conduct more sophisticated attacks against multiple systems or networks and possibly, to modify or create basic hacking tools. The organization possesses an elementary target analysis, command and control, and learning capability.

Third is complex-coordinated: the capability for a coordinated attacks capable of causing mass-disruption against integrated, heterogeneous defenses (including cryptography). The organization has the ability to create sophisticated hacking tools. They possess a highly capable target analysis, command and control, and organization learning capability.

The Monterey team estimated that it would take a group starting from scratch 2-4 years to reach the advanced-structured level and 6-10 years to reach the complex-coordinated level, although some groups might get there in just a few years or turn to outsourcing or sponsorship to extend their capability.

The study examined five terrorist group types: religious, New Age, ethno-nationalist separatist, revolutionary, and far-right extremists. They determined that only the religious groups are likely to seek the most damaging capability level, as it is consistent with their indiscriminate application of violence. New Age or single issue terrorists, such as the Animal Liberation Front, pose the most immediate threat, however, such groups are likely to accept disruption as a substitute for destruction. Both the revolutionary and ethno-nationalist separatists are likely to seek an advanced-structured capability. The far-right extremists are likely to settle for a simple-unstructured capability, as cyberterror offers neither the intimacy nor cathartic effects that are central to the psychology of far-right terror. The study also determined that hacker groups are psychologically and organizationally ill-suited to cyberterrorism, and that it would be against their interests to cause mass disruption of the information infrastructure.

Thus, at this time, cyberterrorism does not seem to pose an imminent threat. This could change. For a terrorist, it would have some advantages over physical methods. It could be conducted remotely and anonymously, and it would not require the handling of explosives or a suicide mission. It would likely garner extensive media coverage, as journalists and the public alike are fascinated by practically any kind of computer attack. Indeed cyberterrorism could be immensely appealing precisely because of the tremendous attention given to it by the government and media.

Cyberterrorism also has its drawbacks. Systems are complex, so it may be harder to control an attack and achieve a desired level of damage than using physical weapons. Unless people are injured, there is also less drama and emotional appeal. Further, terrorists may be disinclined to try new methods unless they see their old ones as inadequate, particularly when the new methods require considerable knowledge and skill to use effectively.

Terrorists generally stick with tired and true methods. Novelty and sophistication of attack may be much less important than assurance that a mission will be operationally successful. Indeed, the risk of operational failure could be a deterrent to terrorists. For now, the truck bomb poses a much greater threat than the logic bomb.

The next generation of terrorists will grow up in a digital world, with ever more powerful and easy-to-use hacking tools at their disposal. They might see greater potential for cyberterrorism than the terrorists of today, and their level of knowledge and skill relating to hacking will be greater. Hackers and insiders might be recruited by terrorists or become self-recruiting cyberterrorists, the Timothy McVeigh=s of cyberspace. Some might be moved to action by cyber policy issues, making cyberspace an attractive venue for carrying out an attack. Cyberterrorism could also become more attractive as the real and virtual worlds become more closely coupled, with a greater number of physical devices attached to the Internet. Some of these may be remotely controlled. Terrorists, for example, might target robots used in telesurgery. Unless these systems are carefully secured, conducting an operation that physically harms someone may be easy as penetrating a Web site is today.

Although the violent pursuit of political goals using exclusively electronic methods is likely to be at least a few years into the future, the more general threat of cybercrime is very much a part of the digital landscape today. In addition to cyberattacks against digital data and systems, many people are being terrorized on the Internet today with threats of physical violence. On-line stalking, death threats, and hate messages are abundant. These crimes are serious and must be addressed. In so doing, we will be in a better position to prevent and respond to cyberterrorism if and when the threat becomes more serious.

CYBERATTACKS

Although terrorists have been adept at spreading propaganda and attack instructions on the web, it appears that their capacity for offensive computer network operations may be limited. The Federal Bureau of Investigation (FBI) reports that cyberattacks attributed to terrorists have largely been limited to unsophisticated efforts such as e-mail bombing of ideological foes, denial-ofservice attacks, or defacing of websites. However, it says, their increasing technical competency is resulting in an emerging capability for network-based attacks.

The FBI has predicted that terrorists will either develop or hire hackers for the purpose of complementing large conventional attacks with cyberattacks. During his testimony regarding the 2007 Annual Threat Assessment, FBI Director Robert Mueller observed that "terrorists increasingly use the Internet to communicate, conduct operational planning, proselytise, recruit, train and to obtain logistical and financial support. That is a growing and increasing concern for us." In addition, continuing publicity about Internet computer security vulnerabilities may encourage terrorists' interest in attempting a possible computer network attack, or cyberattack, against U.S. critical infrastructure. The Internet, whether accessed by a desktop computer or by the many available handheld devices, is the medium through which a cyberattack would be delivered. However, for a targeted attack to be successful, the attackers usually require that the network itself remain more or less intact, unless the attackers assess that the perceived gains from shutting down the network entirely would offset the accompanying loss of their own communication. A future targeted cyberattack could be effective if directed against a portion of the U.S. critical infrastructure, and if timed to amplify the effects of a simultaneous conventional physical or chemical, biological, radiological, or nuclear (CBRN) terrorist attack.

The objectives of a cyberattack may include the following four areas:

1. loss of integrity, such that information could be modified improperly;
2. loss of availability, where mission-critical information systems are rendered unavailable to authorised users;
3. loss of confidentiality, where critical information is disclosed to unauthorised users; and
4. physical destruction, where information systems create actual physical harm through commands that cause deliberate malfunctions.

Publicity would also potentially be one of the primary objectives for a terrorist cyberattack. Extensive media coverage has shown the vulnerability of the U.S. information infrastructure and the potential harm that could be caused by a cyberattack. This might lead terrorists to believe that even a marginally successful cyberattack directed at the United States would garner considerable publicity.

Some suggest that were such a cyberattack by an international terrorist organization to occur and become known to the general public, regardless of the level of success of the attack, concern by many citizens and cascading effects might lead to widespread disruption of critical infrastructures. For example, reports of an attack on the international financial system's networks could create a fiscal panic in the public that could lead to economic damage.

According to security experts, terrorist groups have not yet used their own computer hackers nor hired hackers to damage, disrupt, or destroy critical infrastructure systems.

Yet reports of a recent disruptive computer worm that has spread through some government networks, including that of the National Aeronautics and Space Administration, have found a possible link to a Libyan hacker with the handle "Iraq Resistance" and his online hacker group "Brigades of Tariq ibn Ziyad," whose stated goal is "to penetrate U.S. agencies belonging to the U.S. Army." References to both the hacker and group have been found in the worm's code. However, this does not provide conclusive evidence of involvement, as e-mail addresses can be spoofed and code can be deliberately designed to implicate a target while concealing the true identity of the perpetrator.

The recent emergence of the Stuxnet worm may have implications for what potential future cyberattacks might look like. Stuxnet is thought to be the first piece of malicious software (malware) that was specifically designed to target the computer-networked industrial control systems that control utilities, in this case nuclear power plants in Iran. Although many experts contend that the level of sophistication, intelligence, and access required to develop Stuxnet all point to nation states, not only is the idea now in the public sphere for others to build upon, but the code has been released as well. An industrious group could potentially use this code as a foundation for developing a capability intended to degrade and destroy the software systems that control the U.S. power grid, to name one example.

Cyberspace Attacks

Governments are particularly concerned with terrorist and state-sponsored attacks against the critical infrastructures that constitute their national life support systems. The Clinton Administration defined eight: telecommunications, banking and finance, electrical power, oil and gas distribution and storage, water supply, transportation, emergency services, and government services. There have been numerous attacks against these infrastructures. Hackers have invaded the public phone networks, compromising nearly every category of activity, including switching and operations, administration, maintenance, and provisioning (OAM&P).

They have crashed or disrupted signal transfer points, traffic switches, OAM&P systems, and other network elements. They have planted "time bomb" programs designed to shut down major switching hubs, disrupted emergency 911 services throughout the eastern seaboard, and boasted that they have the capability to bring down all switches in Manhattan. They have installed wiretaps, rerouted phone calls, changed the greetings on voice mail systems, taken over voice mailboxes, and made free long-distance calls at their victims' expense — sticking some victims with phone bills in the hundreds of thousands of dollars. When they can't crack the technology, they use "social engineering" to con employees into giving them access.

In March 1997, one teenage hacker penetrated and disabled a telephone company computer that serviced the Worcester Airport in Massachusetts. As a result, telephone service to the Federal Aviation Administration control tower, the airport fire department, airport security, the weather service, and various private airfreight companies was cut off for six hours.

Later in the day, the juvenile disabled another telephone company computer, this time causing an outage in the Rutland area. The lost service caused financial damages and threatened public health and public safety. On a separate occasion, the hacker allegedly broke into a pharmacist's computer and accessed files containing prescriptions.

Banks and financial systems are a popular target of cyber criminals. The usual motive is money, and perpetrators have stolen or attempted to steal tens of millions of dollars.

In one case of sabotage, a computer operator at Reuters in Hong Kong tampered with the dealing room systems of five of the company's bank clients.

In November 1996, he programmed the systems to delete key operating system files after a delay long enough to allow him to leave the building. When the "time bombs" exploded, the systems crashed. They were partially restored by the next morning, but it took another day before they were fully operational. However, the banks said the tampering did not significantly affect trading and that neither they nor their clients experienced losses.

In another act of sabotage against a critical infrastructure, a fired employee of Chevron's emergency alert network disabled the firm's alert system by hacking into computers in New York and San Jose, California, and reconfiguring them so they'd crash. The vandalism was not discovered until an emergency arose at the Chevron refinery in Richmond, California, and the system could not be used to notify the adjacent community of a noxious release. During the 10-hour period in 1992 when the system was down, thousands of people in 22 states and 6 unspecified areas of Canada were put at risk.

An overflow of raw sewage on the Sunshine Coast of Australia in June was linked to a 49-year-old Brisbane man, who allegedly penetrated the Maroochy Shire Council's computer system and used radio transmissions to create the overflows. The man faced 370 charges that included stealing, computer hacking, and use radio communications equipment without authority.

Government computers, particularly Department of Defense computers, are a regular target of attack. Detected attacks against unclassified DoD computers rose from 780 in 1997 to 5,844 in 1998 and 22,144 in 1999.

Politically and Socially Motivated Cyberattacks

There are a few indications that some terrorist groups are pursuing cyberterrorism, either alone or in conjunction with acts of physical violence. In February 1998, Clark Staten told the Senate Judiciary Committee Subcommittee on Technology, Terrorism, and Government Information that it was believed that "members of some Islamic extremist organizations have been attempting to develop a 'hacker network' to support their computer activities and even engage in offensive information warfare attacks in the future."

In November 1998, the *Detroit News* reported that Khalid Ibrahim, who claimed to be a member of the militant Indian separatist group Harkat-ul-Ansar, had tried to buy military software from hackers who had stolen it from Department of Defense computers they had penetrated. The attempted purchase was discovered when an 18-year-old hacker calling himself Chameleon attempted to cash a $1,000 check from Ibrahim. Chameleon said he did not have the software and did not give it to Ibrahim, but Ibrahim may have obtained it or other sensitive information from one of the many other hackers he approached. Harkat-ul-Ansar declared war on the United States following the August cruise-missile attack on a suspected terrorist training camp in Afghanistan run by bin Laden, which allegedly killed nine of their members.

The Provisional Irish Republican Army employed the services of contract hackers to penetrate computers in order to acquire home addresses of law enforcement and intelligence officers, but the data was used to draw up plans to kill the officers in a single "night of the long knives" if the British government did not meet terms for a new cease-fire. As this case illustrates, terrorists may use hacking as a way of acquiring intelligence in support of physical violence, even if they do not use it to wreak havoc in cyberspace.

Potential Threat

To understand the potential threat of cyberterrorism, two factors must be considered: first, whether there are targets that are vulnerable to attack that could lead to violence or severe harm, and second, whether there are actors with the capability and motivation to carry them out.

Looking first at vulnerabilities, several studies have shown that critical infrastructures are potentially vulnerable to cyberterrorist attack. Eligible Receiver, an exercise conducted by the Department of Defense in 1997 with support from National Security Agency penetration testing teams, found the power grid and emergency 911 systems had weaknesses that could be exploited by an adversary using only publicly available tools on the Internet. Although neither of these systems were actually attacked, study members concluded that service on these systems could be disrupted. Also in 1997, the President's Commission on Critical Infrastructure Protection issued its report warning that through mutual dependencies and interconnectedness, critical infrastructures could be vulnerable in new ways, and that vulnerabilities were steadily increasing, while the costs of attack were decreasing.

Although many of the weaknesses in computerized systems can be corrected, it is effectively impossible to eliminate all of them. Even if the technology itself offers good security, it is frequently configured or used in ways that make it open to attack. In addition, there is always the possibility of insiders, acting alone or in concert with other terrorists, misusing their access capabilities. According to Russia's Interior Ministry Col. Konstantin Machabeli, the state-run gas monopoly, Gazprom, was hit by hackers in 1999 who collaborated with a Gazprom insider. The hackers were said to have used a Trojan horse to gain control of the central switchboard which controls gas flows in pipelines, although Gazprom, the world's largest natural gas producer and the largest gas supplier to Western Europe, refuted the report.

Consultants and contractors are frequently in a position where they could cause grave harm. This past March, Japan's Metropolitan Police Department reported that a software system they had procured to track 150 police vehicles, including unmarked cars, had been developed by the Aum Shinryko cult. At the time of the discovery, the cult had received classified tracking data on 115 vehicles. Further, the cult had developed software for at least 80 Japanese firms and 10 government agencies. They had worked as subcontractors to other firms, making it almost impossible for the organizations to know who was developing the software. As subcontractors, the cult could have installed Trojan horses to launch or facilitate cyberterrorist attacks at a later date. Fearing a Trojan horse of their own, last February, the U.S. State Department sent an urgent cable to about 170 embassies asking them to remove software, which they belatedly realized had been written by citizens of the former Soviet Union.

Future Prospects

In August 1999, the Center for the Study of Terrorism and Irregular Warfare at the Naval Postgraduate School in Monterey,

California, issued a report titled "Cyberterror: Prospects and Implications." Their objective was to articulate the demand side of terrorism. Specifically, they assessed the prospects of terrorist organizations pursuing cyberterrorism. They concluded that the barrier to entry for anything beyond annoying hacks is quite high, and that terrorists generally lack the wherewithal and human capital needed to mount a meaningful operation. Cyberterrorism, they argued, was a thing of the future, although it might be pursued as an ancillary tool.

The Monterey team defined three levels of cyberterror capability. First is simple-unstructured: the capability to conduct basic hacks against individual systems using tools created by someone else. The organization possesses little target analysis, command and control, or learning capability.

Second is advanced-structured: the capability to conduct more sophisticated attacks against multiple systems or networks and possibly, to modify or create basic hacking tools. The organization possesses an elementary target analysis, command and control, and learning capability.

Third is complex-coordinated: the capability for a coordinated attacks capable of causing mass-disruption against integrated, heterogeneous defenses (including cryptography). The organization has the ability to create sophisticated hacking tools. They possess a highly capable target analysis, command and control, and organization learning capability.

The Monterey team estimated that it would take a group starting from scratch 2-4 years to reach the advanced-structured level and 6-10 years to reach the complex-coordinated level, although some groups might get there in just a few years or turn to outsourcing or sponsorship to extend their capability.

The study examined five terrorist group types: religious, New Age, ethno-nationalist separatist, revolutionary, and far-right extremists. They determined that only the religious groups are likely to seek the most damaging capability level, as it is consistent with their indiscriminate application of violence. New Age or single issue terrorists, such as the Animal Liberation Front, pose the most immediate threat, however, such groups are likely to accept disruption as a substitute for destruction. Both the revolutionary and ethno-nationalist separatists are likely to seek an advanced-structured capability. The far-right extremists are likely to settle for a simple-unstructured capability, as cyberterror offers neither the intimacy nor cathartic effects that are central to the psychology of far-right terror. The study also determined that hacker groups are psychologically and organizationally ill-suited to cyberterrorism, and that it would be against their interests to cause mass disruption of the information infrastructure.

Thus, at this time, cyberterrorism does not seem to pose an imminent threat. This could change. For a terrorist, it would have some advantages over physical methods. It could be conducted remotely and anonymously, and it would not require the handling of explosives or a suicide mission. It would likely garner extensive media coverage, as journalists and the public alike are fascinated by practically any kind of computer attack. Indeed cyberterrorism could be immensely appealing precisely because of the tremendous attention given to it by the government and media.

Cyberterrorism also has its drawbacks. Systems are complex, so it may be harder to control an attack and achieve a desired level of damage than using physical weapons. Unless people are injured, there is also less drama and emotional appeal. Further, terrorists may be disinclined to try new methods unless they see their old ones as inadequate, particularly when the new methods require considerable knowledge and skill to use effectively. Terrorists generally stick with tired and true methods. Novelty and sophistication of attack may be much less important than assurance that a mission will be operationally successful. Indeed, the risk of operational failure could be a deterrent to terrorists. For now, the truck bomb poses a much greater threat than the logic bomb.

The next generation of terrorists will grow up in a digital world, with ever more powerful and easy-to-use hacking tools at their disposal. They might see greater potential for cyberterrorism than the terrorists of today, and their level of knowledge and skill relating to hacking will be greater. Hackers and insiders might be recruited by terrorists or become self-recruiting cyberterrorists, the Timothy McVeigh's of cyberspace.

Some might be moved to action by cyber policy issues, making cyberspace an attractive venue for carrying out an attack. Cyberterrorism could also become more attractive as the real and virtual worlds become more closely coupled, with a greater number of physical devices attached to the Internet. Unless these systems are carefully secured, conducting an operation that physically harms someone may be easy as penetrating a Web site is today.

FEDERAL GOVERNMENT EFFORTS TO ADDRESS CYBER TERRORISM

A number of U.S. government organizations appear to monitor terrorist websites and conduct a variety of activities aimed at countering them. Given the sensitivity of federal government Programmes responsible for monitoring and infiltrating websites suspected of supporting terrorismrelated activities, much of the information regarding the organizations and their specific activities is deemed classified or law enforcement-sensitive and is not publicly available. The information listed below represents a sampling of what has been publicly discussed about some of the federal government organizations responsible for monitoring and infiltrating jihadist websites.

It should be noted that the actions associated with the organizations listed below could be conducted by employees of the federal government or by civilian contract personnel.

- *Central Intelligence Agency (CIA)*: development, surveillance, and analysis of websites, commonly referred to as honey pots, for purposes of attracting existing and potential jihadists searching for forums to discuss terrorism-related activities.
- *National Security Agency (NSA)*: surveillance of websites and rendering them inaccessible.
- *Department of Defence (DOD)*: surveillance of websites focused on discussions of perceived vulnerabilities of overseas U.S. military facilities or operational capabilities and disabling those that present a threat to operations.
- *Department of Justice (DOJ)*: development of polices and guidelines for creating, interacting within, surveilling, and

rendering inaccessible websites created by individuals wishing to use the Internet as a forum for inciting or planning terrorism-related activities.

- *Federal Bureau of Investigation (FBI)*: monitoring of websites and analysis of information for purposes of determining possible terrorist plans and threats to U.S. security interests.
- *Department of Homeland Security (DHS)*: monitoring of websites and analysis of information for purposes of determining possible threats to the homeland.

Numerous other federal government organizations have cyber security responsibilities focused on policy development, public awareness campaigns, and intergovernmental and private sector coordination efforts. Information gleaned from the agencies may at times be used to help inform and advise non-federal government entities responsible for safeguarding a geographic area or activity that has been discussed in an online jihadist forum.

Federal Government Monitoring and Response

A number of reasons exist that may provide justification for the federal government to monitor websites owned, operated, or frequented by individuals suspected of supporting international jihadist activity that pose a threat to U.S. security interests.

Such websites may be used for purposes of spreading propaganda, recruiting new members or enticing existing participants, communicating plans counter to U.S. interests, or facilitating terrorist-related activities. Quite often the jihadist websites are the first indicators of extreme elements of the jihadist community identifying a controversial issue for purposes of inciting action harmful to U.S. interests. For example, a recent controversy in the United States about a proposed burning of copies of the Quran on the ninth anniversary of the September 11, 2001, attacks led to increased chatter on international jihadist websites. The FBI reportedly disseminated an intelligence bulletin specifically noting online threats to the pastor and church planning to conduct this event and more general threats to U.S. global interests. When assessing whether to monitor, infiltrate, or shut down a Web site suspected of inciting participants to take harmful actions against

U.S. security interests, numerous competing interests should be considered. First, the federal government would determine whether the Web site is owned by a U.S. corporation and whether U.S. citizens may be participating in the Internet forum. Such a determination is necessary to ensure that proper procedures are adhered to with respect to upholding the rights afforded by the U.S. Constitution's First and Fourth Amendments, in particular.

Second, once it is confirmed that a suspected jihadist Web site is being used to facilitate terrorism-related activities, the national security community may consider the short- and long-term implications of a variety of operational responses. Options include permanently or temporarily shutting down the Web site, passively monitoring the Web site for intelligence-gathering purposes, or covertly engaging the members of the forum with the desire to elicit additional information for purposes of thwarting a potential terrorism-related activity and/or building a stronger criminal case. Different agencies may weigh each option differently, creating a need to achieve interagency consensus prior to action.

DOD has been considering establishing a computer network monitoring database for government and private networks. Organizations would provide information on a voluntary basis, and the data collected would be shared with all participants. However, privacy concerns and questions of DOD's proper role in federal cyber security make the implementation of such a Programme unlikely in the current political climate.

A memorandum of agreement signed in October 2010 between DHS and DOD represents an effort to increase coordination of operations and plans to protect civilian critical infrastructure as well as military networks. The partnership could be used as a means through which DOD would have a greater role in defending privately owned critical infrastructure using the EINSTEIN 2 and 3 network monitoring systems developed by DHS.

10

Hacking and Spam Attacks

HACKING

Hacking means finding out weaknesses in a computer or computer network, though the term can also refer to someone with an advanced understanding of computers and computer networks. Hackers may be motivated by a multitude of reasons, such as profit, protest, or challenge. The subculture that has evolved around hackers is often referred to as the computer underground but it is now an open community. While other uses of the word hacker exist that are not related to computer security, they are rarely used in mainstream context. They are subject to the long standing hacker definition controversy about the true meaning of the term hacker. In this controversy, the term hacker is reclaimed by computer programmers who argue that someone breaking into computers is better called a cracker, not making a difference between computer criminals (black hats) and computer security experts (white hats). Some white hat hackers claim that they also deserve the title hacker, and that only black hats should be called crackers.

Classifications

Several subgroups of the computer underground with different attitudes use different terms to demarcate themselves from each other, or try to exclude some specific group with which they do not agree. Eric S. Raymond (author of The New Hacker's Dictionary) advocates that members of the computer underground should be called crackers. Yet, those people see themselves as hackers and even try to include the views of Raymond in what they see as one wider hacker culture, a view harshly rejected by Raymond himself. Instead of a hacker/cracker dichotomy, they give more emphasis to a spectrum of different categories, such as white hat, grey hat, black hat and script kiddie. In contrast to Raymond, they usually reserve the term cracker for more malicious activity. According to a cracker or cracking is to "gain unauthorised access to a computer in order to commit another crime such as destroying information contained in that system". These subgroups may also be defined by the legal status of their activities.

White Hat

A white hat hacker breaks security for non-malicious reasons, perhaps to test their own security system or while working for a security company which makes security software. The term "white hat" in Internet slang refers to an ethical hacker. This classification also includes individuals who perform penetration tests and vulnerability assessments within a contractual agreement. The EC-Council, also known as the International Council of Electronic Commerce Consultants has developed certifications, courseware, classes, and online training covering the diverse arena of Ethical Hacking.

Black Hat

A "black hat" hacker is a hacker who "violates computer security for little reason beyond maliciousness or for personal gain". Black hat hackers form the stereotypical, illegal hacking groups often portrayed in popular culture, and are "the epitome of all that the public fears in a computer criminal". Black hat hackers break into secure networks to destroy data or make the network unusable for those who are authorised to use the network. They choose their targets using a two-pronged process known as the "pre-hacking stage".

- *Part 1: Targeting*: The hacker determines what network to break into during this phase. The *target* may be of particular interest to the hacker, either politically or personally, or it may be picked at random. Next, they will port scan a network to determine if it is vulnerable to attacks, which is just testing all ports on a host machine for a response. Open ports—those that do respond—will allow a hacker to access the system.

- *Part 2: Research and Information Gathering*: It is in this stage that the hacker will visit or contact the target in some way in hopes of finding out vital information that will help them access the system. The main way that hackers get desired results from this stage is from "social engineering", which will be explained below. Aside from social engineering, hackers can also use a technique called "dumpster diving". Dumpster diving is when a hacker will literally search through users' garbage in hopes of finding documents that have been thrown away, which may contain information a hacker can use directly or indirectly, to help them gain access to a network.

- *Part 3: Finishing The Attack*: This is the stage when the hacker will invade the preliminary target that he/she was planning to attack or steal. Many "hackers" will be caught after this point, lured in or grabbed by any data also known as a honeypot (a trap set up by computer security personnel).

Grey Hat

A grey hat hacker is a combination of a Black Hat and a White Hat Hacker. A Grey Hat Hacker may surf the Internet and hack into a computer system for the sole purpose of notifying the administrator that their system has been hacked, for example. Then they may offer to repair their system for a small fee.

Elite Hacker

A social status among hackers, *elite* is used to describe the most skilled. Newly discovered exploits will circulate among these hackers. Elite groups such as Masters of Deception conferred a kind of credibility on their members.

Script Kiddie

A script kiddie (or skiddie) is a non-expert who breaks into computer systems by using pre-packaged automated tools written by others, usually with little understanding of the underlying concept—hence the term script (i.e. a prearranged plan or set of activities) kiddie (i.e. kid, child—an individual lacking knowledge and experience, immature).

Neophyte

A neophyte, "n00b", or "newbie" is someone who is new to hacking or phreaking and has almost no knowledge or experience of the workings of technology, and hacking.

Blue Hat

A blue hat hacker is someone outside computer security consulting firms who is used to bug test a system prior to its launch, looking for exploits so they can be closed. Microsoft also uses the term BlueHat to represent a series of security briefing events.

Hacktivist

A hacktivist is a hacker who utilises technology to announce a social, ideological, religious, or political message. In general, most hacktivism involves Web site defacement or denial-of-service attacks.

Attacks

A typical approach in an attack on Internet-connected system is:
- *Network enumeration*: Discovering information about the intended target.
- *Vulnerability analysis*: Identifying potential ways of attack.
- *Exploitation*: Attempting to compromise the system by employing the vulnerabilities found through the vulnerability analysis.

In order to do so, there are several recurring tools of the trade and techniques used by computer criminals and security experts.

Security Exploits

A security exploit is a prepared application that takes advantage of a known weakness. Common examples of security exploits are SQL injection, Cross Site Scripting and Cross Site Request Forgery which abuse security holes that may result from substandard programming practice. Other exploits would be able to be used through FTP, HTTP, PHP, SSH, Telnet and some web-pages. These are very common in Web site/domain hacking.

Techniques

- *Vulnerability scanner*: A vulnerability scanner is a tool used to quickly check computers on a network for known weaknesses. Hackers also commonly use port scanners. These check to see which ports on a specified computer are "open" or available to access the computer, and sometimes will detect what Programme or service is listening on that port, and its version number.

- *Password cracking*: Password cracking is the process of recovering passwords from data that has been stored in or transmitted by a computer system. A common approach is to repeatedly try guesses for the password.

- *Packet sniffer*: A packet sniffer is an application that captures data packets, which can be used to capture passwords and other data in transit over the network.

- *Spoofing attack (Phishing)*: A spoofing attack involves one Programme, system, or Web site successfully masquerading as another by falsifying data and thereby being treated as a trusted system by a user or another Programme. The purpose of this is usually to fool Programmes, systems, or users into revealing confidential information, such as user names and passwords, to the attacker.

- *Rootkit*: A rootkit is designed to conceal the compromise of a computer's security, and can represent any of a set of Programmes which work to subvert control of an operating system from its legitimate operators. Usually, a rootkit will obscure its installation and attempt to prevent its removal through a subversion of standard system security. Rootkits may include replacements for system binaries so that it becomes impossible for the legitimate user to detect the presence of the intruder on the system by looking at process tables.

- *Social engineering*: When a Hacker, typically a black hat, is in the second stage of the targeting process, he or she will typically use some social engineering tactics to get enough information to access the network. A common practice for hackers who use this technique, is to contact the system administrator and play the role of a user who cannot get access to his or her system. Hackers who use this technique have to be quite savvy and choose the words they use carefully, in order to trick the system administrator into giving them information. In some cases only an employed help desk user will answer the phone and they are generally easy to trick. Another typical hacker approach is for the hacker to act like a very angry supervisor and when the his/her authority is questioned they will threaten the help desk user with their job. Social Engineering is so effective because users are the most vulnerable part of an organization. All the security devices and Programmes in the world won't keep an organization safe if an employee gives away a password. Black Hat Hackers take advantage of this fact. Social Engineering can also be broken down into four sub-groups. These are intimidation, helpfulness, technical, and name-dropping.

  - *Intimidation:* With the angry supervisor, the hacker attacks the person who answers the phone with threats to their job. Many people at this point will accept that the hacker is a supervisor and give them the needed information.

  - *Helpfulness:* Opposite to intimidation, helpfulness is taking advantage of a person natural instinct to help someone with a problem. The hacker will not get angry instead act very distressed and concerned. The help desk is the most vulnerable to this type of Social Engineering, because they generally have the authority to change or reset passwords which is exactly what the hacker needs.

- *Name-Dropping:* Simply put, the hacker uses the names of advanced users as "key words", and gets the person who answers the phone to believe that they are part of the company because of this. Some information, like web page ownership, can be obtained easily on the web. Other information such as president and vice president names might have to be obtained via dumpster diving.
- *Technical:* Using technology to get information is also a great way to get it. A hacker can send a fax or an e-mail to a legitimate user in hopes to get a response containing vital information. Many times the hacker will act like he/she is involved with law enforcement and needs certain data for record keeping purposes or investigations.
- *Trojan horses*: A Trojan horse is a Programme which seems to be doing one thing, but is actually doing another. A trojan horse can be used to set up a back door in a computer system such that the intruder can gain access later. (The name refers to the horse from the Trojan War, with conceptually similar function of deceiving defenders into bringing an intruder inside.)
- *Viruses*: A virus is a self-replicating Programme that spreads by inserting copies of itself into other executable code or documents. Therefore, a computer virus behaves in a way similar to a biological virus, which spreads by inserting itself into living cells. While some are harmless or mere hoaxes most computer viruses are considered malicious.
- *Worms*: Like a virus, a worm is also a self-replicating Programme. A worm differs from a virus in that it propagates through computer networks without user intervention. Unlike a virus, it does not need to attach itself to an existing Programme. Many people conflate the terms "virus" and "worm", using them both to describe any self-propagating Programme.
- *Keyloggers*: A keylogger is a tool designed to record ('log') every keystroke on an affected machine for later retrieval.

Its purpose is usually to allow the user of this tool to gain access to confidential information typed on the affected machine, such as a user's password or other private data. Some keyloggers uses virus-, trojan-, and rootkit-like methods to remain active and hidden. However, some key loggers are used in legitimate ways and sometimes to even enhance computer security. As an example, a business might have a keylogger on a computer used at a point of sale and data collected by the keylogger could be used for catching employee fraud.

INTERNET HACKING AND SURVEILLANCE OVERVIEW

As technology continues to advance, social and ethical issues arise in regards to privacy and security of personal information. Many people are aware of widespread issues in computer technology, such as surveillances and attacks. One major form of infringement on privacy and security is hacking, an unauthorised access into a system in order to gain information. Hacking includes a wide range of activities such as monitoring, thievery, exploitation, altering, vandalism, and destruction of computer systems, all of which endanger individuals' rights to privacy and security. Although this intrusion is frequently associated with negativity, some aspects of hacking can be useful and beneficial towards society. Businesses can benefit from ethical hacking, and law enforcement officials can benefit from the skills and knowledge of convicted hackers.

The subtopic of this chapter describes how the U.S., government can benefit from a form of passive hacking called "Carnivore" or "DCS 1000", an Internet surveillance system that eavesdrops on the public's electronic transmissions. Finally, the rest of the chapter discusses how this dynamic nature of technology challenges individuals, businesses, and the government to consider new social and ethical standards regarding personal privacy and security.

Practical Uses and Considerations

Computer hacking is performed to monitor, modify, and/or use the informational content for one's own gain, whether for fun or fraudulent purposes. A hacker can gain access to a wide range of personally identifiable information that endanger and damage the privacy of individuals, businesses, and government.

Information that can be hacked into includes: personal health, financial, and inter-banking information; social security numbers; driver's license data; utility grids; emergency information systems; controls for dams and locks; military communications; and other sensitive information that travels on communication networks such as the Internet. Although not every attack results in theft or security loss, hackers often cost companies a great deal of time and money.

The hacking process is performed by a hacker, a person that uses programming skills to gain illegal access to a computer, a network or a file. This hacker is classified according to his/her primary intentions and level of damage done to individuals and/ or businesses. He or she may be benign and has the intention to simply monitor or learn more about the system, without planning to destroy, change, or leave anything behind. Another type of hacker, the information thief, causes more damage because he/she gains access to company or customer information systems, retrieves individuals' personal information, and puts them to his/her own use.

This type of hacker provides or sells the stolen information to others for many purposes, including credit card and financial theft, corporate blackmail, or espionage. Lastly, the intention of the functionality thief is to gain knowledge from the interception of web services, then to proceed to alter, wreck, or crash the systems' operation. This type of hacking ranges from basic fun pranks to more serious crimes with the intent of revenge, damage, or the achievement of political and defence corruption. A hacker uses various methods of penetrating through systems to monitor and retrieve personal information, or to crash a system itself.

Different methods are briefly discussed here. First, a denial of service attack (DOS) overloads a network with such a great amount of traffic that it crashes, denying users access to the service. An example of a DOS attack would be the loss of service to a web mail service provider.

Second, a hacker may also use Internet Protocol (IP) spoofing as a way of disguising his/her real identity. This method allows a hacker to gain unauthorised access to computers by sending a message to a computer with an IP address showing that the message is from a trusted host. To accomplish this, a hacker must use different tools to find an IP address of a trusted host, and then alter the packet headers so it appears that the packets are coming from the host.

Third, another technique called Google hacking finds easily exploitable targets and sensitive data on the web by using Google, a powerful search engine used by many people. Google has gained popularity and offers many features, including "language and document translation; web, image, newsgroups, catalog, and news searches". These features also come with a price, as many hackers use the value of this search engine for bad intentions.

Fourth, one of the more common methods of hacking, phishing, imitates the e-mails of legitimate companies. It links recipients to fraudulent web sites that were designed to trick people into sharing their personal information. This may include "personal financial data such as credit cards numbers, account usernames and passwords, and social security numbers." Phishers are usually able to convince up to 5 per cent of targets. Some big name companies that a hacker may imitate are Citibank, eBay, Visa, Washington Mutual, Wells Fargo, AOL, and Yahoo.

Both Google hacking and phishing can often be used simultaneously. Lastly, the phishing method is a form of social engineering. With social engineering, a hacker can gain unauthorised access to a computer by deception, tricking the user into providing passwords and other needed information. One popular form of this is the use of deceptive mass e-mails, such as pretending to be a system administrator who needs people's passwords for important network access. The widespread fraud and privacy abuses trigger people's concerns about their own security and the use and control of their personal information. If an identify theft impersonates an authorised user, he or she can inflict damage to the real user's personal records, credit history, and reputation.

Moreover, there exists the fear of political or national threat in which an intruder can break into, damage, steal, and/or act on private information from computer systems worldwide. From a business perspective, hacking causes financial loss when an intruder accesses a company's web site and web service, linking to sensitive records containing customers' credit card information, address, and phone numbers. A hacker may be able to alter or damage the data, or use the information to sell to other people or companies. Competitors may also hack a company's web service to gain reports about potential clients, further using the list of leads for their own business benefit. Hacking also negatively impacts E-commerce, as consumers lose their trust in the Internet as a reliable and secure commerce medium.

The result is a loss of sales opportunities for businesses due to the reduction of online transactions. Additional consequences of hacking include time, money, and human miscommunication costs. A loss of time and money occurs in order to discover, test, apply, and train employees with technology needed to keep computer and network systems secured. The security processes used to ensure privacy include the continuous assessment of systems' security to identify risks, the evaluation of policies and protection, and the implementation of detection systems such as technology encryptions and firewalls. These processes not only contribute to money costs, but also take away valuable time and may slow down regular businesses.

A human miscommunication crisis can also occur and lead to erroneous proceedings. When the victim does not acknowledge that the wrongful incident is a result of hacking, he or she may blame the incorrect person or company that did not actually commit the crime. From another perspective, hacking may be considered ethical and beneficial to society if it is proven legitimate. Increasingly, businesses and authorities are willing to work with hackers to prevent online attacks and make improvements in computer securities. This type of hacking can be justifiable as long as the hacker has good intentions and commits no theft, vandalism, or breach of confidentiality. The exploration of systems by the benign hacker can be useful because it allows new findings and learning of others' capabilities.

Some hackers can avoid prosecution and criminal charges by trading in their abilities to help the government protect sensitive computer systems against other hackers, thieves and terrorists. Furthermore, in some cases the government may be willing to pay hackers to search the Internet for vulnerable computer systems, track criminals' online activities, and help make sensitive government networks more secure. Another positive aspect of hacking is called ethical hacking, a method used to determine the strength, reliability, and vulnerability of Internet security measures. Ethical hackers use simulations to purposely attack, exploit, or expose the systems to hackers in order to test the security of networks, servers, and applications. This type of hacking is useful in finding and fixing unknown security leaks.

Ethical hacking makes it possible for businesses to be better prepared in the case that a real hacking incident occurs. It allows businesses to reduce or prevent the time and costs used to fix damages. It also puts pressure on companies to frequently update their computer systems in order to create and revise more secured networks. For example, vendors like Microsoft have a separate department that works solely to prevent people from hacking into their programmes. By detecting the methods hackers use, Microsoft has been able to evolve programmes to stop this dilemma.

Analysis of Internet Surveillance Via "Carnivore" or DCS 1000"

On July 11, 2000, the U.S., Federal Bureau of Investigation (FBI) announced its use of an Internet surveillance system called "Carnivore", or "DCS (Digital Collection System) 1000." The system is a computerbased application installed with an Internet Service Provider (ISP) to intercept and collect the electronic transmissions of criminal suspects. The FBI uses Carnivore as a form of passive hacking tool to keep track of individuals that execute their criminal plans through cyberspace.

By installing these "black boxes" on the main network, the government can increase law enforcement by connecting directly to the public's Internet traffic. This surveillance has been beneficial since, it has helped secure the convictions of thousands of felons.

However, opposing viewpoints exist within the society since, the usage of such a system generates ethical and privacy concerns. From the beginning of Carnivore's invention, the main mechanics have been kept a closely guarded secret. No information about the first version was made to the public, but there were speculations that this first version was in fact a readily available commercial programme called Etherpeek.

In 1997, the second version was created with the name of Omnivore. According to the very little reports given by the FBI, Omnivore's purpose was to "look through e-mail traffic traveling over a specific ISP and capture e-mail from a targeted source, saving it to a tape-backup drive or printing it in real-time". This system was used until 1999, when it was replaced by a more advanced structure called the Dragonware Suite. This structure contained added features, such as the capability to download files and web pages from suspected criminals, and better developed software to search e-mail messages. Dragonware encompasses three parts: Pacleteer, Coolminer, and Carnivore.

Packeteer, on which there has been no official information released, appears to be an application for reassembling packets into cohesive messages or web pages. Coolminer, on which there has also been no official information released, is most likely an application for extrapolating and analysing data found in the messages. Although there has been no official information on Paketeer or Coolminer, the Carnivore feature has been used since, the Cold War, where the U.S., Navy was able to "tap into Soviet undersea fibre optic lines by using special submarines, and gain complete knowledge of that set of communication". Since, then, Carnivore has thrived to become a main form of government Internet surveillance today.

Implementation and Usage

Carnivore uses a Windows NT/2000-based system that captures information through a form of packet sniffing. A packet sniffer is a form of technology used by computer administrators to monitor networks, perform diagnostic tests, and troubleshoot problems. Sniffing programmes exist in two forms, either as commercial packet sniffers used to help maintain networks, or as underground packet sniffers used to break into computers. In the case of Carnivore, a packet sniffer is a programme that plugs into computer networks and enables a person to view all traffic information passing through.

Each packet is "sniffed" as the programme carries information to the viewer, without interfering with any of the information. A packet sniffer can be set up in two ways: unfiltered, which captures all the packets, or filtered, which captures only the packets that comprise of specific data. In the case of Carnivore, a filtered system is used to capture only the targeted individuals' transmission. After the intended packet is found, the data is copied and then stored in memory or on a hard drive. The process of setting up the Carnivore system involves four stages: installation, filtration, segregation, and collection.

Before any of the stages, the FBI needs to receive judicial approval. Once approved, they check to see if the suspect's Internet Service Provider has the technology to comply with the court order. If not, the FBI cooperates with the ISP technicians to place Carnivore in the network where the suspect's communication packets can be isolated. Once cooperation with the ISP is achieved, the initial filtering is set up. During this process, Carnivore monitors all the ISP traffic from both targeted and non-targeted individuals, then proceeds to filter the packets at the ISP's designated speed. Carnivore takes a picture each second, searching for the suspect's information.

If the suspect's information does not exist, the packet automatically disappears and is not collected, stored, or saved. If there are traces of information, Carnivore proceeds to the third stage. The third stage consists of segregating the suspect's information. Once detection has been made, the packets containing some traces of the suspect's information are then segregated for additional filtration and storage. This leads ultimately to the last stage of collection, which involves more filtering of the suspect's information. Carnivore then collects and processes the final information that can be used according to the court order, discarding any non-retrievable information. A defence method that individuals can use to protect their privacy is through encryption technology. A personal computer (PC) can encrypt messages with codes that are difficult to break.

Officials may monitor a suspect's online communications and sniff up the data, but they are not able to understand this encrypted information. The most popular encryption uses online key systems, known as the public-key encryption. A user issues a public key that others can use to send the user a message, which can be decoded only with the user's private key. To overcome this, law-enforcement officials have advocated the use of different software that use a "back door" feature to read the encrypted e-mail or files of criminals. However, it can be argued that allowing back door software would actually weaken codes used for Internet security, which hackers and criminals could exploit. Nonetheless, the point still stands that if material is encrypted, the individual is protected from the government's intrusion to some extent because it is generally difficult to break the encryption.

The Positive Aspects of Internet Surveillance

Millions of people around the world use the Internet. With the infinite knowledge and possibilities it provides, the Internet can definitely be utilised to connect people to one another and/ or make everyday tasks easier. However, many people are unaware of the prospective perils the Internet has. "The rise of the Internet, with e-mail, instant messages, and more, has opened gigantic pipelines for all to use, including criminals". These criminals view the internet as the perfect way to commit crimes, to con individuals, or to affect millions of people through cyber-terrorism. Criminals also use e-mail to spread information to other criminals since, the process is convenient and fast.

This is where the Carnivore system comes in: it keeps an eye on these hazardous people to put a stop to their evil intentions. That in itself, Carnivore is a form of passive hacking used to detect the "real" illegal hackings and other wrongdoings. Carnivore is used by the FBI in five areas: cyber-terrorism, information warfare, child pornography, fraud, and virus writing. Terrorism is a great threat throughout the world. Particularly in the United States, cyber-terrorism can be devastating because of the society's reliance on computers. Cyber-terrorists have the capability to shut down national infrastructures like energy usage, transportation, water, and telecommunications as a means to intimidate and harm the society.

Carnivore attempts to stop or hinder terrorism by monitoring and supervising the Internet activities of known terrorist groups, with procedures equivalent to tapping phones lines. While testifying on the worldwide threat of terrorism, George Tenet, the Director of Central Intelligence, states that "terrorist groups, including Hizbollah, HAMAS, the Abu Nidal organisation, and Bin Laden's al Qu'ida organisation, are using computerised files, e-mail, and encryption to support their operations". These organisations have yet to succeed terrorising America through cyber terrorism; however, the potential threat is still greatly present. This is the very reason the FBI sees Carnivore as a necessity, because the system makes it possible for officials to monitor activity and prevent any catastrophic tragedies from occurring.

There have already been early signs of promise, such as when the FBI discovered that e-mail was a major method used for communication for a terrorist group. Thus, the FBI was able to stop this group from stealing explosives from National Guard Armories in several southern states. It was also discovered that this same terrorist group used the Internet to download information on Ricin, the 3rd deadliest toxin in the world. In instances like this, Carnivore can follow the steps of terrorists and stop them before they strike. Next, Carnivore is helpful when tracking down those individuals that intend to use information warfare against the United States.

Information warfare is a subcategory of cyber-terrorism. Since, many nations cannot measure up to America's power in terms of military strength, they seek information warfare as retaliation. "This type of war attempts to exploit our 'Achilles heel,' a national dependence on information technology in government, commercial, and private operations." A book published by two Chinese military officials explains that the use of unconventional techniques, such as spreading computer viruses, is the only way to neutralise the United States. Moreover, the Russian government has been known to think along the same lines.

Russian government officials acknowledge that attacking America's computer infrastructure could lead to the same result as using weapons of mass destruction; either way hurts the United States immensely. Another crime that Carnivore prevents is child pornography. Even though this is not a national security threat, it is destructive to communities and society.

The offenders may download graphics from child pornography web sites and/or use the Internet as a device to arrange meetings between themselves and young children. This can lead to violent and sometimes deadly consequences. "Between 1995 and 2001, the FBI investigated over 800 cases involving offenders crossing state lines to carry out an illegal sexual relationship and more than 1,800 cases involving the exchange of child pornography over the Internet".

It is vital to track these people because they have the tendency to victimise repeatedly. Studies have shown that a child molester typically abuses approximately 70 children in his or her lifetime. With the help of Carnivore, the FBI devised a plan to capture these sexual predators through processes such as "Innocent Images." This site is intended to capture those who distribute child pornography with the Internet. A FBI agent will go undercover as a child over the internet and lure sex offenders to meet with them, allowing the agent to arrest and prosecute the criminal. Fraud is an issue that countless Americans have encountered. The Internet is ideal for fraud for three reasons.

First, people can be easily targeted with the amount of features that it offers, such as chat rooms, instant messages, e-mails, and forums. A person can look up names, addresses, and e-mail addresses through a directory and start sending out spam e-mails.

Secondly, individuals can remain anonymous. When a person creates a web site selling defective materials that do not actually work, he or she may experience fewer, if any, consequences because his or her real identity is kept secret. It is difficult to trace the real identity of the creators of millions upon millions of web sites that can be found. "The critical difference in fraud committed over the

Internet is that the perpetrator can 'virtually' vanish, leaving consumers wondering to whom or where to turn to for help".

Thirdly, those that commit fraud do not face expenses with obtaining a toll-free number, mail, and/or hiring people to maintain the mail. Since, they can sign up for free e-mail with companies like Yahoo and Hotmail and obtain a screen name for instant messages with AIM, these previous expenses are no longer necessary. According to the North American Association, Internet related fraud estimates to be about $10 billion per year. In one meticulous case in 2000, 19 individuals implemented an insider trading scheme, where a person with stock information passed along tips to firms through chat rooms.

These 19 people were accused of fraud and discovered to have pocketed several million dollars worth of illegal money. Had Carnivore been in place at the time of this occurrence, they may have been caught sooner than through traditional methods. Finally, the spreading of computer viruses is becoming increasingly perilous. Viruses can be detrimental to company and government computer systems, hurting individuals who simply open an e-mail. Viruses such as the Melissa Macro Virus and the Explore.Zip worm have destroyed individuals' computer files and programmes around the world. They can entirely shut down e-mail systems and delay communications. For example, in some incidents, Microsoft had to put a halt to all outgoing e-mails throughout the company.

A hacker can also spread a virus to a company to destroy its database, which often holds immeasurable valuable information. This can be costly and some of the data lost may never be recovered. All things considered, this new programme will eventually be able to do exactly what it was invented to do: monitor, track, and prevent criminals from breaking the law; protect potential victims from facing harmful consequences, and give society assurance that the world is safer place. Even with the loopholes found in Carnivore currently, the overall benefits this plan offers can outweigh its negative aspects. Since, this programme has recently been revealed and is relatively new, the public will have to wait and see if the FBI and government officials can keep their word on its potentials.

INDIVIDUAL HACKING ATTACKS

Accessing Systems

The first type of attacks is aimed at enabling access to protected data and computer systems. This can be achieved if the victim computer is vulnerable to a security weakness that can be exploited by the attacker. Software and techniques for this purpose can be acquired through different channels: many specialized security forums discuss the known weaknesses of different operating systems and other software. If the designated victim computer is not immune against all current (and known) software flaws (socalled "patching"), this information can be used to gain access to it. However, even if all known patches have been applied to a computer system, this does not mean that the system is protected against all possible attacks. So-called "Zero-Day-Exploits", i.e. software flaws that have not yet been disclosed to the manufacturer (and therefore not yet been patched), can be acquired via the black market. Such software enables access to a system even though the system administrators have followed all publicly known security measures.

Once an attacker has gained access to a computer system, several possibilities lie ahead. First, the system can simply be shut down, thereby making it unavailable to legitimate users. However, the system can be restarted by administrators immediately, giving the attackers only a very short moment of success. Nevertheless, even a very short interruption can be hazardous for some systems, such as control systems for power plants or in medical environments. Furthermore, an outage can be combined with a conventional attack, e.g. to handicap rescue workers after a bomb attack. Furthermore, the information on a system can be altered, thereby giving it a new meaning, e.g. to mislead people relying on that information, or destroyed. Finally, some attacks can be conducted without anybody noticing, making countermeasures extremely difficult.

Altering Information

The second possibility is to change information that is being stored on the computer system. This can lead to so-called "defacements" that often take place after a web server has been compromised,. In the case of a defacement, a web page (usually an entry page) is replaced with another page that informs the visiting user that this particular web server has been hacked (and most likely also provides information about who has done it). In doing so, the attackers can easily demonstrate their capabilities and the weakness of the victim. In addition, the impression is created that the attacker will be able repeat his action at any given point in time and even with other, even more highly protected systems. Therefore, defacements of web servers that belong to security agencies, the military, or other important services are popular targets for attackers. The group "Pentaguard", for example, demonstrated its capabilities in 2001 when it simultaneously defaced a multitude of government and military websites in the U.K, Australia, and the United States. This attack was later evaluated as one of "the largest, most systematic defacements of worldwide government servers on the Web". Terrorist organizations had also already used this technique in the past. Al-Qaeda, for example, hacked the website of Silicon Valley Landsurveying Inc. in order to deposit a video file showing the hijacked (and later beheaded) Paul Marshal Johnson. By publishing the link to the stored video, the organization could simultaneously demonstrate its technical as well as conventional dangerousness. In another case, pro-Palestinian hackers used a coordinated attack to break into 80 Israel-related sites and deface them. Instead of defacing a web server, all other information stored on a computer system can also be affected, i.e. deleted or altered. If, for example, vital data, such as the U.S. Social Security database, financial institutions' records, or secret military documents, were able to be irreversibly damaged, grave social disorder and a long-lasting lack of trust in all government institutions could be the consequence. Studies, such as the exercise "Eligible Receiver", and recent attacks have shown that even top-secret military computers and sensitive nuclear research centers are not immune against all attacks.

Silent Operations

The shutting down of a computer or the defacement of a web page each have the advantage that the success of the attack becomes immediately known to both operators and users of the affected system. However, if an attacker does not aim at a demonstration of his powers, but rather tries to gather information, secrecy is of essence. Therefore, the third possibility for an attacker to proceed after gaining access to a computer is simply to search for useful information and try to leave few or no traces at all. This form of action also has another advantage: whereas a security flaw that has been detected can be fixed after an intruder has been detected, an unknown security weakness allows the attacker to use it not only once but for a longer period of time. Hence, apart from the above-mentioned "Zero-Day-Exploits", other forms of custommade software are of also interest.

A mode of operation that could also be put to use by a terrorist organization can be observed in a case that a security company has tested. The company prepared USB sticks with a custom-designed, newly developed Trojan horse program that could not be detected by virus scanners. Twenty of these sticks were "lost" on the premises of a credit union. Of these, 15 sticks were found by employees – and promptly connected to the company network where the Trojan started to collect passwords and other valuable information and e-mailed this data back to the offenders. Such an attack would be a powerful way for a terrorist organization to initiate counterespionage.

Another way to introduce such software could be through legal channels. This was observed in the year 2000, when Japan's Metropolitan Police Department used a software system to track 150 police vehicles, including unmarked cars. It turned out that this software had been developed by the Aum Shinrikyo cult – the same group that gassed the Tokyo subway in 1995. It turned out that members of the cult had developed software for at least eighty firms and ten government agencies. The cult had been able to work largely undetected because the software developers were engaged as subcontractors, thus enabling personnel clearance to be easily circumvented.

Large-Scale Attacks

If the information inside a computer is not of essence, but the aim is simply to make its services unavailable, the use of large-scale attacks might be preferred over a hacking attack. Large-scale attacks are often committed with the help of hundreds or thousands of other computers (so-called Distributed-Denial-of-Service-Attacks or DDoS-Attacks). In these cases, viruses and Trojan horses are used to control other computers.

These computers are turned into so-called "zombies" that are forced to report to a botnet on a regular basis. These zombies are, in turn, controlled by a bot-master that instructs them, for instance, to forward thousands of requests to a particular site in order to make it inaccessible to its users. In 2006, more than 60,000 active bot-infected computers were observed per day. Furthermore, over 6 million distinct bot-infected computers were detected in 6 months. These "zombies" were controlled by less than 5,000 command-and-control-servers. It can therefore be safely assumed that the persons in control of these bot-nets are not hobby hackers, but well experienced and organized groups.

For terrorist groups, however, it is not necessary to acquire these skills or to organize bot-nets by themselves as bot-nets can also be rented. Prices for attacks range from about 150 to 400 US-dollars, depending on the target and the duration of the attack.

Some bot-net-operators even offer discounts for multiple orders. Also – as a nontechnical alternative – the same effect as that achieved with a bot-net attack can be obtained if enough human supporters are available who can take over the part of will-less "zombies" in bot-net attacks.

This can be observed in an online demonstration that was launched against the German airline "Lufthansa" in 2001. In order to call attention to the involvement of the company in the deportation of illegal alien residents, supporters were asked to open the web page of the company at the same date and time. Over 13,000 people followed the call.

The Lufthansa server was unable to reply to the sudden peak of requests so that the web page became unavailable to customers during this time frame. This technique is also known as "swarming", "virtual blockade", or "virtual sit-in" and it shows that even technically non-adept organizations can use the power of distributed attacks against targets in the Internet.

However, for a terrorist organization, the operation of a bot-net could also be an interesting option, since it can be used in a variety of ways. Two main options seem to be realistic: the use of bot-nets for email campaigns and for aggressive attacks on other Internet sites. In the first option, the "zombie" computers can be used to send out massmailings with terrorist content (e.g. propaganda). These mails are difficult to trace back since they do not originate from the computer of the terrorist organization, but from thousands of computers linked to the bot-net. Furthermore, this service can also be rented out to other companies wishing to cover their tracks in order to forward spamemails and willing to pay for this service. Therefore, by using this first option, the botnet can also be used as a source of income for the organization. When using a bot-net for the second option, i.e. utilization for attacks on other targets in the Internet, a terrorist organization can benefit from the large diversification of attackers in a bot-net. Such aggressions can hardly be traced back and, in addition, the defense against such attacks is often not possible.

Manifold examples of the use of bot-nets to bring down other services in the Internet can be found. Among them are actions that can be classified as terrorist or part of a cyber war. For example, six different Hizbollah sites, the Hamas site, and other Palestinian information sites were brought down by a so-called "FloodNet" attack of pro- Israeli hackers. The service virtually "flooded" the respective servers with pings resulting in the unavailability of the servers for all other requests. Even after a relaunch with a slightly different spelling, the sites were still unreachable as the hackers immediately adjusted the attack to the new name. The targets of such attacks can be chosen freely, i.e. any system that is reachable over the Internet can be the victim of a (distributed or simple) denial-of-service-attack. Therefore, the internal and external communication systems of NATO troops were the victim of an attack during the allied air strikes on Kosovo and Serbia as well as the thirteen root servers for the Internet domain name systems (DNS).

Hybrid Attacks

Many of the attacks described above can result in violence against persons or property and they can generate fear within a population. However, this depends largely on the chosen target and the actual effect that the attack was able to accomplish. Therefore, some authors claim that a conventional bomb attack is – in many ways – easier to plan and conduct and that the results can be better foreseen. However, even in cases of conventional bomb attacks, the losses can be increased if hybrid attacks are launched, i.e. an attack that is aimed at a physical target is combined with one or both of the abovementioned electronic forms of attack.

The bomb attack can be aimed at any given target. For example, it is often chosen to bring forth a high number of casualties. In this case, a supplementary digital attack could be launched that is aimed at the communication devices of police or ambulances in order to hinder an effective coordination of rescue teams,. Another possibility would be for attackers to choose to launch an assault on the economic stability of a country. In this case, a hybrid attack against national financial networks (such as Fedwire or Fednet) or against transfer networks (such as SWIFT) could be launched. It is estimated that such an attack could wreak havoc on the entire global economy. Another possibility would be to directly attack the infrastructure that forms the basis of the Internet. To achieve this, offenders could assault any system whose operation is of the essence for the functioning of the Internet. One example would be the domain name service (DNS). The DNS is responsible for the translation of domain names (such as www.mpicc.de) into IP-numbers (such as 194.94.219.193). This task is necessary for many transactions, e.g. the opening of a web page or the sending of an email. If an attacker was able to disturb this service, large parts of Internet-based services would be inaccessible. Therefore, a DDoS attack on the thirteen root servers of the DNS in October 2002 was described as an attack against the "heart of the Internet network." However, due to built-in safeguards, no slowdowns or even outages were caused. The same is true for a recent attack which took place in February 2007: even though the aggression lasted for almost twelve hours, the influence was hardly noticeable.

Such attacks against the infrastructure are possible not only by digital, but also by conventional means. For example, many transcontinental data connections rely on transatlantic cable connections between Europe and the United States. Whereas European cable ends are widely spread between many different countries, they are often bundled on the American side (e.g. in New Jersey and Rhode Island). An attack on one or two of these connections could have a serious impact on Internet connections in general. In the past, this was observed when cables were damaged accidentally. For example, after an underground cable between China and the USA was severely damaged, according to a survey, 97% of Chinese users reported problems of accessing foreign web pages and 57% claimed that their life and work was being affected by the damage. Another focus of a conventional attack against IT infrastructures could be to target one or more of the central so-called peeringpoints that interconnect different networks in the Internet.

The German peeringpoint DE-CIX in Frankfurt, for example, is said to handle 80% of German and 35% of European Internet traffic. The London Internet Exchange LINX is the world's largest Internet peeringpoint. In 2006, it was at the center of a planned assault. However, Scotland Yard arrested suspects beforehand. An MI5-website is reported to have said that "without these services, the UK could suffer serious consequences, including severe economic damage, grave social disruption, or even large-scale loss of life." Since this report is focused on the use of the Internet by terrorists, there will be no further analysis of possible targets for conventional attacks. The examples above show, however, that terrorists can severely damage targets in the Internet even without any technical knowledge.

Attacks on Human Life

Often, attacks on computer systems are considered less dangerous than conventional attacks with bombs because damages to computers are said to "only" lead to economic losses. However, these days, computers are no longer exclusively used to "crunch numbers" and store huge amounts of data. Instead, a new type of service has quietly evolved: SCADA systems are used to measure and control other systems and can therefore lead to effects not only in the "virtual", but also in the "real" world. Often, these systems are also connected to the Internet – in one way or another: according to informal sources, 17% of SCADA malfunctions are caused by a direct Internet access to the SCADA system. Other possibilities include VPN-, modem- or trusted connections, e.g. remote access to allow maintenance work. Even though such possibilities for remote access are not advisable for security reasons, the need to cut costs and the ability to remotely control several SCADA systems centrally, instead of having one person control one system on-site, led many companies to establish such structures.

Furthermore, many of the control systems are based on standard Windows- and UNIX operating systems. Therefore, some hackers claim that it would take them only about a week to get into most of the existing control systems. The effect of a combination of SCADA systems that are connected to the Internet and security weaknesses could be observed in 2003 when 21 power plants were brought down and other critically important institutions in the United States, including Edwards Air Force Base, the test center for B-2 and B-1 bombers, also affected. As far as is publicly known, these breakdowns were the result of the W32.Lovsan worm that was using the same port to exploit a weakness on individual personal computers being used by the plants to communicate with each other. The collision resulted in a large power-down in the United States and Eastern Canada.

However, even though 60 million households are said to have been without electricity, no panic erupted; there were only a few injuries, and hospitals and emergency services continued to function properly. Therefore, some authors question whether cyber attacks are really of the same class as conventional attacks carried out with bombs. From a terrorist's point of view, it generally should not matter which weapon is used to commit an attack – as long as the attack is efficient, causes fear in the public, and is repeatable (at least in general) at any given point in time. Therefore, attacks that endanger human life often receive larger media coverage than those that only affect computer systems. Some of these attacks only have a nexus to electronics, e.g. bomb attacks that are triggered by RFID chips contained in newer passports. Other forms of computer attacks that endanger human life have – for the most part – only been discussed and not yet taken place (or this has not become known to the public). Two different options are mainly being discussed: attacks on SCADA systems connected to potentially dangerous machinery with an immediate outcome and those that lead to a long-term effect.

Attacks with an Immediate Outcome

Most scenarios that are under discussion and that could directly result in lost lives have not yet taken place or they have not become known to the public. The following are especially considered to be potential target scenarios for terrorist attacks with an immediate danger to human lives: launching attacks on hydroelectric dams, tampering with control systems for railways or air traffic, and gaining control over systems supervising power plants.

Probably the most discussed scenario of cyberterrorism with an immediate danger for human lives is an attack on a hydroelectric dam. The consequences of (accidentally) damaged dams have been observed in the past, e.g. when, in 1975, the Banqiao and Shimantan dams on tributaries of the Huang He (Yellow) River in China failed, dozens of lower dams were damaged, and at least 85,000 people died. If terrorists were able, for example, by way of hacking into a SCADA system controlling a dam, to create a similar effect by deliberately opening the floodgates, again hundreds or even thousands of people would be at risk. The vulnerability of such systems could also be observed in 1996, when an individual used simple explosive devices to destroy the master terminal of a hydroelectric dam in Oregon. Although the structure of the dam was not affected by the attack, the power-generating turbines were completely disabled and had to be switched to manual control. However, attacks via digital channels have also been on the rise. In 1998, for example, a 12-year-old was able to break into a computer system that runs Arizona's Roosevelt Dam. Federal authorities afterwards reported that he had complete command of the SCADA system controlling the dam's massive floodgates.

A similar incidence – albeit without a threat to human life – took place in the year 2000, when the police arrested a man who used a stolen computer and radio transmitter to control the sewage treatment in Queensland, Australia. The culprit had manipulated the system over a period of two months, letting hundreds of thousands of gallons of putrid sludge ooze into parks and rivers. According to an employee of the Australian Environmental Protection Agency "marine life died, the creek water turned black and the stench was unbearable for residents." However, the perpetrator's motive was not to generate fear in the public, but to bargain for a consulting contract in order to fix the problems he had caused. Nevertheless, the case shows that physical damage can be caused by manipulating SCADA systems.

It is easy to imagine what could happen if a terrorist were to gain control over a system that is set up to prevent the collision of airplanes. In 1997, a juvenile was able to access the communication systems of Worcester, Mass. Airport. The action disrupted the telephone service to the Federal Aviation Administration Tower at the Airport, the Airport Fire Department, and other related services such as airport security, the weather service, and various private airfreight companies. Furthermore, the main radio transmitter and the circuit which enables aircrafts to send an electronic signal to activate the runway lights on approach were disabled. Fortunately, no accidents were caused by the attack. However, the incident clearly shows the potential danger and the vulnerability of systems that are responsible for protecting human lives. In a worst case scenario, colliding trains or airplanes could possibly cost hundreds of lives.

Finally, other scenarios with the possibility for mass mortality have also had an impact on the discussion about possible targets for cyberterrorists. In particular, the chance of terrorists controlling nuclear power plants or military missile control centers has been a subject discussed by many authors. The above-mentioned power-down of 2003 has shown that digital attacks can indeed have an impact on such systems. However, many of these situations rely on the failure of all other security measures at the same time. Air traffic controllers and pilots are especially trained as regards "situational awareness" and use computers only as an aid. So, for a successful attack, it would be necessary to manipulate pilots and/or controllers as well as intrude into the computer system. Furthermore, military facilities that are able to launch missiles are often not connected to the Internet, but "air-gapped" instead, making a remote launch simply impossible.

There are, however, no grounds for a complete all-clear. One reason is that it is not reasonable or sufficient to distinguish exclusively between "computer only" and "human only" scenarios. If organizations have (or can buy) the aid of an insider – either in the form of active participation or in the form of gathering otherwise protected information – many security measures can be dangerously compromised. The second reason is that the military also makes use of increased connectivity and remote controlling in order to save the lives of soldiers. New weapons are being developed that rely on remote control. For example, semi-autonomous military robots often provide a communication channel for human controllers – sometimes even over the Internet. This, for example, is the case with "RoboGuard", a guard robot that can be equipped with infrared- sensors and weaponry. Finally, many software products also used by military services rely on civilian technology and established operating systems, thereby opening additional loopholes for security risks.

Attacks with a Long-Term-Effect

The situations mentioned above can result in a one-time catastrophe. In order to create long-lasting panic and fear within the population, however, long-term effects and uncertainty may be even more suitable for terrorist organizations. Scenarios that are being discussed in this field include the manipulation of machinery, for example, in the production of food or medication. However, it is doubtful whether such scenarios are realistic. If, for example, the production chain of a food company were altered to create poisonous food, it seems likely that quality control would detect changes in the composition at an early stage. In addition, a sudden increase in the use of different ingredients would likely draw attention. Finally, the taste of the altered product would likely change.

Other possible targets include the weapons-production process, where manipulation could lead to useless ammunition. This would be effective especially, because testing is hardly possible and defects would be noticed only after it is too late. However, since these production areas are usually high-risk areas, security measures are high, and production computers are seldom linked to public networks the risk of a digital effect in this area can be considered very low.

Terrorist-Related Contents

From the beginning, one great strength of the Internet has always been its use for communication. However, widespread success began with the establishment of the WWW and the possibility for everyone to disseminate information. Today, terrorists have also begun to use the Internet not only to launch attacks, but also to exploit it for new possibilities in a "war of ideas." The use of the Internet is especially of interest for the presentation of terrorist viewpoints, the propagation of threats and propaganda, and the possibility to it for fundraising.

Presentation of Terrorist Views

In general, terrorists and terrorist organizations have to work undercover which makes the communication of their views, aims, and ambitions extremely difficult. "Conventional" ways to spread ideas are leaflets and "mouth-to-mouth" propaganda. However, both alternatives are time-consuming and risky and they do not reach a large group of people. Additionally, terrorists are faced with the problem of how to communicate with (and possibly influence) the media or other people and organizations who might not actively be looking for such information but who would be interested in it once introduced to it.

With the help of the Internet, the situation has changed. Almost every organization of importance now has its own website and the number of terrorist websites is steadily rising: Whereas in 1999, two of 30 deemed foreign terrorist organizations had their own websites (according to the United States Department of State), in 2005 more than 4,500 terrorist-related websites were known to exist. Many websites contain detailed information on leaders, the history of the organization, aims, or recent successes. The information is put together in such a way that the different "target groups", e.g. supporters, enemies, or mass media, can easily find relevant information. Some websites even offer cartoon-style design and children stories in order to reach already the youngest. Also, information is provided in different languages so that even foreigners can compare their media news with the views of the respective organization. The website of the Revolutionary Armed Forces of Colombia (FARC – http://www.farcep.org [last visited: September 2007]), for example, offers information in English, Italian, Portuguese, Russian, and German.

For an overview of terrorist websites and their languages of operation. As regards content, terrorists are not restricted to presenting information on their organization alone. Everything is virtually possible, from a mere presentation of viewpoints to a general glorification of terrorism or justification of recent acts of violence (or threats to perform new acts) even up to and including the incitement of further terrorist acts by the reading audience and recruits. The honoring of "martyrs" and communication with families of terrorists has even already taken place. The website alneda. com, for example, has published the names and home phone numbers of 84 al- Qaeda fighters who have been captured. Presumably, the aim of this action was to allow sympathizers to contact their families and let them know whether they were alive. Other websites contain obituaries of suicide bombers, effectively glorifying them and encouraging others to follow this path. The Internet has therefore become the most important means by which terrorist organizations communicate with their supporters and other interested parties.

The most popular terrorist sites attract tens of thousands of visitors each month. Of course, governments try to shut down such websites and prevent the spreading of information. However, the "censorship resistance" of the Internet is often used. For example, when Jordanian officials removed an article from 40 print copies of The Economist on sale in Jordan, an online copy was printed, photocopied, and faxed to 1,000 Jordanians, thereby circumventing local censors. Furthermore, websites are often stored on servers that are physically located in different countries than the one the organization is acting from. For example, several websites of al Qaeda are physically stored in the USA and Canada.

Threats and Propaganda

As mentioned above, terrorist websites are not restricted to a presentation of views alone. Instead, terrorists can also use the Internet to send threats to enemies and spread propaganda. The possibility to use multimedia technology especially enables an organization to burn images into the memories of the viewing audience in an impressive way. The assassination of Daniel Perl for example, showed the impact of psychological warfare as conducted by these new means. Also, other more recent, messages are no longer sent as mere text messages. Instead, professional-looking videos are being produced, e.g. in the case of threats against German and Austrian involvement in Afghanistan. These videos were subtitled in German and sent to a website called "Global Islamic Mediafront (GIMF). A high-ranking member of the German Office for the Protection of the Constitution is quoted as having said that this video is seen as a form of "psychological warfare" because it does not make direct threats, but instead creates an atmosphere of unease. Other messages are directly forwarded to TV stations which incorporate the material and broadcast it in their programs. Therefore, some attacks are staged and filmed from several angles at the same time so that the material can be better used for the distribution to the media, websites, and the production of DVDs.

The use of terrorist websites, however, also has two big disadvantages. First, most websites are only visited by people who are actively seeking such information. Therefore, organizations have to find new ways to also reach other people, e.g. mass media. Secondly, websites serve as a "single point of failure": If the website is closed down, all information contained there must be moved to another site and the new name spread among those who wish to visit the site and get information from it.

Terrorists have started to fight both problems and added more decentralized approaches to their arsenal. This makes it harder for the government to control content on the one hand. On the other hand, it also makes propaganda available for those capable of being influenced by it or who are open to the views of the organization but not actively seeking it. It is probably for this reason that many propaganda videos have shown up on video-sharing platforms such as YouTube. They depict terrorism in a glorious light and show assault scenes, bombings (often accompanied by modern music), or speeches by agitators. In addition to videos, Internet radio shows are also being launched. Both, video and radio shows allow organizations to spread their body of thought among young viewers who are vulnerable to such influences and may stumble over such material while looking for a new pop song.

Material and information that is spread via the Internet can also be used to influence public opinion. Whereas, in the past, only a few well-established organizations were able to produce newspapers, magazines, or TV shows, the Internet makes it possible for virtually anyone to launch their own periodicals or otherwise use the power of the media. The cost advantage over traditional mass media greatly helps to promote such journals. Al-Qaeda, for example, has launched a weekly bilingual news show containing world news from a terrorist point of view. Viewers of such online journals often cannot identify the source and evaluate whether the news being broadcast is true or false. This, however, has proven to be a double-edged sword in the past.

On the one hand, organizations were able to express their own views under the guise of a seemingly neutral authority, leading to a seemingly prevailing opinion between many "independent" journals. On the other hand, due also to the quick proliferation of fake communiqués, it was not easy to distinguish real terrorist messages from the statements of non-existent groups for some time.

Nevertheless, the risk remains that traditional mass media – thanks to increasing use of the Internet as a source of stories and illustrated footage – can fall for news sites that are set up especially for this purpose. By attractively presenting viewpoints and opinions, terrorist organizations can at least increase their chances of introducing these opinions into mass media products. In this context, semantic attacks are also being discussed. A semantic attack involves subtly changing the content of the web page of a traditional news site, thus disseminating false information. However, it is doubtful whether these attacks would remain unnoticed.

Fundraising and Financing

Some organizations have started to use their websites not only to disseminate information, but also to use it as a source of income for financing (fundraising). This can be done, for example, by selling CDs, DVDs, T-Shirts, badges, flags or books. Other websites give instructions on how to donate money to the organization, for example directly by means of credit card or by providing bank account details. By doing so, organizations can establish a link to supporters and candidates for possible recruitment. The same can be achieved, if terrorists gather user demographics, e.g. from personal information entered on online questionnaires and order forms. Users that are identified as potential sympathizers can then be e-mailed and asked to make donations. Since the websites of the organizations themselves are often at the center of surveillance by security agencies, hundreds of support websites commonly appear and disappear. To allow visitors to find further websites, they are often link by web rings. Yahoo for example has pulled dozens of sites in the Jihad Web Ring, a coalition of 55 Jihad-related sites.

Use of the Internet for Other Purposes

The third sector that is of interest to terrorists, apart from attacks carried out over the Internet and the dissemination of information, is the use of the Internet for seemingly harmless tasks such as sending e-mails or visiting web sites. However, the following section will show that even these simple tasks can be beneficial to a terrorist organization if they are carried out via the Internet. This is especially true for the individual communication between terrorists and terrorist groups and the use of the Internet as a planning and supporting instrument.

Individual Communication

The general benefits of the Internet, such as speed, low cost-level, and wide accessibility, apply especially if it is used for communication purposes. The use of the Internet to communicate goes back to the roots of the Internet itself. Therefore, many tools and programs are in existence and their functionality has already been widely tested. In general, communication can be divided into text-based tools on the one hand, that can either be used in realtime ("chatting") or in delayed mode (e.g. email), and voice-based systems on the other hand.

Text-based systems, such as email, have the advantage that they are widely available and that many companies usually offer these services free of charge. Additionally, they do not require a lot of bandwidth, making it possible to send and retrieve information even over older mobile phones or in areas where Internet-connections are limited. Since email services are offered free of charge by many different companies, terrorist organizations can rely on them and refrain from building up their own service. For example, the organizers of the 9/11 attacks had opened multiple accounts on largely anonymous e-mail services such as "Hotmail.". Text-based, real-time systems, such as IRC, allow for a fast (and largely unsupervised) conversation of two or more persons who are online at the same time. If, however, this is not the case, delayed applications that use a process-and-store mechanism (as with email) have a great advantage: messages can be stored and retrieved at any given point in time; terrorists neither have to be online all the time, nor do they have to entrust third parties with the task of accepting personal messages for them. Finally, many encryption tools have been developed and are freely available for this service. Voice-based systems, however, allow for even faster communication than textbased real-time systems.

Voice-over-IP systems (VoIP) have enjoyed great success since the free-of-charge software "Skype" was introduced. Lately, many manufacturers of messaging systems (such as AIM or Microsoft Messenger) have also included a voice function into their products. Therefore, it is of no surprise that VoIP software has been found in connection with al-Qaeda cells.

Encryption and Anonymity

Information that is exchanged over the Internet is – by nature – digital. This allows for easy encryption and also for opportunities to remain anonymous. With regard to the latter, anonymity services and open proxies can be used. However, in many cases, terrorists must anticipate that their message will be intercepted. Therefore, they must either disguise the message itself or use conventional encryption techniques.

To hide a message, two techniques are especially being discussed. The first is to hide the message with the help of steganography. In this case, a message is hidden inside a picture, sound file, or any other file. This file can then be put on any public website, e.g. a photo could be put on a classic photo site such as webshots.com.

Afterwards, other members of the organization could download the picture and decrypt the message. The entire process is concealed because no one (except for the terrorists) knows that the file contains more information than initially appears. Furthermore, the course of action is completely inconspicuous because it is an everyday event to up- or download a picture from a photo site and does not draw any attention to itself.

Some authors claim that the use of steganography is only a myth. However, even if this technique is not proven, there is a possibility that it could be used by terrorists as well as anybody else. Furthermore, also other techniques could be used to secretly pass messages that cannot be noticed or deciphered by observers. If, for example, code words or certain signals are being agreed upon between different terrorists, it would be sufficient to use this code word in an inconspicuous context.

Therefore, experts currently argue whether the color of the beard of Osama Bin Laden in his latest video is a secret message for his followers. Similar techniques were already used by the group of terrorists conducting the attack on 9/11. The message from Mohammed Atta to the other attackers stated that "19 confirmations for studies in the faculty of law, the faculty of urban planning, the faculty of fine arts, and the faculty of engineering" were obtained. This message could be sent without attracting any attention, even if it was intercepted. For the well-informed, however, the references to the various faculties revealed the different targets for the assassins.

Another method of preventing the content of a message from being revealed is the use of a free mailer e-mail account. To begin with, the use of a free mailer account itself offers a great degree of anonymity and protection in itself, especially if more than one service is used (either alternatively or simultaneously). However, to protect the content of an e-mail, the account is used in an unconventional way: instead of logging in, writing, and sending an e-mail, the password is not known to just one person but to two – sender and recipient. The sender logs onto the account and writes, but does not send, the message. Instead, the message is saved as a draft. Later, the recipient logs onto the same account and reads the message in the draft folder. By means of this technique, the message never leaves the system, so that no traces of an e-mail remain on any system. Thereby, governmental filtering systems were successfully circumvented for a long time. In the meantime, however, this technique is known to secret services around the globe. Therefore, if conventional messages (i.e. unencrypted or not in other ways protected) are being exchanged in this way, terrorist conversations can still be tapped. More difficulties arise, however, if this technique is not used with email accounts, but with online repositories. These storage places accept all kinds of different files, e.g. plain text file, encrypted files, or the above-mentioned seemingly harmless files that contain further information hidden inside.

But even if terrorists decide to send messages as proper e-mails (e.g. because there was no safe channel to exchange the password for the e-mail account), they can do so confidently because any message can be encrypted. Apparently, terrorists are already using all the possibilities that computers and networks offer, "starting from encryption techniques to password-protected repositories somewhere in the virtual world."

This statement by the President of the German Federal Police (Bundeskriminalamt) Jörg Ziercke was confirmed when thousands of encrypted messages were found by federal officials on the computers of arrested Al-Qaeda terrorists Abu Zubaydah and Ramzi Yousef; the latter of which was tried for the previous bombing of the World Trade Center. Good encryption programs are available to the public as opensource software. Thus, terrorists can be sure that no hidden "backdoor" is contained in the program. Furthermore, if the right encryption parameters are used, even up-to-date technology is not able to decrypt the message without the proper key.

Yet, apparently not all terrorists use encrypted messages. For example, the organizers of the 9/11 attacks indeed used e-mail, but did not see the need to encrypt their messages. In some cases, this might not be careless, but the intended purpose. If, for example, terrorists want the content of their communication to become known, they send it in unencrypted form in the hopes that the message will be intercepted by the appropriate authorities. Since it is common knowledge that the surveillance of telecommunication is on the rise, such information could be purposefully disseminated in order to conceal other – real – attack plans that concentrate on other targets.

Planning and Supporting

According to a terrorist training manual, public sources can provide up to 80% of all required information on an opponent. Officials agree and state that the combination of all unclassified information available in the Internet "adds up to something that ought to be classified". Terrorists can therefore heavily rely on publicly available information in the Internet for the planning of attacks and for the support of their mission. Examples of this field of application are especially the use of publicly available information and the collection of specialized information for training purposes.

Publicly Available Information

An often cited example of publicly available information which is useful for terrorists is the satellite maps that are provided, for example, by Google, Microsoft, or NASA. In former times, these images were only available to experts. Now, they are a common good and accessible for anybody, including terrorists. In the eyes of governments around the world, at least part of such information poses a threat to national security because it allows the examination of otherwise protected areas from a bird's eye view. Therefore, it is reasonable that officials have begun to ask providers of digital maps to disclose certain – security-relevant – information, e.g. defensive fortifications or military development and production areas. But even maps of publicly accessible areas can be of interest because they can easily be combined with other data, such as street names. As a result, for example, escape routes can be planned with great precision, even before a territory is inspected in person.

In many cases, the information that is contained on the website of possible targets (e.g. companies or government institutions) is also of interest to terrorists. In one case, for example, maps, time schedules for shuttle busses, and a copy of the official telephone directory of a military base were available via the official website. This information could be gathered by terrorists and used for the preparation of a conventional attack. The same is true for much other information that can be accessed via the Internet. For example, reports of security weaknesses in airports or transport companies could draw the attention of terrorists to possible targets. In summary, the amount of sensitive data that can be discovered at the various corporate websites can be constituted as "a gold mine for potential attackers.". According to some authors, terrorist organizations have even started to use databases to gather, sort, and evaluate the details of potential targets in the United States. Actual findings on terrorists' computers have shown that publicly available information of all kinds are indeed being downloaded and used for planning purposes.

Training

Since so much information that can be abused is available over the Internet, some authors claim that the Web has become "an open university for jihad". Some information that is of great interest – especially for new terrorists – has even been precompiled, e.g. information on bombs, poisons, or many other dangerous goods. The "Mujahadeen Poisons Handbook", for example, contains various "recipes" for homemade poisons and poisonous gases for use in terrorist attacks. Comparable information can also be found in other collections, such as the "Terrorist's Handbook", the "Anarchist Cookbook", the "Encyclopedia of Jihad", the "Sabotage Handbook", and the famous "How to make Bombs", all of which are freely available. Modern terrorists amend these handbooks by adding extra information, e.g. on hostage taking, guerrilla tactics, and special bombs. Some excerpts, e.g. from the virtual training manual of al-Qaida Al Battar, have been published by the U.S. Department of Justice. The danger that appears to originate from many of these compilation should, however, not be overestimated. Even though the documents are clearly labeled, many of them contain the same information that can be found in most standard chemistry books for university students. Then again the Internet offers some advantages over traditional libraries. For example, contents can be gathered without causing any suspicion and without attracting a librarian's attention. Furthermore, new information can be added at any time and collections can be mirrored between different locations. This (and the possibility to use anonymity services for retrieving the information) enables terrorists to circumvent censorship and deletion.

Support

As explained above, the Internet can serve as a huge library for terrorists. Combined with the possibilities to interact fast and anonymously with each other new opportunities for a support between terrorists and terrorist groups arise. This can happen in three different ways: (1) supporters find instructions on what contributions are currently needed by an organization; (2) organizations offer help to individuals; and (3) organizations help each other. The first possibility is that individuals support a terrorist organization. This can happen in many of the ways that are being described above, e.g. through financing. But also support of electronic attacks has already taken place. Recently, for example, software called "the electronic jihad program" has been discovered on jihadi web sites. The program can be downloaded by interested followers. It is designed as to allow individuals to easily participate in attacks on different web sites over a windows-like interface. In order to encourage other users, usernames of participants and the hours spent for attacking websites are being collected and put on public "high score"-lists. The publishers of this software obviously hope that with a spreading use of the Internet continually more users engage in such a form of "electronic jihad."

The second form of support goes into the opposite direction, i.e. terrorist organizations support individuals in their efforts. This form of support can especially take place in the above mentioned way of compiling information for special purposes like instructions on hostage taking or on building bombs. This form of support is seemingly on the rise. Al-Qaeda, for example, is said to run a "massive and dynamic online library of training materials" which is supported by experts who can answer questions either on message boards or in chat rooms. Topics that are covered in this database are said to range from weapons and poisons to navigation instruments and even to camouflaging and masquerading. Such a "terrorist's helpdesk" could enable small groups of terrorists all over the globe to act fast and competent. Information on the third form of support – support between different organizations – is hardly available. However, at least the technical infrastructure is available that allows loosely interconnected groups to maintain contact with one another. Even terrorist groups that fight for different political goals and that are located in different geographical areas could communicate with each other and exchange information, such as on weapons or tactics.

DISTRIBUTED DENIAL OF SERVICE ATTACKS

Distributed Denial of Service attacks ("DDoS") are a natural development in the search for more effective and debilitating denial of service attacks. Instead of using just one computer to launch an attack, the hacker enlists numerous computers to attack the target computer from numerous launch points. Prior to an attack, the hacker places a daemon, or a small computer program, on an innocent third-party computer. These third-party computers are often referred to as "zombies" or "soldiers." The "slave" daemons are remotely controlled by the "master" program to launch attacks against certain servers. By distributing the source of attacks across a wider array of zombie computers, the attacker has made it more difficult for the target server to block off the attack routes.

Trinoo (June 1999)

On August 17, 1999, a Trinoo network of at least 227 systems was used to flood a single server at the University of Minnesota, including more than 100 compromised computers at the University of Washington. The attack rendered the system inoperable for two days.

There has been speculation that Trinoo was one of the programs that brought down Yahoo and other major Internet sites in February 2000. Trinoo is used to create distributed denial of service UDP flood attacks. There is concern that Trinoo could enlist common desktop computers in a DDoS attack by loading a daemon on the local computer through an e-mail attachment. According to one estimate, Trinoo networks are "being set up on hundreds, perhaps thousands, of systems that are being compromised by remote buffer overrun exploitation."

After the attacker has placed the daemons on the intermediary computers, master programs are set up on other computers to act as commanders to call "the troops" into action. The attacker only needs to access the master programs, via telnet, to launch the massive, coordinated attacks. Both the slave and master programs are password controlled to prevent system administrators from taking control of the Trinoo network. Once the attacker has accessed the master, he only needs to enter the IP address of the targeted server in a "dos IP" command to wake up the daemon "zombies" that begin launching their massive queries at the target. The attacker is also able to launch attacks against multiple targets using the "mdos" command. Finally, the attacker can set a time limit for the DoS attack.

Tribe Flood Network (August 1999)

Tribe Flood Network, ("TFN"), is a DDoS program written by a German hacker that is capable of launching ICMP, SYN Flood, UDP Flood and Smurf attacks. In late August, 1999, DDoS attackers began to shift from Trinoo to TFN. Using TFN, a single attacker can launch an attack from dozens of computers on which the attacker has surreptitiously placed the TFN daemon. The attacker remotely controls the TFN client network using a variety of connection methods, including telnet TCP connections. Unlike various versions of Trinoo, TFN clients do not require a password to be activated, although the client sends commands to the daemon in an ICMP packet. However, there is no telnet TCP or UDP-based communication between the client and the daemon, making detection of the client's call to action more difficult to detect on the client, or master, system.

Tribe Floodnet 2k (January 2000)

Tribe Floodnet 2k ("TFN2K") is an updated version of the TFN DDoS attack tool. According to Mixter, the German hacker who wrote the program, TFN2K still contains the popular features of the original TFN, including the client/server functionality, stealth, and encryption techniques. However, Mixter added several new features that make the system more robust and deadly, including remote one-way command instructions to the distributed servers who go on to launch the attacks. Also, TFN2K boasts stronger encryption between the client and the server.

Stacheldraht (October 1999)

The most recent advance in DDoS attacks has come in the form of Stacheldraht, a German word for "Barbed Wire." Stacheldraht has the ability to automatically update the daemon programs, reducing the attacker's risk of intrusion. Stacheldraht was based on the source code from Tribe Flood Network, with at least two significant new features. The communication between the attacker and the Stacheldraht masters are encrypted and the daemons can be automatically updated by the masters. One of the weaknesses of TFN was the attacker's connection to the master program located on the remote computers.

Stacheldraht combines Trinoo's master/daemon control features with TFN's ICMP flood, SYN flood, UDP flood, and Smurf attacks. The attackers control the master computers through encrypted clients, and each master can control up to 1000 daemons that are installed on innocent third-party computers. The attack begins in the preparation stage, called the "mass-intrusion phase," where large numbers of computers are compromised. The attacker places the Stacheldraht daemons on the compromised systems and the daemons lie in wait for the command to attack. The third-party computers are also victims in these attacks because the systems have been compromised and they use up bandwidth and processing power.

Tracking Down the Attackers

The Federal Bureau of Investigation ("FBI") has had a very difficult time locating the origin of the attackers because of the networked nature of the Internet, the spoofing of the DoS packets, and the procedural difficulty of organizing an investigation that involves countless jurisdictions. One method used to track the attacker is to start from the targeted server and locate the immediate server that sent the packet. However, because the packet was carrying "false identification," each subsequent router along the network could lead the investigator astray.

Because the packet's "false papers" hide the true origin of the packet, it is difficult to reconstruct the origin of the spoofed packets after the fact. In order to determine where the packet came from, the investigators must set up a filer, or "trace and trap," before they arrive at that particular router. This is complicated by fact that the packet could cross as many as thirty different routers owned by ten different companies in several different legal jurisdictions. In the February, 2000 attacks on the major Internet sites, the authorities have identified several university computers that were compromised and used to attack the targeted servers.

Bibliography

Ahuja, Vijay: *Network and Internet Security*. Academic Press, Inc.: Boston, 1996.

Amoroso, E. : *Fundamentals of Computer Security Technology*, Prentice Hall, Englewood Cliffs, 1994.

Askari Rizvi: *Nuclear Terrorism and South Asia*, Albuquerque, NM: Sandia National Laboratories, February 2003.

Cadoree, Michelle: *Computer Crime and Security*. Washington, D.C.: LC Science Tracer Bullet, 1994.

Charlotte Waelde, *Law and the Internet: Regulating Cyberspace*. Hart Pub, 1997.

Daniel J.: *Bandits on the Information Superhighway*. O'Reilly & Associates, Inc.: Sebastopol, 1996.

David Post : *The Rise of Law in Cyberspace*, 48 Stan, L. Rev. 1367, 1996.

Friedman, G.: *The Future of War of Cyber Crimes*, N.Y., Random House, 1996.

Froomkin, Michael : *The Essential Role of Trusted Third Parties in Electronic Commerce*, 75 Ore. L. Rev. 49, 1996.

Herman H.: *The Computer, From Pascal to von Neumann*. Princeton, NJ, Princeton University Press, 1972.

Hoffman, Bruce: *Inside Terrorism and Internet Crime*, New York: Columbia University Press, 1998.

James Keller: *Public Access to the Internet*, Cambridge, MA: The MIT Press, 1995.

Joel Moses: *The Computer Age, A Twenty-Year View.*Cambridge, MA, The MIT Press, 1979.

John C.: *Dvorak Predicts: An Insider's Look at the Computer Industry*, New York: McGraw Hill, 1994.

Kaplan, David: *Computer Virus Attack*, New York: Crown Publishers, 1996.

Keane J.: *Democracy and Cyber Crimes*, London, Verso, 1988.

Kurz, Raymond, *Internet and the Law: Legal Fundamentals for the Internet User*. Rockville, MD.: Government Institutes, 1996.

Laliberte, S. : *Security by Example Defend I.T.* New York, Addison Wesley, 2004.

Laquer, Walter: *Terrorism Attack from Computer Hacking*, Oxford: Oxford University Press, 1999.

McMahon, David: *Cyber Threat: Internet Security for Home and Business*. Warwick Publishing Inc.: Toronto, 2000.

McQuade, S.: *Understanding and Managing Cybercrime*, Boston: Allyn & Bacon, 2006.

Peter T.: *Manager's Guide to Internet Security*. CSI: San Francisco, 1994.

Posen, B.R.: *The Sources of Cyber Crime*, Ithaca, 1984, Cornell Univ. Press.

Rosen, P.: *Policy of Cyber Laws*, Ithaca, Cornell University Press, 1996.

Schroeer, Dietrich: *Science, Technology, and the Cyber Crimes*, Ontario: John Wiley & Sons, 1984.

Steve J.: *The Cybernetics Group*, Cambridge, MA, The MIT Press, 1991.

Susan, J.: *Crime, Space and Society*, Cambridge, England, Cambridge University Press, 1986.

Verton, D. : *Black Ice: The invisible Threat of Cyber-terrorism*, New York: McGraw-Hill/Osborne, 2003.

Vijay K. Gurbani: *Internet & TCP/IP Network Security*. McGraw-Hill: New York, 1996.

Yar, M.: *Cybercrime and Society*, London: Sage, 2006.

Zanini, M.: *Countering the New Terrorism*, Santa Monica, CA: RAND, 1999.

Index

□□□

* 9 7 8 8 1 9 3 1 4 2 2 3 3 *